No one else

can match the effectiveness, the simplicity, or the appeal of the

SPECTRUM READING SERIES

Students gain meaningful practice— independently

With the SPECTRUM READING SERIES students not only get the practice they need in essential reading skills, they also enjoy being able to do it on their own.

In grades one through six, each lesson features an illustrated story followed by exercises in comprehension and basic reading skills. Because the same format is used consistently throughout, your students will have little trouble doing the lessons independently. And each two-page lesson can be finished easily in one class period.

Students develop and refine key reading skills.

- **Comprehension** exercises help students go beyond understanding of facts and details to drawing conclusions, predicting outcomes, identifying cause and effect, and developing other higher level comprehension skills.
- **Vocabulary development** builds on words from the reading selections. In addition to learning synonyms, antonyms, and words with multiple meanings, students develop sight vocabulary and learn to use context as a clue for meaning.
- **Decoding** exercises refine students' abilities to "attack" and understand new reading words.
- **Study skills** are developed by helping students apply their reading skills to new tasks, such as using reference materials, reading graphs, and applying other everyday life skills.

Reading selections captivate and motivate.

Students get their best reading practice by actually reading. That's why the selections in the SPECTRUM READING SERIES, in addition to offering practice in skills, also motivate students to read—just for fun.

Students quickly become friends with the characters in these entertaining stories. And they enjoy new levels of reading success—thanks in part to carefully controlled vocabulary and readability as well as beautiful illustrations.

The program adapts completely to any teaching situation.

The SPECTRUM READING SERIES can be used in many different ways.

- For the whole class . . . for intensive reinforcement of reading skills or to supplement a basal reading program.
- For reading groups . . . to provide skills practice at the appropriate levels.
- For individual use . . . to help build a completely individualized program.
- For at-home practice . . . to expand on skills learned in the classroom.

 Children's Publishing

Send all inquiries to: McGraw-Hill Children's Publishing • 8787 Orion Place • Columbus, Ohio 43240-4027

ISBN 1-57768-463-X

7 8 9 10 11 12 POH 06 05 04 03 02

The McGraw-Hill Companies

Index of Skills for *Reading Grade 3*

Numerals indicate the exercise pages on which these skills appear.

Knowing the Words

Abbreviations— 91, 93, 101, 149

Antonyms—9, 25, 35, 49, 59, 73, 97, 121, 129, 137, 139, 151, 161

Classification—3, 13, 29, 45, 53, 63, 99, 115, 123, 135, 143, 153

Homographs—19, 21, 23, 29, 39, 61, 93, 107, 113, 127, 155, 159, 165

Homophones—11, 15, 17, 51, 63, 79, 87, 109, 113, 127, 145, 169

Multiple meanings—7, 31, 43, 47, 55, 71, 89, 103, 119, 157, 163, 167

Sight vocabulary—*All lessons*

Synonyms—15, 27, 37, 49, 65, 77, 85, 95, 105, 117, 125, 131, 133, 137

Word meaning from context—*All activity pages*

Working with Words

Base words and endings—17, 27, 59, 71, 81, 97, 107, 117, 141

Compound Words—13, 31, 45, 55, 69, 85, 111, 127, 133, 149

Contractions—5, 25, 43, 49, 69, 99, 115, 139, 157

Irregular spellings—19, 27, 73, 83, 115, 145, 155, 169

Possessives—15, 31, 57, 77, 89, 105, 141, 151

Prefixes and suffixes—21, 41, 59, 67, 81, 109, 131, 133, 139, 147, 161, 169

r-Controlled vowels—5, 25, 57, 67, 77

Singular and plural—3, 9, 41, 75, 83, 97, 99, 135, 147

Syllables—23, 33, 73, 85, 105, 121, 127, 151

Variant sounds—17, 33, 45, 69, 107, 135, 149, 161

Vowel digraphs and diphthongs—9, 11, 55, 75, 87, 111, 123, 145, 167

Reading and Thinking

Cause and effect—5, 7, 15, 17, 19, 21, 25, 29, 33, 35, 37, 43, 47, 51, 55, 65, 71, 73, 75, 79, 81, 87, 89, 93, 99, 105, 107, 109, 113, 115, 117, 123, 129, 133, 137, 143, 149, 151, 161, 165, 167, 169

Character analysis—7, 19, 21, 31, 43, 65, 89, 91, 109, 135, 151, 155, 169

Comparison and contrast—5, 7, 19, 31, 35, 51, 69, 89, 101, 103, 109, 111, 113, 127, 143, 153

Context clues—3, 11, 19, 23, 25, 31, 37, 39, 41, 49, 53, 57, 65, 71, 75, 79, 85, 91, 97, 99, 101, 103, 105, 115, 119, 121, 127, 129, 137, 141, 147, 149, 161

Drawing conclusions—9, 11, 13, 15, 17, 23, 27, 29, 31, 35, 39, 41, 45, 47, 49, 53, 57, 61, 69, 73, 77, 81, 83, 87, 89, 95, 97, 101, 103, 105, 107, 111, 117, 119, 121, 123, 125, 127, 129, 131, 133, 137, 139, 141, 143, 147, 149, 153, 159, 161, 165, 167, 169

Fact and opinion—111, 113, 117, 123, 139, 145, 155, 163

Facts and details—3, 5, 11, 13, 17, 19, 23, 27, 29, 33, 35, 37, 39, 43, 47, 49, 51, 53, 55, 59, 63, 67, 71, 75, 77, 81, 83, 85, 87, 89, 95, 99, 101, 103, 107, 109, 115, 117, 119, 121, 123, `31, 133, 137, 139, 145, 147, 151, 153, 159, 165, 167, 169

Main idea—3, 7, 11, 15, 21, 27, 33, 41, 43, 47, 51, 55, 59, 65, 71, 77, 85, 87, 91, 95, 97, 101, 103, `05, 107, 113, 115, 119, 123, 125, 127, 131, 133, 137, 139, 143, 145, 147, 151, 157

Predicting outcomes—5, 11, 13, 17, 23, 25, 29, 33, 39, 47, 51, 55, 59, 67, 73, 77, 79, 83, 85, 87, 95, 105, 107, 113, 115, 117, 121, 123, 125, 129, 135, 151, 155, 161, 165, 167

Reality and fantasy—3, 13, 25, 45, 57, 95, 97, 131, 135, 147, 157

Sequence—5, 9, 13, 19, 25, 31, 37, 45, 49, 55, 61, 67, 75, 81, 89, 99, 109, 111, 121, 129, 133, 135, 141, 149, 153, 163

Word referents—9, 21, 45, 69, 93, 151, 159, 163

Learning to Study

Alphabetical order—7, 29, 47, 61, 93, 129, 143, 165

Dictionary use— 35, 37, 39, 79, 95, 101, 103, 113, 119, 125, 137, 143, 153

Following directions—*All activity pages*

Parts of a book—51, 53, 63, 65, 91, 145, 163, 169

Reference materials—155, 157 159, 167

SPECTRUM READING
Grade 3

Table of Contents

Office Surprise

What would you do with an old, broken robot?

1   "Carlos, would you like to run over to the office with me for a few minutes?" Mrs. Garza asked.

2   Carlos put down the clock he was trying to fix. "Sure, Mom. I like going to your office on Saturdays."

3   Mrs. Garza wrote ads to help people sell things. She used lots of signs and devices in her ads.

4   While his mom worked, Carlos looked around. He wandered into a storeroom filled with old signs. At first he didn't see anything interesting. Then something made him catch his breath. Hidden in a corner was an old, dusty robot. It was nearly as big as Carlos. It had two metal arms with silver fingers. Its head was round and had two green lights for eyes. Carlos pushed some buttons on the robot's chest, but nothing happened.

5   Carlos hurried to his mother's office and said, "Mom, there's a robot . . ." He stopped when he noticed that his mother was talking to her boss, Mrs. Chung.

6   "Oh, that old thing," Mrs. Chung said. "We used it once, but it's just junk now. It's time to get rid of it."

7   "I wish I could buy it," Carlos said dreamily. "I'd love to have a robot."

8   "It isn't worth much," Mrs. Chung said. "I could sell it to you for ten dollars."

9   "Ten dollars?" Carlos asked, grinning. "I already have about six dollars. I could earn the rest. May I, Mom?"

10   "Well, for a person who likes to fix things, I guess a broken robot sounds just right," his mom said, smiling.

11   Carlos ran back to the storeroom. "You won't have to stay here much longer," he said to the robot. "As soon as I save enough money, I'm taking you home with me."

Knowing the Words

Write the words from the story that have the meanings below.

1. announcements of
    something for sale _____
    (Par. 3)

2. equipment _____
    (Par. 3)

3. machine that
    obeys commands _____
    (Par. 4)

In each row below, circle the three words that belong together.

4. run   walk   sleep   wander

5. machine   snack   robot   device

6. fingers   arms   dust   chest

Working with Words

A word that means one of something is **singular.** A word that means more than one is **plural.** Most singular words are made plural by adding *s.* Most words that end in *s, ss, x, ch,* and *sh* are made plural by adding *es.* Form the plural of each word below by adding *s* or *es.*

1. button _____   4. robot _____

2. boss _____   5. clock _____

3. wish _____   6. circus _____

Reading and Thinking

1. Check the answer that tells what the story is mainly about.

    _____ finding a robot

    _____ going to the office

    _____ fixing a clock

2. What day of the week is it in this
    story? _____

3. What do you think will happen when

    Carlos saves up ten dollars? _____

    _____

4. Some things are real, and some are make-believe. Write **M** next to the two sentences that tell about make-believe things.

    _____ Robots are machines.

    _____ Robots can think for themselves.

    _____ Robots have feelings.

    _____ Robots can obey commands.

Write the best word to complete each sentence below.

5. Andrea had six square _____
    on her good coat, but one fell off.
    (zippers, buttons, dollars)

6. There was a typewriter in each

    _____. (office,
    automobile, meadow)

7. The bike was _____
    by some bushes. (written, wanted, hidden)

The Ride Home

Would you wave at a robot?

1 Carlos raced to the storeroom where the robot he had just paid for was kept. "In here, Dad," he said, feeling excited.

2 Mr. Garza looked at the dusty piece of metal and tried to smile. "You didn't tell me it was so big."

3 "It's almost as big as I am," Carlos said proudly. He tried to roll the robot, but the wheels were stuck. "Could you grab it under the arms, Dad?" he asked. "I'll carry this end."

4 Together they carried the robot to the van. People stopped to stare. "This is my very own robot," Carlos told them.

5 Mr. Garza opened the back of the van. "Dad, you wouldn't make my new friend ride in there, would you?" Carlos cried.

6 Mr. Garza noticed that people were watching. He slammed the door shut. "Put it in the backseat," he grumbled.

7 Carlos sat in the backseat beside the robot. He moved the robot's arm and made it wave at people on the street. Everyone pointed and laughed. Carlos smiled back. "Isn't it wonderful, Dad?"

8 Mr. Garza frowned at Carlos. "I don't know," his father said. "I feel silly driving around town with a waving robot." Carlos sat back in his seat. Then he made the robot give his father a friendly wave. Mr. Garza laughed. "Well, I must admit this is a ride I'll never forget."

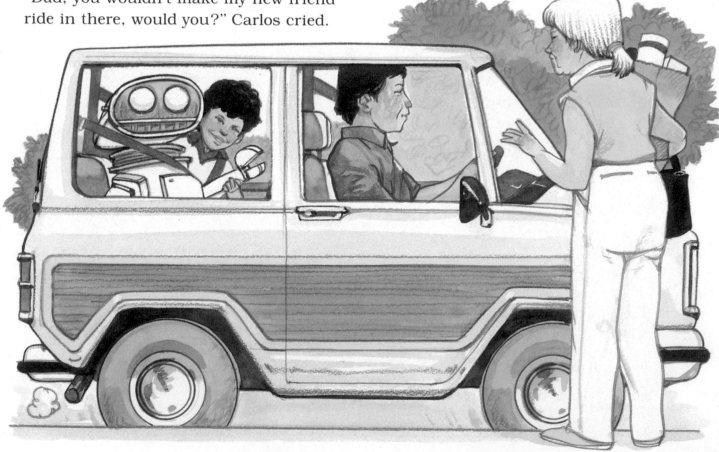

4

Knowing the Words

Write the words from the story that have the meanings below.

1. said in a low voice _____
   (Par. 6)

2. say something is true _____
   (Par. 8)

Working with Words

A **contraction** is a short way to write two words. An apostrophe (') shows that one or more letters have been taken out. Write a contraction from the story for each pair of words below.

1. it is _____
   (Par. 3)

2. I will _____
   (Par. 3)

3. would not _____
   (Par. 5)

4. is not _____
   (Par. 7)

5. do not _____
   (Par. 8)

Circle the correct letters to complete each word and write them in the blank.

6. Get into the c____ and put on your seat belt.

   or   ir   ar

7. Did you f ____ get to sweep the floor?

   or   ir   ar

8. Meet us at the corn ____ after the show.

   or   ar   er

Reading and Thinking

1. Number the sentences to show the order in which things happened.

   ____ Carlos made the robot wave.

   ____ Carlos and his dad went to the storeroom.

   ____ Carlos and his dad took the robot to the van.

   ____ Carlos tried to roll the robot.

2. How big was the robot? _____

   _____

3. Carlos and his dad had to carry the robot because _____

   _____.

4. Tell two ways that a robot is different from a child. _____

   _____

   _____

5. What do you think Carlos will do as soon as he gets the robot home? ____

   _____

5

Robot Commands

What do you think it would take to make a robot move?

1 "It's great," Marie said when she saw her brother's new project.

2 "I'm going to fix it," Carlos said, looking at the robot in the driveway.

3 Marie smiled and said, "I think a robot is harder to fix than a clock."

4 First, Carlos dusted off his new friend. Next, he oiled the wheels and arms. Then Carlos removed the cover from the robot's back. Inside he saw an old battery and some broken wires. Carlos replaced the wires with wires from an old radio. He took the battery from his camping lantern and put it inside the robot. Finally, Carlos was ready to test it. He pressed some buttons on the robot's chest. The robot just sat there.

5 "Why don't you move?" Carlos yelled. Just then the robot's lights flashed on. It started to roll. For a moment, Carlos stood there with his mouth open. Then he saw that the robot was going toward a neighbor's rose bed.

6 Carlos ran after the robot. "Don't go in there," he yelled, but it kept going.

7 Carlos was getting frantic. "Quit! Stop! Don't!" he yelled all at once.

8 The robot halted just before it hit the first rosebush. Carlos rolled the robot back to his own yard. "I'm glad I got you to work," he said, "but I'm going to have to watch what I say around you."

Knowing the Words

Write the words from the story that have the meanings below.

1. something being worked on _____
   (Par. 1)

2. try out _____
   (Par. 4)

3. very upset _____
   (Par. 7)

Check the meaning that fits the underlined word in each sentence.

4. Jane passed her math <u>test</u>.

   _____ something to measure what a person knows

   _____ try out

5. The dog walked through the <u>bed</u> of daisies.

   _____ piece of furniture

   _____ place for flowers

6. I forgot to wear my <u>watch</u>.

   _____ something that keeps time

   _____ look for

Reading and Thinking

1. Check the answer that tells what the story is mainly about.

   _____ bringing the robot home

   _____ stopping the robot

   _____ getting the robot to work

2. How do you think Carlos felt when he tried to get the robot to move?

   _____

   _____

3. How do you think fixing a robot might be like fixing a radio? _____

   _____

4. Carlos pressed buttons on the robot's chest because _____

   _____.

Learning to Study

Number each list of words below in alphabetical order.

1. _____ dusted

   _____ friend

   _____ camping

   _____ battery

2. _____ wires

   _____ lights

   _____ robot

   _____ yell

3. _____ smile

   _____ fix

   _____ mouth

   _____ removed

4. _____ yard

   _____ watch

   _____ stop

   _____ pressed

7

A Special Helper

Read to find out what happens when a robot helps with chores.

1 Carlos dashed into the house. "Mom! Dad! Marie! My robot works!"

2 Everyone hurried outside. They clapped as Carlos demonstrated how the robot moved and stopped. Carlos believed he was the luckiest kid in the whole world.

3 After his family had gone back into the house, Carlos patted the robot on the back. "You're good at taking orders. Maybe you can help me with my chores."

4 Carlos went inside and came back with two wastebaskets. He took one of them to the trash can and took off the can's lid. "Empty," Carlos said, pouring the trash into the can. He put the lid back on.

5 "Now it's your turn," Carlos said. He gave the other wastebasket to the robot. "Empty," he commanded. The robot turned the wastebasket over. All the trash landed on the grass. Carlos picked up the trash and stuffed it back into the wastebasket.

6 "Let's try again," Carlos said. He put the wastebasket into the robot's hands and turned it toward the trash can. "Move," he ordered. The robot rolled to the trash can. It stopped when Carlos told it to. "Empty," Carlos said. The robot turned the wastebasket over. The trash landed on the lid of the trash can.

7 "Oh, no, I forgot about the lid," Carlos moaned. "We've both got a lot to learn, robot."

Knowing the Words

Write the words from the story that have the meanings below.

1. showed by example _____
   (Par. 2)

2. commands _____
   (Par. 3)

3. small jobs _____
   (Par. 3)

Words with opposite meanings are called **antonyms.** Match each word from the first list with its antonym from the second list.

4. _____ moved   **a.** full

5. _____ empty   **b.** stopped

6. _____ outside   **c.** inside

Working with Words

Circle the correct word in **( )** and write it in the blank.

1. Chris _____ a beach ball to the lake. (tank, took)

2. Nan lives in a _____ down the street. (hose, house)

3. _____ we will see a full moon tonight. (Merry, Maybe)

Form the plural of each word below by adding *s* or *es.*

4. grass _____   7. dish _____

5. hand _____   8. back _____

6. lid _____   9. ax _____

Reading and Thinking

1. Number the sentences to show the order in which things happened.

   _____ Carlos showed his family what the robot could do.

   _____ The robot dumped the trash on the ground.

   _____ Carlos showed the robot how to empty the trash.

   _____ The robot dumped the trash on the lid of the trash can.

Write **T** if the sentence is true.
Write **F** if the sentence is false.

2. _____ Carlos was excited because his robot followed orders.

3. _____ Carlos kept his robot's tricks a secret.

4. _____ Carlos had to be careful when he gave orders to the robot.

5. _____ The robot could not hear well.

Words such as *he, she, you, it, we,* and *they* are used in place of other words. Read these sentences. *The robot was made of metal. It had green eyes.* In the second sentence, *it* is used in place of *the robot.*

Read each set of sentences below. Fill in each blank.

6. Carlos yelled to his family. He wanted them to see the robot.

   He stands for _____.

7. Marie liked the robot. She liked to see Carlos having fun.

   She stands for _____.

9

What's your name?

What do you think would be a good name for Carlos's robot?

1   Every day Carlos taught his robot more commands. When he said "Right" the robot turned right, and it turned left when Carlos said "Left." Carlos even taught the robot to shake hands when he said "Shake."

2   "I think you are ready to meet my sister," Carlos said. He held the door open while giving the robot orders. The robot rolled into the kitchen, bumping into things on the way.

3   Marie was preparing supper. "Meet my sister, Marie," Carlos said to the robot. "Shake." Marie had a bowl of ice in her right hand. The robot did not wait for her to set the bowl down. It just grabbed and shook Marie's hand. Ice flew out of the bowl and scattered across the floor.

4   Marie chuckled and said, "I think your robot needs a little more work, Carlos. Have you named it yet?"

5   "Not yet," Carlos answered. "It needs a very special name. Something that tells what a terrific helper it is." Carlos sat down at the table to think. After a while, he said, "I know, I'll name it Mosh, which is short for *my* *own* *special* *helper*. What do you think, Mosh?"

6   Mosh's eyes lit up. "Did you see that, Marie?" Carlos asked, getting excited. "Mosh's eyes lit up, so I guess that means my robot likes that name."

7   "Carlos, that robot is just a machine," his sister said. "It doesn't

have feelings. You understand that, don't you?"

8   "That's what she thinks," Carlos whispered to Mosh. Mosh winked back.

Knowing the Words

Write the words from the story that have the meanings below.

1. wonderful _____
   (Par. 5)

2. things such as
   happiness, sadness,
   and anger _____
   (Par. 7)

3. said with
   a quiet voice _____
   (Par. 8)

Some words sound alike but have different spellings and meanings. Write the word with the correct meaning to complete each sentence below.

4. Ann can hardly _____ for the show to begin. (wait, weight)

5. Please don't _____ on that paper. (right, write)

6. _____ will go to the playground. (Eye, I)

Working with Words

Circle the correct word in ( ) and write it in the blank.

1. Phyllis _____ her puppy a trick. (taught, that)

2. Please _____ for me while I get my jacket. (want, wait)

3. Do you know where Muffy has

   hidden her _____?
   (boil, bowl)

Reading and Thinking

1. Check the answer that tells what the story is mainly about.

   _____ fixing supper

   _____ talking to Marie

   _____ naming the robot

2. What name was given to the robot?

   _____Why was it given

   that name? _____

   _____

3. What other commands do you think

   the robot could be taught? _____

   _____

Write **T** if the sentence is true.
Write **F** if the sentence is false.

4. _____ The robot did exactly what it was told to do.

5. _____ The robot could talk.

6. _____ The robot knocked the ice out of Marie's hand.

7. _____ Carlos thinks Mosh has feelings.

Write the best word to complete each sentence below.

8. Gilda was _____ a flat tire on her bike. (bumping, fixing, preparing)

9. Please _____ off that sand before you come inside. (wait, shake. whisper)

A New Friend

How do you meet new people?

1 "Mosh, I miss my old friends," Carlos said, feeling blue. "I wonder if I'll ever meet any kids in this new neighborhood. At least I have you. Come on, I'll teach you to play tag."

2 Carlos and Mosh went into the backyard. Carlos tapped Mosh on the arm and said, "When I do that, you're 'it.' When I say 'tag,' you have to catch me and touch me." Then Carlos ran away from Mosh and yelled, "Tag!" The robot started rolling.

3 Just then, Mrs. Wilson, a neighbor, came out to pick flowers. Mosh rolled up behind Mrs. Wilson and tagged her.

4 Mrs. Wilson was so startled that her flowers went flying. Carlos ran over to her. "I'm sorry, Mrs. Wilson. I guess my robot thought you were playing tag."

5 "Oh, that's OK. It just surprised me," Mrs. Wilson said, chuckling. Carlos helped her gather the flowers. When he finished, he looked around for Mosh.

6 "Now where's Mosh?" Carlos cried, running to the front yard. Down the street, he could see Mosh chasing a girl. Carlos ran, yelling, "Stop, Mosh!"

7 The girl looked at Carlos and asked, "Is that yours?"

8 "Yes, we were playing tag," Carlos answered.

9 "Gee, I wish I had a robot," the girl said. "Did you just move here?"

10 Carlos nodded and said, "My name is Carlos. What's yours?"

11 "I'm Susan," the girl replied. "May I play tag with you and your robot?"

12 Carlos smiled and ordered, "Mosh, tag." Mosh began chasing the children. The three of them played all afternoon.

13 On the way home, Carlos asked, "Mosh, did you run away intentionally so I could meet a new friend?" Mosh just winked.

Knowing the Words

Write the words from the story that have the meanings below.

1. sad _____
(Par. 1)

2. for a
reason _____
(Par. 13)

In each row below, circle the three words that belong together.

3. girl   robot   boy   child

4. street   sidewalk   yard   driveway

5. chase   run   ask   roll

6. start   down   behind   beside

7. sat   yell   look   cry

Working with Words

A **compound word** is made by combining two smaller words. Write a compound word using the underlined words in each sentence.

1. A <u>house</u> for a <u>dog</u> is a

_____.

2. A <u>yard</u> in <u>back</u> of a house is a

_____.

3. A <u>room</u> where you can <u>store</u> things

is a _____.

4. Days at the <u>end</u> of the <u>week</u> are

called the _____.

5. A <u>cup</u> used for <u>tea</u> is a

_____.

Reading and Thinking

1. Number the sentences to show the order in which things happened.

____ Mrs. Wilson picked flowers.

____ Mosh learned to play tag.

____ Carlos met Susan.

____ Mosh chased a girl.

2. Who is Mrs. Wilson? _____

_____

Write **T** if the sentence is true.
Write **F** if the sentence is false.

3. ____ Mrs. Wilson was angry.

4. ____ Mosh chased the girl away.

5. ____ Carlos was glad Mosh chased the girl.

6. What do you think it meant when Mosh winked at the end of the story?

_____

_____

7. Write **R** next to the two sentences that tell about real things.

____ Flowers can fly by themselves.

____ Robots can roll.

____ Children can meet new friends.

8. What do you think Carlos and Mosh did after they got home? _____

_____

Too Much Trash!

Read to find out how being in a hurry gets Carlos into trouble.

1   "Come on, Mosh, we have to put the trash cans next to the curb," Carlos said. "The trash won't be picked up if the cans aren't out in front of our house. Let's hurry because I want to get back to the broken alarm clock my dad gave me."

2   Carlos pulled one big trash can down the driveway. Mosh pulled the other can. Then Carlos hurried back inside to work on the clock. He got so busy he forgot everything else.

3   Suddenly Carlos jumped up. "I forgot Mosh!" he cried. He dashed out the door and came to a quick halt. Carlos couldn't believe his eyes. Every trash can in the neighborhood was out in front of the Garzas' house. He saw Mosh dragging the last can from the end of the block.

4   "Mosh, stop! These cans don't belong here," Carlos said angrily. "Take them back right now!"

5   The robot turned off its lights and stood still. Mosh refused to move. Carlos stopped to think about Mosh's behavior. He thought to himself, "This is no ordinary robot. Could it have feelings?"

6   "I guess it was my fault, too," Carlos said. "I told you the trash wouldn't be picked up if it wasn't in front of our house. I was only talking about our trash, not the neighbors'."

7   Carlos examined each trash can to try and figure out where each one belonged. Then he returned them to the right houses. He was worn out by the time he got home.

8   "I'm sorry I got mad at you, Mosh," Carlos said later. "It's just that sometimes you can be *too* helpful."

Knowing the Words

Write the words from the story that have the meanings below.

1. edge of the
   street _____
   (Par. 1)

2. mistake _____
   (Par. 6)

3. looked at
   closely _____
   (Par. 7)

Words that mean the same, or nearly the same, are called **synonyms.** Circle the pair of synonyms in each row.

4. hurried   whispered   dashed   picked

5. guess   sorry   halt   stop

6. busy   mad   happy   angry

7. big   small   large   quick

Write the word with the correct meaning to complete each sentence below.

8. Have you seen _____
   trash can? (hour, our)

9. I did not _____ the
   phone ring, did you? (here, hear)

Working with Words

An 's at the end of a word may be used to show that something belongs to someone. Add 's to each name in ( ) and write the new word in the blank.

1. _____ clock (Dad)

2. _____ lights (Mosh)

3. _____ room (Marie)

Reading and Thinking

1. Check the answer that tells what the story is mainly about.

   _____ fixing a clock

   _____ moving trash cans

   _____ getting angry

2. Mosh moved all of the neighbors'

   trash cans because _____

   _____.

3. Why do you think Mosh turned off its

   lights and would not move? _____

   _____

   _____

4. Was Carlos still angry at the end of the story? Explain your answer.

   _____

   _____

5. What do you think Mosh did after

   Carlos said he was sorry? _____

   _____

15

Where's my shirt?

What would you do if you went to get dressed and someone else's clothes were in your drawer?

1 "Carlos, are you done putting away the clean clothes so soon?" Marie asked.

2 "I taught Mosh how to do it," Carlos bragged. "I'm teaching Mosh to help me with all my work."

3 "Great, then you can spend your time doing things over when they're done wrong," Marie teased.

4 Carlos woke up the next day to see his dad standing by the bed. "Carlos, you put away the clothes yesterday, didn't you? Do you really expect me to build houses wearing this?" He was holding one of Marie's fancy pink blouses. "I don't think it will fit," he said. He tried to look angry, but there was a twinkle in his eyes.

5 Mrs. Garza came into the room. "Carlos, don't you think I would look silly wearing this to the office?" She had on Carlos's baseball T-shirt with her skirt.

6 Carlos couldn't help laughing at his mother's outfit. "I'm sorry. I taught the robot to put the clothes away. I guess it got mixed up."

7 Just then a cry came from the hallway. Marie stomped into Carlos's room. "I can't go shopping in Dad's work shirt. Where's my . . ." Marie stopped when she saw her mom wearing Carlos's shirt. "What's going on?" she asked.

8 Mr. Garza chuckled and said, "Our clothes are a little mixed up thanks to Mosh." Then Mr. Garza turned to Carlos and said, "Looks like your day will be spent getting our clothes back in the right places."

9 "That will take hours," Carlos moaned. He looked over at Mosh and frowned. He wasn't sure, but the robot looked as if it were almost laughing.

Knowing the Words

Write the words from the story that have the meanings below.

1. women's shirts _____
   (Par. 4)

2. sparkle _____
   (Par. 4)

3. set of
   clothes _____
   (Par. 6)

4. walked heavily _____
   (Par. 7)

Write the word with the correct meaning to complete each sentence below.

5. We rode our bicycles _____
   an hour this morning. (for, four)

6. Please _____ the screen
   door. (clothes, close)

7. This dark _____ came from
   a cherry tree. (would, wood)

8. Gina has _____ sharpened
   pencils. (two, to)

Working with Words

Say *city.* Circle the words below that have the sound *c* stands for in *city.*

1. fancy   can   since   clothes
2. center   expect   except   force

A word without any ending is a base word. The base word of *asked* is *ask.* Circle each base word below.

3. mixed   6. laughing
4. wearing   7. going
5. frowns   8. looked

Reading and Thinking

Write **T** if the sentence is true.
Write **F** if the sentence is false.

1. _____ Carlos's chore was to put away
   the clean clothes.

2. _____ Mr. Garza was too big for
   Marie's blouse.

3. _____ Mr. Garza was very angry.

4. _____ Carlos was not happy at the
   end of the story.

5. Whose shirt was Mrs. Garza

   wearing? _____

6. Marie stomped into Carlos's room

   because _____

   _____.

7. What do you think Carlos might do

   after he puts the clothes away? _____

   _____

The Big Push

Have you ever tried to use a machine that wasn't working quite right?

1   Carlos picked Mosh up off the ground. "I'm sorry, Mosh, I didn't mean to pitch the ball hard enough to knock you over. I guess you're not ready for baseball yet."

2   "I think I would like some lunch now," Susan said. "I'll go make some sandwiches for us while you two wait here."

3   After Susan left, Carlos sat on the swing. "I think it's time I taught you to push me in a swing, Mosh," he said. "Push just a little to get me started. Then, each time I swing back to you, push me away again."

4   Mosh pushed Carlos gently at first, then harder. Carlos thought he was going to fly right out of the swing. "Stop," Carlos told Mosh. But instead of stopping, Mosh pushed harder. Carlos felt dizzy. Again, he ordered the robot to stop, but Mosh kept pushing.

5   Carlos was getting worried. How would he ever get off this swing? Just then Susan came back with the sandwiches. "Can you get Mosh to stop?" Carlos yelled to her.

6   Susan told Mosh to stop, but the robot pushed the swing harder and harder. Then Susan remembered Mosh's battery. She jerked the cover off the robot's back and took out the battery. Mosh stopped instantly. Carlos waited for the swing to stop. His legs trembled as he got off.

7   "There must be something wrong with Mosh," Susan said.

8   When Carlos looked inside Mosh, he found some loose wires. "These wires must have come loose when the baseball hit it," he said.

9   Carlos fixed Mosh. Then he said to the robot, "You are as good as new now. I won't ever ask you to push me in a swing again, though. If you had pushed me any harder, I would have been the first kid in space."

Knowing the Words

Write the words from the story that have the meanings below.

1. right away _____
(Par. 6)

2. shook _____
(Par. 6)

Some words are spelled the same but have different meanings. For example, *can* might mean "something that food comes in" or "able to do something."

Look at the list of words below. For each pair of sentences, one word from the list will correctly complete both. Choose the correct word to fill in the blanks for each pair of sentences.

fly   left   like

3. That kite looks just _____ mine.

I really _____ to watch circus performers.

4. Do you have any money _____?

Do you write with your _____ hand?

5. How do you think birds _____?

The _____ walked on the table.

Working with Words

Fill in each blank with the correct letters to make a word.

kn   igh   wr   ph

1. _____ong   3. _____ee

2. r_____t   4. micro_____one

Reading and Thinking

1. Number the sentences to show the order in which things happened.

_____ Susan removed Mosh's battery.

_____ Carlos taught Mosh to push a swing.

_____ Mosh was knocked down by a baseball.

_____ Carlos fixed Mosh's wires.

2. Check two words that tell how Carlos probably felt when Mosh wouldn't obey him.

_____ frightened   _____ amused

_____ bored   _____ confused

3. Mosh wouldn't stop pushing the

swing because _____

_____.

4. What did Susan do to get Mosh to

stop? _____

5. Check two sentences that tell how Carlos and Susan are alike.

_____ They both own a robot.

_____ They are both children.

_____ They had trouble with Mosh.

Write the best word to complete each sentence below.

6. Do you _____ when you are scared? (command, tremble, push)

7. Barb felt _____ when she got off the ride. (ready, new, dizzy)

19

More Than Just Worms

How can you tell that seeds have been planted in a certain area?

1 "I'm glad you are going fishing with us today," Carlos said to Susan. "We will be leaving in a couple of hours, so let's dig up some worms now. Mosh can help, and it won't take long."

2 Carlos got a small shovel and a can for the worms. "Do not dig where grass or flowers are growing, Mosh," Carlos explained. He showed the robot how to dig up the worms and put them into the can. "You finish this. Susan and I will get the rest of the stuff ready."

3 The children went into the house and packed a picnic lunch. When they were finished, Susan looked out the window. "I hate to say this, but Mosh is digging up Mrs. Wilson's garden," she said.

4 Carlos dashed outside. "Mosh, stop!" he yelled. He rushed over to Mrs. Wilson's yard. "I know you can't see anything growing, but Mrs. Wilson planted seeds here this morning."

5 Carlos knew he had to tell Mrs. Wilson. He knocked on her door. When Mrs. Wilson opened the door, Carlos said shyly, "My robot accidentally dug up your seeds. Mosh was digging worms for our fishing trip. I'll buy more seeds and stay home to plant them."

6 "Those seeds can wait a day," Mrs. Wilson said. "I wouldn't want you to miss out on a fishing trip. I know how much fun that is." She gave a little sigh. "I haven't been fishing in years."

7 "Would you like to go with us?" Carlos asked.

8 Mrs. Wilson's face lit up. "I would love to. I think I still have my old fishing pole somewhere around here."

9 "Don't worry about worms," Carlos said. "Thanks to Mosh, we have enough to catch every fish in the lake."

Knowing the Words

Write the words from the story that have the meanings below.

1. not done on
   purpose _____
   (Par. 5)

2. bother _____
   (Par. 9)

Choose the correct word below to fill in the blanks for each pair of sentences.

can   yard

3. This _____ does not have a label on it.

   I _____ finish my homework in fifteen minutes.

4. A deer is in the _____.

   Joan bought a _____ of ribbon.

Working with Words

A **suffix** is a group of letters added to the end of a word that changes the meaning of the word. The suffix **-ly** helps tell how something was done. *Shyly* means "done in a shy way."

Add **-ly** to the words below. Use the new words to complete the sentences.

accidental   sad   loud

1. Gretchen watched _____ as her friend rode away.

2. Steve _____ spilled his apple juice.

3. Agnes laughed _____

Reading and Thinking

1. Check the answer that tells what the story is mainly about.

   _____ digging for worms

   _____ going fishing

   _____ talking to Mrs. Wilson

2. Mosh dug up Mrs. Wilson's garden

   because _____

   _____.

3. What kind of person do you think Carlos is? Explain your answer.

   _____

   _____

Read each set of sentences below. Fill in each blank.

4. The seeds were planted yesterday. They haven't started growing yet.

   They stands for _____.

5. Lucy and I are the same age. We go to school together.

   We stands for _____.

21

Surprise!

What would you expect to find in a suitcase?

1   "Carlos, would you get my suitcase when you get the fishing poles?" asked Marie. "I'm staying over at Jane's tonight."

2   Carlos got the fishing poles and Marie's suitcase. He gave the suitcase to Mosh and said, "Would you take this to Marie while I take these poles out to the car? Then look for something with a lid to put these worms in. We don't want them to crawl all over the car."

3   After Carlos put the poles in the car, he came back inside to help Mosh with the worms. "OK," he said to the robot, "what did you find to put the worms in?" Mosh didn't move. Carlos looked around, but he didn't see the worms anywhere.

4   Just then a scream came from Marie's room. "Carlos Garza, get in here this second!"

5   Carlos's face turned pale. "Mosh, you didn't put them in Marie's suitcase, did you?" he gasped. Carlos hurried into Marie's bedroom.

6   Marie spoke angrily as she pointed to her suitcase. "This is the worst thing that pile of bolts has ever done!"

7   "I'm sorry," Carlos apologized. "Mosh was just trying to find something with a lid on it."

8   "Those worms have probably ruined my suitcase. What am I going to do?" Marie cried.

9   "Take my suitcase," Carlos offered. "I'll clean this one out. It will be as good as new."

10   Carlos took Marie's suitcase outside and opened it up. He was putting the worms back into the can when Susan came by with her fishing pole. She gave Carlos a strange look. "I've never seen anyone carry their worms in a suitcase before," she said with a chuckle.

11   Carlos grumbled, "Mosh still has a lot to learn."

Knowing the Words

Write the words from the story that have the meanings below.

1. breathed in
   quickly _____
   (Par. 5)

2. said you
   were sorry _____
   (Par. 7)

Choose the correct word to fill in the blanks for each pair of sentences.

> spoke   second

3. The alarm clock will ring any

   _____ now.

   Tracy sits in the _____ seat
   in the first row.

4. Donna _____ in a whisper.
   The wheel on Ann's bike has a

   broken _____.

Working with Words

Words are sometimes easier to read if they are divided into parts called **syllables.** Some words have two consonants between two vowels. These words can be divided into syllables between the consonants, as in *ex/pect.*

In each word below, draw a line to divide the word into syllables.

1. welcome
2. perhaps
3. forgive
4. awful

5. temper
6. blossom
7. traffic
8. borrow

Reading and Thinking

Write **T** if the sentence is true.
Write **F** if the sentence is false.

1. _____ Mosh put the worms in Marie's suitcase.

2. _____ Marie was upset when she saw the worms.

3. _____ Susan thought it was funny to see the worms in the suitcase.

4. What two things did Mosh do while Carlos put the fishing poles in the

   car? _____

   _____

5. Why do you think Marie called Mosh

   a pile of bolts? _____

   _____

6. What do you think Carlos will do after he cleans out the suitcase?

   _____

   _____

Write the best word to complete each sentence below.

7. The baby was _____
   through the grass. (putting, finding, crawling)

8. Jenny _____ the can of soup. (opened, grumbled, stayed)

9. Rose wore a _____ blue blouse. (round, pale, plenty)

The Fishing Trip

How long do you think it takes to catch a fish?

1 "Dad, can Mosh go fishing with us?" Carlos asked. "After all, Mosh dug up the worms for us."

2 "All right," his dad sighed. "Just try to keep Mosh out of trouble for a few hours."

3 When they got to the lake, Carlos and Susan took Mosh to one side of the dock. Mr. Garza and Mrs. Wilson sat on the other side. Carlos showed Mosh how to throw the line into the water. To Carlos and Susan's surprise, Mosh started making a high-pitched whistling noise. A few seconds later, Mosh's pole was bent over like a rainbow.

4 "You've got a fish, Mosh. Pull it in!" Carlos cried. He helped Mosh pull in the fish. Mosh threw the line back into the lake. The funny whistling noise started again. Soon Mosh, Carlos, and Susan all had fish pulling on their lines.

5 "Hey!" Carlos said excitedly, "Mosh knows how to call the fish."

6 "Carlos, I'm sure there are just more fish on your side of the dock," his dad said.

7 "Can we trade sides to see?" Carlos asked. He, Susan, and Mosh traded places with Mr. Garza. Mrs. Wilson stayed on the side with Mosh just in case Carlos was right.

8 As soon as they had their hooks in the lake, Mosh began to make the noise. "I've got one!" Mrs. Wilson cried.

9 Mr. Garza kept looking back at all the fish the others were catching. He still hadn't caught one fish. Finally, he took his pole and moved next to Mosh. Carlos looked at his father and smiled. Mr. Garza winked.

10 "This is pretty good luck, isn't it?" Carlos said. "Mosh sure is a special robot. Do you think it could've been used in a fishing ad?"

Knowing the Words

Write the word from the story that has the meaning below.

1. high sounding _____
(Par. 3)

Circle the pair of antonyms (opposites) in each row.

2. pushing crying pulling whistling

3. soon bent side straight

4. later other right wrong

5. started winked finished cried

Working with Words

Write a contraction from the story for each pair of words below.

1. you have _____
(Par. 4)

2. I am _____
(Par. 6)

3. I have _____
(Par. 8)

4. had not _____
(Par. 9)

5. could have _____
(Par. 10)

Circle the correct letters to complete each word and write them in the blank.

6. Did Jennifer or Mary go f____st?

or ir ar

7. Will you ____der spaghetti?

or ir ar

8. Let's go ov____ to my house.

er ar or

9. Do you h____ any strange noises?

are ear ore

Reading and Thinking

1. Number the sentences to show the order in which things happened.

____ Mrs. Wilson caught a fish.

____ Carlos showed Mosh how to fish.

____ Carlos and Susan traded places with Carlos's dad.

____ Mr. Garza sat next to Mosh.

2. Write **R** next to the two sentences that tell about real things.

____ Worms are used to catch fish.

____ Rainbows can be used to catch fish.

____ Fish can be on one side of a dock and not the other.

3. The fish were biting because _____

_____.

4. What do you think will happen when Carlos's dad is sitting next to Mosh?

_____

_____

_____

Write the best word to complete each sentence below.

5. The fish on Lin's _____ was a foot long. (water, hook, lake)

6. Pat put the boat next to the

_____. (dock, noise, rainbow)

25

Sara and Bill

Read to find out how Mosh teaches a lesson without saying a word.

1 "Dad, Mrs. Wilson's grandchildren are visiting her. Their names are Sara and Bill," Carlos said.

2 "Hmm, those are the names I saw on those papers in our yard," Mr. Garza said. "Will you please go out and clean up the mess?"

3 "Sure," Carlos answered. "Come on, Mosh." Carlos showed the robot how to help pick up the papers and put them in the trash can. Soon the yard was clean.

4 That afternoon Carlos went over to get to know Sara and Bill. Mrs. Wilson served them lemonade at the picnic table. As soon as Sara put her cup down, Mosh picked it up and took it over to the trash can. Mosh did the same when Bill put his cup down.

5 "Mosh doesn't have to do that," Mrs. Wilson said. "Sara and Bill can clean up their own messes."

6 "Yeah, we don't need a dumb robot to pick up our stuff," Sara snapped.

7 "What about all your papers that blew into our yard?" Carlos asked.

8 Sara looked innocently at Carlos. "What papers?" she asked.

9 Before Carlos could answer, Mosh came across the yard with the trash can. The robot turned it over. All the papers went on Sara's lap. "What are you doing?" Sara cried, surprised.

10 Mrs. Wilson looked at the papers. "Why, Sara, aren't these your pictures?

And these papers have your name on them, Bill. It appears that Carlos and Mosh really have been cleaning up after you. Say you're sorry and then clean up this mess," she said, frowning.

11 Sara and Bill were not happy with Carlos when he left, but he didn't care. He put his arm around his one-of-a-kind friend. "Good going, Mosh," he said. "Actions *do* speak louder than words."

Knowing the Words

Write the words from the story that have the meanings below.

1. said in a
   mean way _____
   (Par. 6)

2. without fault _____
   (Par. 8)

3. looks like _____
   (Par. 10)

Synonyms are words that have the same or nearly the same meaning. Circle the pair of synonyms in each row.

4. paper   stuff   garbage   trash

5. cleaned   served   put   gave

Working with Words

When a word ends with a vowel and a consonant, the consonant is usually doubled before adding **-ed** or **-ing.** For example, *snap + ed = snapped.*

Double the last consonant in the word in ( ). Then add **-ed** or **-ing** to the word to make a word that completes each sentence.

1. Are you _____ that book on the shelf? (put)

2. Joan _____ on the ice. (slip)

3. Lou is always _____ that toy around. (drag)

Fill in each blank with the correct letters to make a word.

        wr   igh   mb

4. du _____ 5. _____ite 6. h_____

Reading and Thinking

1. Check the answer that tells what the story is mainly about.

   _____ drinking lemonade

   _____ learning a lesson

   _____ going to Mrs. Wilson's

2. What did Mrs. Wilson serve to the

   kids? _____

3. Why did Mosh throw Sara and Bill's cups away as soon as they were

   finished? _____

   _____

4. What do you think Carlos meant when he called Mosh a "one-of-a-

   kind friend"? _____

   _____

5. Why do you think Mosh dumped the

   papers in Sara's lap? _____

   _____

Disappearing Newspapers

People are calling to say they didn't get the newspapers. What do you think happened to the papers?

1 "Let's get these newspapers ready to go, Mosh," Carlos said. "Since we're still new at this, I want to prove that we can do a good job."

2 Carlos rolled up his papers and put rubber bands around them. Mosh put them into the bag. Then Carlos delivered the papers to the people on his route. He did not notice that Mosh had followed him with the trash can. As soon as Carlos finished, he took his bag home and then ran to Susan's house.

3 When Carlos got home, Marie was quite upset. "Why didn't you deliver your papers today?" she asked. "A lot of people have called to complain."

4 "What do you mean?" Carlos asked, puzzled. "I did that before I went to my friend's house."

5 "Well, the phone has not stopped ringing for the last two hours," Marie said. "Everyone says the same thing. They didn't get their papers today."

6 "Gee, fifty papers can't just vanish," Carlos mumbled. He took a walk around his route. He could not find one newspaper. Then he remembered that he had just taught Mosh to put papers in the trash. Carlos raced home. When he looked inside the trash can, he saw a pile of neatly folded newspapers.

7 Carlos found Mosh. "Did you put all of those papers in the trash?" he asked. The robot's green eyes flashed.

8 "Mosh," Carlos said, trying to be patient, "I know I told you that papers belong in the trash, but I meant ones that people don't want anymore. People like to read their newspapers before they throw them away. Now I have to deliver them all again."

9 Carlos put the papers back into his bag. "You stay here, Mosh," he said. "I'm too tired to let you help me right now."

Knowing the Words

Write the words from the story that have the meanings below.

1. talk about things that are wrong _____
(Par. 3)

2. confused _____
(Par. 4)

3. said in a low voice _____
(Par. 6)

4. calm _____
(Par. 8)

In each row below, circle the three words that belong together.

5. taught   learned   remembered   have

6. hour   deliver   newspaper   route

7. phone   ring   trash   talk

Choose the correct word below to fill in the blanks for each pair of sentences.

ring   saw

8. I _____ Jill at school.

This _____ is too dull.

9. We hear the bell _____ every day at noon.

This _____ does not fit my finger.

Reading and Thinking

1. Where did Carlos find the newspapers? _____

2. The papers had to be delivered twice because _____ _____.

Write **T** if the sentence is true.
Write **F** if the sentence is false.

3. _____ Mosh helped deliver the papers.

4. _____ Carlos had not been delivering papers for very long.

5. _____ Susan told Carlos where he could find the newspapers.

6. What do you think Carlos did after he delivered the papers again? _____
_____

Learning to Study

Number each list of words below in alphabetical order.

1. _____ rush
_____ remember
_____ robot
_____ ring

2. _____ trash
_____ tell
_____ too
_____ that

3. _____ finish
_____ flash
_____ friend
_____ found

4. _____ mumble
_____ many
_____ Mosh
_____ meant

Car Wash

Have you ever been surprised by someone with a hose?

1 "Carlos, if you help me baby-sit for Sara and Bill, I'll share the money with you," Marie said.

2 Carlos paused to think. "Well, I do need money to buy a new battery for Mosh," he said.

3 "Great," Marie said happily. "Let's go!"

4 Marie and Carlos walked over to Mrs. Wilson's. At noon, Marie went inside to fix some lunch. Carlos stayed outside with a book. He wanted to keep an eye on Sara and Bill.

5 "We're going to play car wash," Sara announced. "Do you want to play?"

6 "No, thanks," Carlos said. "I'll just sit here and read my book."

7 Sara and Bill pretended they were washing everything in the yard. They washed the lawn chairs, the picnic table, and the birdbath.

8 Then Sara yelled, "Look at that dirty car!"

9 Carlos looked up and saw Bill pointing the hose at him. "I'm glad that hose isn't turned on," Carlos chuckled. He went back to reading. Then he thought, "I wonder where Sara is?" Carlos looked up just in time to see water shoot out of the hose and spray all over him.

10 Carlos jumped up and tried to run away, but it was already too late. He was soaked. "Turn that off!" Carlos screamed. "Sara, why did you do that?"

11 "I'm sorry," Sara said. "I really didn't think the water would spray that far."

12 "The water did cool me off," Carlos admitted, "but from now on, please wash your pretend cars with pretend water."

Knowing the Words

Write the word from the story that has the meaning below.

1. stopped for
   a moment _____
   (Par. 2)

Check the meaning that fits the underlined word in each sentence.

2. Sue tried to <u>fix</u> the clock.

   _____ prepare

   _____ repair

3. The <u>wash</u> was hung on the fence.

   _____ clean with water

   _____ clothes being cleaned

Working with Words

Write a compound word using the underlined words in each sentence.

1. A place where a <u>bird</u> can take a <u>bath</u>

   is a _____.

2. The <u>time</u> when you eat <u>lunch</u> is

   called _____.

An 's at the end of a word is used to show that something belongs to one person or thing. To show that something belongs to more than one person or thing, an apostrophe (') is added to the end of a plural word that ends in s.

Circle each group of words below that shows that more than one person or thing owns something.

3. book's pages   5. kids' games

4. cars' wheels   6. Sara's chair

Reading and Thinking

1. Number the sentences to show the order in which things happened.

   _____ Carlos was sprayed with water.

   _____ Marie and Carlos agreed to baby-sit.

   _____ Marie started to fix lunch.

   _____ Sara apologized.

2. What kind of a person do you think

   Sara is? Explain your answer. _____

   _____

3. Write two ways in which Sara and Bill's car wash was different from a

   real car wash. _____

   _____

4. Who turned the water on when

   Carlos got sprayed? _____

5. Did Carlos stay mad at Sara? _____

   How do you know? _____

   _____

Write the best word to complete each sentence below.

6. Jane _____ the sponge
   in the sink. (asked, soaked, pretended)

7. Ruth _____ when the bee
   stung her. (cried, chuckled, ate)

31

Rabbit-Sitting

Read to find out what happens when Mosh becomes jealous of a rabbit.

1   Carlos set the rabbit cage in his room. "I'm glad Susan asked me to watch Fluffy while she is at camp," Carlos said to Mosh.

2   Mosh rolled over to the cage to investigate. The rabbit backed up into a corner and shook. "Get away, Mosh. You are scaring Fluffy," Carlos explained.

3   When Carlos took Fluffy out of the cage, Mosh tried to pet the rabbit. "Don't, Mosh," Carlos said, "you might hurt her." Mosh rolled into a corner and turned off its lights.

4   Carlos played with Fluffy all morning. He locked the rabbit in the cage when he went to eat lunch. When he came back, the cage was empty. Carlos was frantic as he searched all over the house for the missing rabbit. He could not find Fluffy anywhere.

5   Carlos rushed back to his room. "Mosh, did you let that rabbit out of the cage?" he asked. "Why would you do such a thing? Were you trying to play with Fluffy or were you jealous because I was playing with her instead of with you?"

6   Mosh turned around and faced the wall. Carlos thought, "This robot is amazing. It has feelings!" He couldn't help smiling. "So that's it! You are jealous," he said, slightly amused. "Mosh, that rabbit will never take your place. I like her, but I love you. You're my own special helper, remember? Now show me what you did with Fluffy."

7   Mosh rolled over to the closet and opened the door. Inside was a cozy bed made of towels. Fluffy was safely asleep.

8   Carlos grinned. "Let's get her back into the cage," he said. "Or maybe it would be safer to leave Fluffy out and lock you in the cage," he teased.

Knowing the Words

Write the words from the story that have the meanings below.

1. look into _____
(Par. 2)

2. wanting something that
someone else has _____
(Par. 5)

3. a little bit _____
(Par. 6)

4. cloths used
for drying _____
(Par. 7)

Working with Words

Some words that have one consonant between two vowels are divided into syllables after the first vowel. The first vowel sound in these words is most often long, as in *bā/by*.

Other words that have one consonant between two vowels are divided after the consonant. In these words, the first vowel is most often short, as in *wăg/on*.

The words below have been divided into syllables. Put a mark above the first vowel in each word to show if the vowel stands for a long or short sound. Mark the long vowels with ‾ over the letter. Mark the short vowels with �‿.

1. nev/er   **4.** clos/et   **7.** si/lent

2. co/zy   **5.** sev/en   **8.** po/ny

3. pal/ace   **6.** pi/lot   **9.** la/dy

Say *gentle*. Circle the words below that have the sound *g* stands for in *gentle*.

10. cage   get   page   hedge

11. giant   age   agree   gum

12. gift   edge   engine   garden

Reading and Thinking

1. Check the answer that tells what the story is mainly about.

_____ playing with Mosh

_____ camping out

_____ taking care of Fluffy

2. Why did Fluffy sit in the corner of her cage and shake? _____

_____

3. Mosh put the rabbit in the closet because _____

_____.

4. Did Mosh hurt the rabbit? _____

How do you know? _____

_____

5. What do you think Carlos and Mosh did after they put Fluffy back in her cage? _____

_____

A Pet for Carlos

Have you ever been frightened by something you thought you saw?

1   "I miss Susan's rabbit," Carlos sighed. "I wish I had a soft, furry pet. It's too bad that I'm not allowed to have pets." Suddenly Carlos snapped his fingers and said, "I know, I'll make Mosh my pet."

2   Carlos wrapped Mosh in an old brown rug. Then he put one of Marie's shaggy winter hats over Mosh's head. "You look great, Mosh," Carlos said when he finished. "Let's show Marie."

3   Marie was in the den reading a magazine. She looked up as Carlos and Mosh entered the room and asked, "What are you two doing now?"

4   "Mosh is my new pet," Carlos said proudly.

5   "Pet!" Marie laughed. "It looks more like a monster that you should keep hidden."

6   Carlos decided to call Tommy, a friend from his old neighborhood. He wanted to tell Tommy all about Mosh. "I wish you could move here, too," Carlos said.

7   When Mosh heard the word *move,* he rolled out the door. Carlos heard screaming outside. He looked out and saw kids running in all directions, looking very frightened. "A monster!" he heard one child yell.

8   Carlos quickly said good-bye to Tommy and hung up the phone. He dashed outside and saw Mosh rolling down the sidewalk. The kids were all running away from the disguised robot. "Mosh, stop!" Carlos yelled when he caught up with it. He pulled off Mosh's hat so everyone would see it wasn't really a monster.

9   "I don't know why people were afraid of you," Carlos said. "I think you make a great pet. I guess people just aren't used to seeing pets with wheels."

Knowing the Words

Write the words from the story that have the meanings below.

1. covered with hair _____
   (Par. 1)

2. dressed up so you
   can't be recognized _____
   (Par. 8)

Circle the pair of antonyms (opposites) in each row.

3. neighbor   friend   beast   enemy

4. quickly   loudly   slowly   sadly

5. shaggy   soft   hard   gentle

6. great   huge   terrible   old

Learning to Study

The word you look up in a dictionary is called an **entry word.** Many words that have endings are not listed as entry words. To find these words, look up the base word to which the ending is added. To find the word *sighed*, look up *sigh.* Write the word under which each of these words would be listed in a dictionary.

1. wheels _____

2. reading _____

3. rolled _____

4. wanted _____

5. screaming _____

6. suddenly _____

7. directions _____

Reading and Thinking

1. How was Mosh like a pet when Carlos finished dressing it up?

   _____

   _____

2. What did Marie say Mosh looked

   like? _____

3. Mosh rolled out the door because

   _____.

Write **T** if the sentence is true.
Write **F** if the sentence is false.

4. _____ Mosh was dressed up to look like an animal.

5. _____ Carlos missed his friend.

6. _____ Carlos watched Mosh roll out of the house.

7. _____ The kids were afraid of Mosh's wheels.

The First Day of School

How would you feel about going to a new school?

1 "I'm kind of nervous about going to a new school," Carlos told Susan as they walked to school. "Look, everyone is staring at me."

2 Susan looked around. "They aren't staring at you. Look behind you."

3 Carlos looked back. "Oh, no," he moaned. "Mosh, you can't come to school! What am I going to do? There's no time to take Mosh back home."

4 "We can hide Mosh in the closet where the cleaning supplies are kept," Susan suggested. Susan and Carlos went into the building through the back door so that nobody would see them. They put a rag over the robot and hid it in the back of the closet.

5 Carlos forgot about Mosh once school started. He liked his teacher, Mrs. Bell, and the kids in his class. Everything was fine until Mrs. Bell spilled some paint on the floor. She asked a boy named Chad to get the mop. Carlos felt sick.

6 Soon Chad came rushing back into the room. He was pushing Mosh. "Look what I found!" he said, looking surprised. Carlos wanted to hide.

7 "I wonder if our new principal, Mr. Lee, knows anything about this?" Mrs. Bell said aloud.

8 Carlos didn't want Mrs. Bell to take Mosh to the office. He raised his hand and said, "It's mine. It followed me to school today, so I hid it in the closet."

9 "You have your own robot?" Mrs. Bell asked, sounding pleased. "Tell us about it."

10 Carlos told the class that Mosh was a one-of-a-kind robot. He showed them some of the special things Mosh could do. The children listened with interest while Carlos spoke.

11 On the way home from school, Carlos said to Mosh, "Thanks to you, all the kids in school know me already. But from now on, you stay home and try to keep out of trouble while I go to school."

Knowing the Words

Write the word from the story that has the meaning below.

1. things used to
   do a job _____
   (Par. 4)

Synonyms are words that have the same or nearly the same meaning. Circle the pair of synonyms in each row.

2. spill   rush   start   hurry

3. stare   hide   look   push

4. suggest   like   stay   remain

Learning to Study

At the top of each page in a dictionary are two words in dark print called **guide words.** They can help you find other words in the dictionary. The first guide word tells what the first word is on the page. The second guide word tells what the last word is on the page.

The words in a dictionary are listed in alphabetical order. To find a word, decide if it comes in alphabetical order between the guide words on the page. If it does, the word will be on that page. Check two words that could be found on each page that has these guide words.

1. **mop/nobody**
   _____ push
   _____ named
   _____ nervous

2. **paint/robot**
   _____ push
   _____ sound
   _____ principal

3. **closet/door**
   _____ cried
   _____ did
   _____ back

4. **school/teacher**
   _____ surprise
   _____ stare
   _____ thanks

Reading and Thinking

1. Number the sentences to show the order in which things happened.

   _____ Mrs. Bell spilled some paint.

   _____ Carlos showed the class some of the things Mosh could do.

   _____ Mosh followed Carlos and Susan to school.

   _____ Chad found Mosh.

2. Where did Carlos and Susan hide

   Mosh? _____

3. The children hid Mosh because _____

   _____.

Write the best word to complete each sentence below.

4. Alice hung her winter coat in the

   _____. (sink, tent, closet)

5. Do you know the name of the

   _____ at our school? (command, trouble, principal)

Too Cold

Read to find out what Carlos learns about asking Mosh for help.

1   "Carlos, go take your bath and get ready for bed," Marie said. "Hurry! Mom and Dad will be home soon."

2   Carlos was almost finished with a book and didn't want to stop until he knew how the story ended. "Mosh, please go fill the bathtub with water," he said.

3   A few minutes later, Carlos finished the book. He went to check on Mosh. Carlos gasped when he saw the bathtub. "Turn off the water, Mosh! I didn't mean for you to fill it to the top."

4   As he climbed into the bathtub, Carlos scowled. The water was colder than he liked. "Could you get something warm for me to wear when I get out of here?" he asked Mosh.

5   Just as Carlos got out of the tub, Mosh returned with something for Carlos to wear. Carlos looked at it and moaned. "Mosh, I meant something of my own, not my dad's robe."

6   Carlos put on the robe. He hoped he could get to his bedroom without falling. Just as he started down the hall, he heard his parents coming to say good night. Carlos took one step and tripped over the long robe.

7   "Carlos, what are you doing?" his mom asked.

8   Carlos lay on the floor, looking up at his parents. "I asked Mosh to get me something warm to wear. I forgot to say I wanted something of my own."

9   Carlos's mom and dad couldn't help laughing. At last his mom said, "I guess you need to choose your words more carefully when you give Mosh an order."

10   "You can say that again," Carlos said, nodding.

Knowing the Words

Write the words from the story that have the meanings below.

1. investigate _____
   (Par. 3)

2. looked angry _____
   (Par. 4)

Choose the correct word below to fill in the blanks for each pair of sentences.

           top   check

3. Leah watched the _____ spin.

   My paper is on _____.

4. Did you _____ the spelling of the words in that story?

   Brenda wrote a _____ to pay for the movie tickets.

Learning to Study

The meanings of words can be found in the dictionary. Some words have more than one meaning. Look at the words and their meanings below. Answer the questions.

trip **1** to fall **2** journey
try to work at
tub container for water

1. Which word means "container for water"? _____

2. What does the word *try* mean?

   _____

3. What is the first meaning of *trip*?

   _____

Reading and Thinking

Write **T** if the sentence is true.
Write **F** if the sentence is false.

1. ____ Marie was baby-sitting for Carlos.

2. ____ Carlos was happy with the water in the bathtub.

3. ____ Carlos is much shorter than his dad.

4. ____ Carlos's parents were angry with him.

5. What was Carlos doing when Marie told him to go take a bath? _____

   _____

6. What do you think Carlos did after he spoke to his parents? _____

   _____

Write the best word to complete each sentence below.

7. Vickie wrote a funny _____ about a robot. (menu, story, word)

8. Put the shirt in the _____ when you take it off. (drawer, bathtub, garage)

9. I can't understand you when you _____. (laugh, mumble, ask)

10. I think I should _____ my brown pants today. (hurry, hear, wear)

Mosh Speaks

Have you ever tried to fool someone but ended up being sorry you did?

1   "I hope this plan of ours works, Susan," Carlos said as the two of them walked to school with Mosh. "If it does, then Lizzy Wood won't call Mosh a dumb robot any more."

2   "It will work," Susan said. "All you have to do is read the questions from each card in order. The tape player inside Mosh will answer them. Everyone will think Mosh knows how to talk. What could go wrong?"

3   When it was time for sharing, Carlos was chosen to go first. He was so excited that he dropped his cards with the questions on them. Quickly, Carlos picked up the cards and turned on the tape player.

4   "Hi, kids. It's nice to be here today," the voice inside Mosh said. "Carlos, why don't you ask me some questions?"

5   "All right, Mosh, who teaches our class?" Carlos asked.

6   "A kangaroo," answered Mosh. The class roared with laughter. Carlos wished he could stop, but it was too late. The tape was already rolling.

7   "What hops and carries babies in a pouch?" Carlos continued.

8   "Mrs. Bell," Mosh said. The class laughed even harder.

9   "What a dumb robot," Lizzy yelled. Carlos wished he could vanish.

10   "I don't know how he did it, but I think it was clever of Carlos to get Mosh to talk," Mrs. Bell said, smiling.

11   Carlos felt better. But he decided not to play tricks again. He and Mosh got into enough trouble without them.

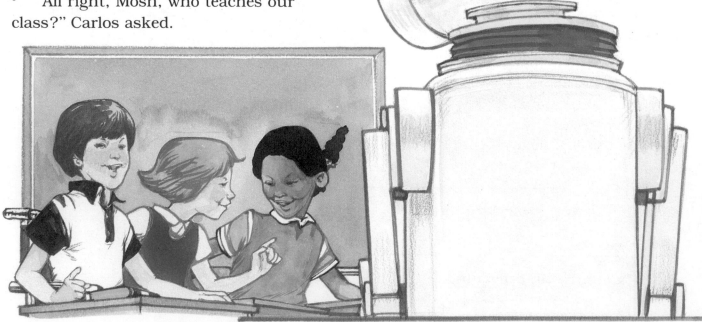

Knowing the Words

Write the words from the story that have the meanings below.

1. a special way
   things are arranged _____
   (Par. 2)

2. doing with others _____
   (Par. 3)

3. small sack _____
   (Par. 7)

Working with Words

A **prefix** is a group of letters added to the beginning of a word that changes the meaning of the word. The prefix **re-** means "again." *Rewire* means "wire again."

Read the words below. Write the correct word next to its meaning.

reread   reorder   reteach   rewrap

1. teach again _____

2. order again _____

3. read again _____

4. wrap again _____

Most words that end in a consonant followed by *y* are made plural by changing the *y* to *i* and adding *es*. The plural of *city* is *cities*. Write the plural form of each word below.

5. baby _____

6. company _____

7. penny _____

Reading and Thinking

1. Check the answer that tells what the story is mainly about.

   _____ trying to fool the class

   _____ teaching Mosh to speak

   _____ dropping the question cards

Write **T** if the sentence is true.
Write **F** if the sentence is false.

2. _____ Carlos was trying to teach Lizzy Wood a lesson.

3. _____ When Carlos picked up his cards, they were not in the right order.

4. _____ Something was wrong with the tape player inside Mosh.

5. _____ Carlos's trick taught him a lesson.

Write the best word to complete each sentence below.

6. During the show, Pat made a penny _____. (sing, vanish, wish)

7. Elsa _____ her books on the way to school. (dropped, played, roared)

8. Please write one _____ to ask our guest. (card, answer, question)

9. Jamie gave a _____ answer. (honor, hollow, clever)

10. The children's _____ filled the room. (laughter, book, tape)

41

Captain Carlos

Have you ever been disappointed? How did you act?

1   "This is the day Mrs. Bell tells who will be the captain of the astronauts in our school play," Susan said to Carlos. "Are you nervous?"

2   "A little," Carlos replied. "I would really like the part, but Lizzy tried out for it, too. She did a very good job."

3   "Well, I'm sure you did a great job, too," Susan said. "And I hope you get to be the captain."

4   That day Mrs. Bell asked if she could talk to Carlos and Lizzy at recess. "I had a hard time deciding who should be the captain in our play," she said. "You were both very good, so I am going to add another part. Carlos, I would like you to be the captain. Lizzy, I would like you to be the first officer."

5   "Will I get to say much?" Lizzy asked as she frowned.

6   "I can tell you're disappointed, Lizzy, but I promise you will have as much to say as Carlos does," Mrs. Bell said calmly. She went on to say, "Carlos, I think Mosh would be good to have in the play, too. What do you think?"

7   "Sure," Carlos agreed. Lizzy sighed and walked away.

8   After school, Carlos walked home with Susan. "I'm so excited about the play!" he said.

9   Just then Lizzy rode up on her bike. "I hope your robot doesn't act up on the night of the play," Lizzy snapped. Then she rode away, leaving Carlos and Susan to wonder what she meant.

Knowing the Words

Write the words from the story that have the meanings below.

1. worried _____
   (Par. 1)

2. what a person in a
   play says and does _____
   (Par. 2)

3. let down;
   unhappy _____
   (Par. 6)

Check the meaning that fits the underlined word in each sentence.

4. Carrie went to the park to <u>play</u>.

   _____ have fun

   _____ a show on stage

5. Did Janice eat <u>part</u> of this apple?

   _____ in a play

   _____ a small piece of something

6. Did you hear the limb <u>snap</u>?

   _____ break suddenly

   _____ speak angrily

Working with Words

Write the two words that were used to form each of these contractions.

1. I'm _____

2. you're _____

3. we'll _____

4. isn't _____

5. don't _____

6. doesn't _____

Reading and Thinking

1. Check the answer that tells what the story is mainly about.

   _____ getting a part in the school play

   _____ Lizzy's part in the play

   _____ walking to school

2. Write two words to describe Lizzy.

   _____

3. Carlos wasn't sure he would get to be the captain in the play because

   _____

   _____.

4. What part was Lizzy asked to play?

   _____

5. Why was Lizzy unhappy? _____

   _____

43

Trouble on Stage

Have you ever been in a play? Read to find out how Carlos's school play went.

1   On the night of the school play, the stage looked like the inside of a spaceship. The curtain opened. Captain Carlos walked onto the stage. "Mosh, bring me the space maps," he called clearly.

2   Mosh rolled out onto the stage and turned around in circles. "Mosh, bring me the space maps," Carlos said even louder.

3   Mosh just moved in bigger circles. Carlos didn't know what to do. Something was terribly wrong with Mosh. Carlos guessed right away that Lizzy had something to do with this.

4   "Mosh, I think you have a little space sickness," Carlos said as if it were part of the play. "Go rest." Carlos pushed Mosh behind the curtain. Then he said, "Send in the first officer with my space maps."

5   "Here are the maps, Sir," Lizzy said loudly. She gave Carlos a mean smile.

6   Carlos was angry. It was bad enough that Lizzy was spoiling the play, but she didn't have to hurt Mosh. Just then Mosh rolled back onto the stage. The robot was acting out of control. Mosh chased Lizzy all around the spaceship.

7   "Captain," Lizzy cried, "do something!"

8   At first, Carlos just watched. He thought Lizzy deserved this. Then he felt sorry for her. "Fear not, First Officer," Carlos said dramatically. Then he took out Mosh's battery. Mosh stopped, and Carlos rolled him behind the curtain again. The play went on as it was written.

9   When the play was over, Lizzy apologized to Carlos. She said she would never hurt Mosh again. "Thanks for helping me out," she added.

10   "You're welcome," Carlos replied. "Do you think we could be friends now?"

11   Lizzy smiled and nodded. "I'd like that," she said.

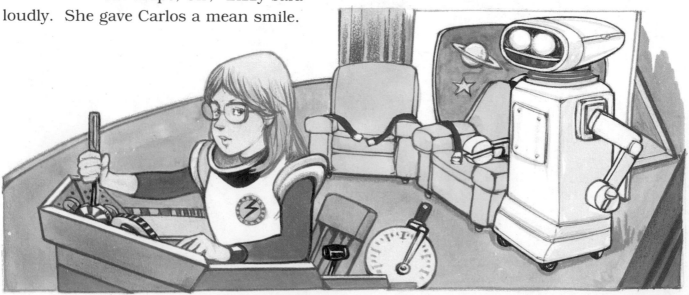

Knowing the Words

Write the words from the story that have the meanings below.

1. awfully _____
(Par. 3)

2. earned _____
(Par. 8)

3. in an
excited way _____
(Par. 8)

In each row below, circle the three words that belong together.

4. stage   curtain   sky   play

5. blast-off   sick   spaceship   maps

6. friends   Mosh   Carlos   stage

Working with Words

Write a compound word using the underlined words in each sentence.

1. A <u>ship</u> used to travel in <u>space</u> is a

_____.

2. <u>Corn</u> that will <u>pop</u> when it is heated

is _____.

3. A game in which a <u>ball</u> is kicked

with the <u>foot</u> is _____.

Circle the correct word in ( ) and write it in the blank.

4. Jeanne drew a _____ on the

card. (circle, correct)

5. The _____ in my glass

melted. (act, ice)

Reading and Thinking

1. Number the sentences to show the order in which things happened.

_____ Mosh chased Lizzy around the stage.

_____ Carlos pulled out Mosh's battery.

_____ Lizzy yelled for help.

_____ Lizzy apologized.

Write **T** if the sentence is true.
Write **F** if the sentence is false.

2. _____ Mosh was disobeying on purpose.

3. _____ Lizzy was frightened when Mosh chased her around the stage.

4. _____ Carlos rescued Lizzy.

5. _____ Carlos planned to take Mosh's battery out during the play.

6. _____ Carlos forgave Lizzy.

7. Write **R** next to the two sentences that tell about real things.

_____ Robots get sick.

_____ Robots can be in plays.

_____ Robots can run on batteries.

Read each sentence and fill in the blank.

8. The people laughed because they enjoyed the play.

They stands for _____.

9. Lizzy screamed when she needed help.

She stands for _____.

45

Mr. Johnson's Offer

Would you want Mosh to help you in a crowded store?

1 Mr. Johnson owned the small grocery store down the street from where Carlos lived. He had asked if Carlos would like to earn some money by passing out cheese samples for two hours on Saturday. Carlos said that sounded like fun and asked if he could bring Mosh. "Sure, I don't see how it could hurt to have your robot here, too," Mr. Johnson said.

2 Carlos put cheese on crackers and Mosh passed them out. Suddenly Carlos heard a scream. "Oh, that Mosh," he sighed. He found Mosh trying to get a lady to take some cheese. Carlos could see the woman didn't want any cheese and was very angry. He said he was sorry and promised it would not happen again.

3 Carlos went back to his job. Soon he heard a crash, and a voice over the loud speaker said, "We need a cleanup in fruits."

4 "Here we go again," Carlos mumbled. He found Mosh in the middle of hundreds of oranges. Mr. Johnson was standing there with his hands on his hips. "Pick these up, then get that thing out of here," he said, pointing to Mosh.

5 Carlos picked up the oranges, and Mosh put them in a neat pile. A crowd gathered to watch them work. Carlos and Mosh started to leave as soon as they were finished.

6 "Wait, Carlos," Mr. Johnson called. He gave Carlos two dollars. "That's for passing out cheese," he said. "And here's an extra two dollars for attracting a crowd. Crowds are good for my business, and that robot knows how to get a crowd."

7 "Would you like us to come back next Saturday?" Carlos asked hopefully.

8 Mr. Johnson shook his head slowly. "No, Carlos, I'd like to keep my store in one piece a little longer," he said with a laugh.

Knowing the Words

Write the words from the story that have the meanings below.

1. part of the body
   where legs begin _____
   (Par. 4)

2. pulling
   toward something _____
   (Par. 6)

3. wishing for something _____
   (Par. 7)

Check the meaning that fits the underlined word in each sentence.

4. Pam ate an orange for lunch.

   _____ a color

   _____ fruit

5. Please point to the problem you are working on.

   _____ show with a finger

   _____ a dot

6. We bought bread at the store.

   _____ place to buy food

   _____ save for later

Reading and Thinking

1. Check the answer that tells what the story is mainly about.

   _____ hundreds of oranges

   _____ an angry woman

   _____ trouble in the grocery store

2. The woman screamed because _____

   _____.

3. What did Carlos put on the crackers?

   _____

4. How might this story have ended if

   Mosh had been left at home? _____

   _____

5. Was Mr. Johnson angry at the end of the story? Explain your answer.

   _____

   _____

   _____

Learning to Study

Number each list of words below in alphabetical order.

1. _____ attract   2. _____ hundred

   _____ ask   _____ hand

   _____ again   _____ hip

   _____ angry   _____ hurt

   _____ ate   _____ hush

47

Lucky Carlos

Carlos thinks he's lucky to have a robot helper. Read to see if you agree.

1 "I'm glad it's Saturday," Carlos said to Marie as he sat at the table. "I've been wanting to work on these walkie-talkies I just bought from Susan. Now I can work all day taking them apart and putting them together again."

2 "No, you can't," Marie replied. "It's your turn to wash the dishes and vacuum the floor. Mom wants it done before she gets home from the office."

3 "Maybe Mosh can help me," Carlos said. "We can be done in fifteen minutes." He showed Mosh how to use the vacuum cleaner. Then Carlos went into the kitchen to wash the dishes. He heard the vacuum roaring in the other room. He felt lucky to have Mosh helping him.

4 Then Carlos heard a loud clattering noise coming from the living room. He rushed in just in time to see Mosh sweeping the table. "Turn it off, Mosh," he yelled. Carlos saw that his walkie-talkies were still on the table, but the tiny screws were gone.

5 "Oh, Mosh, vacuum cleaners are for floors, not tables," Carlos moaned. "I can't put those walkie-talkies back together without the screws. There's only one thing to do."

6 Carlos took the bag full of dirt out of the vacuum cleaner. He took it outside. Carlos dumped the dirt on a newspaper. Then he felt through it with his fingers until he found each tiny screw.

7 Just as he finished, Mrs. Garza drove up. "Carlos, look at your clothes. They are filthy. Why are you going through all that dirt?" his mother asked. "Wait, don't tell me. Mosh is behind this."

8 Carlos nodded and said, "I've just learned the hard way that Mosh doesn't know the best place to use a vacuum cleaner."

Knowing the Words

Write the words from the story that have the meanings below.

1. two-way radios _____
   (Par. 1)

2. very dirty _____
   (Par. 7)

Synonyms are words that have the same or nearly the same meaning. Write **S** after each pair of synonyms. Write **A** after each pair of antonyms (opposites).

3. bought—sold _____

4. yell—whisper _____

5. tiny—little _____

6. glad—happy _____

7. back—front _____

8. filthy—dirty _____

9. loud—soft _____

10. dirt—soil _____

Working with Words

Write the two words that were used to form each of these contractions.

1. it's _____

2. he's _____

3. I'll _____

4. doesn't _____

5. there's _____

6. I've _____

7. let's _____

Reading and Thinking

1. Number the sentences to show the order in which things happened.

   _____ Mosh swept up the screws to the walkie-talkies.

   _____ Carlos searched through the dirt for the screws.

   _____ Mrs. Garza came home.

   _____ Carlos showed Mosh how to clean the carpet.

2. Where was Mrs. Garza when the story began? _____

   _____

3. Check one answer that tells how Mrs. Garza probably got to work.

   _____ in a car

   _____ on a bus

4. What chore was Carlos doing? _____

   _____

Write the best word to complete each sentence below.

5. Adam could not find a broom to

   _____ the sidewalk.
   (empty, feel, sweep)

6. There is a blue _____ in the living room. (dirt, carpet, noise)

7. You cannot _____ the rug with a broom. (vacuum, find, help)

49

Mosh to the Rescue

Do you think it is possible that Mosh could do something right?

1   "I fixed those walkie-talkies you sold me," Carlos said to Susan. "I put one inside Mosh. Now I can give orders from far away."

2   "Let's go outside to see how it works," Susan said.

3   Carlos put Mosh on the sidewalk. Then the kids climbed a tree and waited for someone to appear. They spotted Kevin Price bouncing a ball out in front of his house. One time he bounced the ball too hard and could not catch it. The ball bounced toward the street.

4   "Look," Susan cried, "Kevin's going to run into the street."

5   Carlos knew they couldn't get down from the tree fast enough to stop him. "Tag, Mosh," he yelled into the walkie-talkie. Quickly, the robot started to roll toward Kevin. When Kevin saw Mosh, he turned and ran back toward his house. He was so frightened that he started crying. Carlos and Susan climbed down the tree. They got Kevin's ball and took it to his house.

6   Mrs. Price ran out of the house when she heard Kevin crying. "What happened?" she asked the children.

7   "Mosh stopped Kevin from running into the street," Susan explained. "I hope he isn't too frightened."

8   Mrs. Price hugged her son. "I'm sure he will be OK thanks to you."

9   "Mosh, you make a lot of mistakes, but it's nice to know you can be helpful sometimes," Carlos teased.

10   The robot did not like to be teased about its mistakes. So Mosh turned around and rolled home.

Knowing the Words

Write the word from the story that has the meaning below.

1. saw _____
(Par. 3)

Write the word with the correct meaning to complete each sentence below.

2. Did you _____ tigers and elephants at the zoo? (sea, see)

3. Jeannette has a _____ notebook. (new, knew)

4. We saw a _____ of cows in the pasture. (heard, herd)

Learning to Study

A **table of contents** is one of the first pages in a book. It shows the chapters that are in the book and on what page each one begins. Use the table of contents below to answer the questions.

How to Build a Robot

Table of Contents

1. How many chapters are in this book? _____

2. What is the third chapter called?

_____

3. On what page does the fourth chapter begin? _____

Reading and Thinking

1. Check the answer that tells what the story is mainly about.

_____ saving a child from harm

_____ bouncing a ball

_____ climbing a tree

2. Who was Kevin? _____

_____

3. Why did Kevin run back toward his house? _____

_____

4. Check two sentences that tell about both Susan and Kevin.

_____ They lived near Carlos.

_____ They were playing outside.

_____ They cried when they ran away from Mosh.

5. What might have happened if Mosh had not scared Kevin? _____

_____

Mosh Is Missing

Read to find out what Carlos does when he can't find Mosh.

1   "Where is Mosh?" Carlos cried when he went outside. He turned to Susan and shrugged as he said, "We were only in the house a short time. What could happen to a robot in a few minutes?"

2   Susan and Carlos searched for Mosh. They walked up and down each street in the neighborhood. When they walked behind Lizzy's house, they heard Lizzy talking. The kids peeked through a crack in the fence. They saw Lizzy in the backyard with Mosh. Carlos and Susan heard Lizzy say, "Carlos has so much fun with you that I want to have some fun, too. Let's play tag." Then Lizzy touched Mosh and said, "You're 'it.'" Mosh just stood still.

3   "So, Lizzy wants to have some fun with Mosh," Carlos whispered to Susan. "I'll show her how much fun Mosh can be." Speaking quietly into his walkie-talkie, he said, "Mosh, clean out the garage."

4   Mosh started taking things out of the garage. Soon there were bicycles, tools, shovels, and a ladder lying on the grass.

5   "Oh, no!" Lizzy yelled. "If my parents see this mess, I'll be in big trouble."

6   "I think she's had enough," Carlos giggled. He and Susan walked into Lizzy's yard. "Are you cleaning out the garage, Lizzy?" Carlos asked. "Would you like Mosh to help?"

7   "No, thank you," Lizzy mumbled. "Mosh has been enough help already."

8   "You shouldn't play with things you don't understand. Mosh doesn't take orders from anyone but me," Carlos said. "Let's put these things back in the garage. Then we can play a game of tag."

Knowing the Words

Write the words from the story that have the meanings below.

1. moved shoulders
   up and down _____
   (Par. 1)

2. looked quickly _____
   (Par. 2)

In each row below, circle the three words that belong together.

3. garage   car   sky   driveway

4. curb   concrete   street   grass

5. ladder   minutes   time   clock

6. tag   game   fun   mess

7. shovel   snow   ice   night

Learning to Study

An **index** is a part of a book. It lists a book's topics in alphabetical order. It also lists page numbers so you can find those topics. An index is usually found at the back of a book. Use the index below from a book of games to answer the questions.

        rules, 24
        tag, 6, 12, 21
        tennis, 5, 10–11
        volleyball, 2–4, 11, 13

1. On what pages could you find out

   how to play tag? _____

2. On what pages could you find out

   about tennis? _____

3. On what page could you find rules?

   _____

Reading and Thinking

Write **T** if the sentence is true.
Write **F** if the sentence is false.

1. _____ Carlos was upset when Mosh was missing.

2. _____ Lizzy took Mosh to hurt Carlos's feelings.

3. _____ Carlos told Mosh to take things out of Lizzy's garage to help her.

4. _____ Carlos watched Lizzy put everything back in her garage.

5. How do you think Mosh got in

   Lizzy's yard? _____

6. What game did Lizzy want to play

   with Mosh? _____

Write the best word to complete each sentence below.

7. Agnes _____ all over the house to find her clay. (heard, touched, searched)

8. We rode our _____ to the store. (airplanes, bikes, kites)

A Chilly Experience

What would you do if you had the chance to play in a lot of snow?

1 It had snowed most of the night, so Carlos was listening for school closings on the radio. "There's no school today," he sang as soon as he heard the news.

2 "Before you start playing, I want you and Marie to shovel the snow," Mr. Garza said.

3 Carlos and Marie took turns shoveling. "My hands are cold," Marie said. "Can we get Mosh to help with this?"

4 "We can try," Carlos answered. Mosh came outside, but the robot couldn't move in the snow. Its wheels kept getting stuck. Then Carlos had an idea. "Chains are put on the car tires to get traction," he said. "Maybe chains would work on Mosh's wheels, too."

5 Carlos found two chains from an old swing. He fastened them to Mosh's wheels. The chains kept Mosh from slipping, and the robot had no more trouble moving.

6 "Now I'll teach you how to shovel snow off the sidewalks," Carlos said. He showed Mosh how to scoop up snow with the shovel and dump it off to the side. Mosh learned quickly.

7 "While you're shoveling, I'm going to draw in the snow," Carlos said. He stooped over and drew a picture of a silly face.

8 Carlos stood up and looked at the face. "That looks so good I think I'll draw Mosh now," he said. Just as he stooped over, Mosh rolled by. Before he knew what was happening, Mosh picked up a shovel full of snow and dumped it on Carlos. Most of it landed on Carlos's head. Some slid down his neck and melted inside his coat.

9 Carlos jumped up, looking angry and surprised. Marie laughed and said, "That robot is amazing. This is the first snowstorm, and Mosh already knows how to make a person out of snow."

Knowing the Words

Write the word from the story that has the meaning below.

1. ability to move without slipping _____
(Par. 4)

Check the meaning that fits the underlined word in each sentence.

2. <u>Swing</u> at the baseball with the bat.

_____ strike at

_____ seat that moves back and forth

3. Don't <u>dump</u> that dirt in the driveway.

_____ unload

_____ place for trash

4. I ate a <u>roll</u> with my dinner.

_____ turn over and over

_____ bread

Working with Words

Write a compound word using the underlined words in each sentence.

1. A <u>storm</u> in which <u>snow</u> falls is a

_____.

2. A <u>drift</u> made of <u>snow</u> is a

_____.

Circle the correct word in ( ) and write it in the blank.

3. Three inches of _____ fell yesterday. (saw, snow)

4. Please _____ out two cups of oatmeal. (scoop, skip)

Reading and Thinking

1. Check the answer that tells what the story is mainly about.

_____ drawing in the snow

_____ shoveling snow

_____ getting too cold

2. Number the sentences to show the order in which things happened.

_____ Carlos drew a face in the snow.

_____ Carlos put chains on Mosh's wheels.

_____ Mosh dumped snow down Carlos's back.

_____ Marie's hands got cold.

3. Marie wanted Mosh to help because

_____.

4. Why did Carlos put chains on Mosh's wheels? _____

_____

5. Where did Carlos get the chains for Mosh? _____

6. What was Carlos going to draw in the snow after he drew the silly face?

_____

7. What do you think Carlos did after Mosh threw the snow on him? _____

_____

55

Snowbot

What do you think a snowbot is?

1 Susan called Carlos on the phone at nine o'clock in the morning. "Guess what I heard on the radio," she said.

2 "You heard that school is closed today," Carlos answered. "That's old news, Susan."

3 "Well, that's not all," Susan said. "I heard Mayor Brown say that the city is having a snow sculpture contest today, too. Let's make something."

4 "Sure," Carlos said, sounding excited. "Come on over."

5 When Susan reached her friend's house, Carlos was ready to build. "Well, what should we make?" he asked.

6 "I don't know," Susan said, "but we better hurry. The mayor is judging the sculptures in two hours."

7 Susan and Carlos thought for a few minutes. Finally Carlos said, "I know, let's make a snow robot."

8 "Yeah," Susan agreed. "We can call it a snowbot."

9 The kids worked in the front yard piling up the snow until it was as high as Mosh. Mosh helped with this part, so it didn't take long. Then Mosh modeled while the kids carved arms, hands, wheels, and a head with their gloved hands.

10 They stepped back to take a look at what they had made. "It looks good, but I think we need to give it eyes," Carlos said. "What could we use?"

11 Mosh rolled toward the garage. Soon the robot returned with two old tennis balls and a green marker. The kids knew what they were supposed to do.

12 By the time Mayor Brown came to judge their snow sculpture, it was finished. "I've looked at all the other snow sculptures. This is the most original one I've seen all day. Those are great eyes. You have earned first place," the mayor said, giving each of them a ribbon.

13 Carlos hung his ribbon on Mosh. "Here, Mosh," he said, "I couldn't have won this without you."

Write the words from the story that have the meanings below.

1. leader of a city _____
    (Par. 3)

2. carving; statue _____
    (Par. 3)

3. deciding in a contest _____
    (Par. 6)

Working with Words

Rewrite the following groups of words using *'s* or *s'* to show who owns something. The first one is done for you.

house that belongs to Susan

Susan's house

1. announcement made by the mayor

    _____

2. sculpture that belongs to the kids

    _____

3. eyes that belong to the sculpture

    _____

Circle the correct letters to complete each word and write them in the blank.

4. I felt bett_____ after my nap.

    or   ar   er

5. Snow fell early this m_____ning.

    or   ar   er

6. Who will c_____ve this soap?

    or   ar   er

Reading and Thinking

Write **T** if the sentence is true.
Write **F** if the sentence is false.

1. _____ This story takes place in the winter.

2. _____ The snowstorm knocked down the telephone lines to Carlos's house.

3. _____ Susan made up a new word.

4. _____ The kids took more than two hours to finish their snowbot.

5. Write **M** next to the sentence that tells about something make-believe.

    _____ You could make a robot out of snow.

    _____ Robots can cry like people.

    _____ Tennis balls can be colored green.

Write the best word to complete each sentence below.

6. I made a _____ of a horse in art class. (mayor, marker, sculpture)

7. What color was the _____ that you won? (ribbon, sound, yard)

Pine Street Hill

What do you think it would be like to go sledding with a robot?

1   "Get your sled, Carlos," Susan said. "The mayor closed Pine Street so we can slide down that big hill."

2   Carlos got his sled from the garage. "There's just one thing I don't like about sledding. I don't like dragging the sled back up the hill," he said.

3   "Why don't you have Mosh help with that?" Susan suggested.

4   "That's a great idea," Carlos said. Mosh pulled the sleds to Pine Street. Because of the chains, Mosh rolled easily through the snow. "Take the sleds to the top of the hill, Mosh," Carlos ordered.

5   Mosh rolled up the long hill, dragging the sleds behind it. When they reached the top, Carlos and Susan sat down on their sleds. "It's a lot more fun going down the hill," Carlos told Mosh.

6   Hearing that, Mosh started to go back down the hill. "Get out of the way, Mosh!" Carlos yelled. But the sled was moving faster than Mosh was. It bumped into Mosh and knocked the robot into Carlos's lap. When Carlos leaned over to see around Mosh, the sled turned suddenly and ran into a huge snowdrift.

7   Susan ran over to see if Carlos was all right. "You're not hurt, are you?" she asked.

8   "The next time, you stay at the top while I slide down," Carlos told Mosh.

9   "If Mosh stays at the top, who will pull your sled back up the hill for you?" asked Susan.

10   Carlos thought for a moment before he said, "I'll take care of that." When they got to the top of the hill, Carlos sat down near the front of his sled. He asked Susan to put Mosh on the back.

11   "Hold on, Mosh, here we go!" Carlos cried as the sled bounced down the hill. The other sledders stopped to stare at the sled with its unusual passenger. But Carlos didn't mind. He felt sure that Mosh was having fun, too.

Knowing the Words

Write the word from the story that has the meaning below.

1. someone who rides
   with someone else _____
   (Par. 11)

Circle the pair of antonyms (opposites) in each row.

2. slower   faster   bigger   larger

3. closed   dragged   ordered   opened

4. huge   tiny   under   down

Working with Words

When a word ends with *e*, the *e* is usually dropped before adding **-ed** or **-ing.** For example, *like + ed = liked.*

Add **-ed** or **-ing** to the word in **( )** to make a word that completes each sentence.

1. My mom _____ the cat
   from the tree. (rescue)

2. Why are you _____ at
   the wall? (stare)

3. We should start _____
   the doors now. (close)

The prefix **un-** means "not." *Unsure* means "not sure." Add **un-** to the words below. Use the new words to complete the sentences.

even   happy

4. Barb was _____ about
   losing the game.

5. The top of that table looks

   _____.

Reading and Thinking

1. Check the answer that tells what the story is mainly about.
   _____ rolling through the snow
   _____ running into a snowdrift
   _____ sledding down the hill

2. Where did the kids go sledding?

   _____

3. What helped Mosh roll through the

   snow? _____

4. What might have happened if Carlos and Mosh had not run into a

   snowdrift? _____

   _____

5. What do you think Carlos and Susan did when they were done sledding?

   _____

   _____

The Nightmare

Have you ever had a bad dream?

1 Carlos tossed and turned because he was having a nightmare. In his dream, Carlos was running away from something. He ran into the house. "Close and block the door," Carlos cried out in his sleep. "Don't let it get in!"

2 But the thing in the dream managed to get through the door, so Carlos escaped through the window and ran through the forest until he came to a cave. He ducked inside, hoping the thing wouldn't find him.

3 It was very cold inside the cave. "I need more clothes," Carlos said, still dreaming. "I'm freezing."

4 Carlos felt he was still being followed. He ran into a dark corner. When Carlos turned around, he saw he was being chased by a huge butterfly. Thinking quickly, Carlos knew what he had to do. He had to catch the butterfly.

5 "I need my net," he cried. Carlos grabbed his butterfly net and swung it at the beast. When Carlos looked in his net, he saw a small, blue butterfly.

6 Then Carlos woke up; his room was dark. Something heavy was on top of him, making him very hot. His head was resting on something hard.

7 Carlos turned on his light and looked around the room. It was such a mess he thought he must still be dreaming. The desk was pushed up against the door. All the clothes from his closet were piled on top of him. His butterfly net was lying on his pillow.

8 "What happened in here, Mosh?" Carlos asked. Then he remembered his dream. He must have talked in his sleep.

9 "Thanks for saving me, Mosh," he said, hugging his robot. "But next time, please don't listen to me unless I'm awake."

Knowing the Words

Write the words from the story that have the meanings below.

1. was able _____
    (Par. 2)

2. got out _____
    (Par. 2)

3. monster _____
    (Par. 5)

Choose the correct word to fill in the blanks for each pair of sentences.

duck   light   close

4. Who left the _____ on in the garage?

    The canoe was _____ enough to carry.

5. The _____ flew over the pond.

    Kim needs to _____ to get through the opening.

6. Please _____ the window.

    Do not get too _____ to the parade.

Reading and Thinking

1. Number the sentences to show the order in which things happened.

    _____ Carlos saw the thing that had been chasing him.

    _____ Carlos ran into the house.

    _____ Carlos ran into a cave.

    _____ Carlos woke up.

Write **T** if the sentence is true.
Write **F** if the sentence is false.

2. _____ Carlos was camping out.

3. _____ Carlos woke up during the night.

4. _____ Mosh put the desk in front of the bedroom door.

5. _____ Carlos really caught a butterfly in his net.

Learning to Study

Number each list of words below in alphabetical order.

1. _____ cold
    _____ corner
    _____ cool
    _____ cozy
    _____ comb

2. _____ desk
    _____ deck
    _____ delight
    _____ depend
    _____ deer

3. _____ sleep
    _____ still
    _____ stop
    _____ small
    _____ slip

4. _____ woods
    _____ window
    _____ will
    _____ won
    _____ worry

Birthday Banana Bread

Have you ever tried to follow a recipe?

1   "Today is Dad's birthday, Mosh," Carlos said. "Let's make some of his favorite banana bread and surprise him."

2   Carlos got out a cookbook. "I'll read the recipe, and you follow it. Get out a bowl and spoon while I turn on the oven." Carlos read from the cookbook. "First, mash the bananas in a bowl."

3   The robot threw the bananas into a bowl and was about to mash them with its hands. "Stop!" Carlos yelled. "Let's try this again. Peel the bananas, put them in a bowl, and mash them with the spoon." Carlos watched as Mosh peeled the bananas and put the peeling into the bowl. Again, Carlos told Mosh to stop. Then he showed the robot which part of each banana was supposed to go into the bowl.

4   Then Carlos read, "Add the eggs. No, wait," he said right away. Carlos cracked the eggs open and added them to the mashed bananas. "Now stir that up," he told Mosh.

5   "Last, add flour, milk, and sugar," Carlos said. "Mix everything together. Then pour the batter into the bread pan." Mosh obeyed while Carlos read the rest of the directions to himself.

6   "I'll put this in the oven," Carlos said as he picked up the pan. That is when he saw that Mosh had put the measuring cup in the batter, too. Carlos scooped out the cup and wiped the thick batter off of it.

7   Just then Marie came into the room. "What happened in here?" she gasped.

8   Carlos answered, "Mosh and I made banana bread for Dad's birthday. It was a lot of work, but I think he will be surprised."

9   "If you want it to be a good surprise for Dad," Marie laughed, "you need to give Mosh one more order. Clean up!"

Knowing the Words

Write the words from the story that have the meanings below.

1. directions for preparing food _____
   (Par. 2)

2. mixture _____
   (Par. 5)

3. tool used in cooking _____
   (Par. 6)

In each row below, circle the three words that belong together.

4. cookbook   recipe   milk   directions

5. bowl   peel   spoon   cup

6. flour   sugar   eggs   oven

7. mash   batter   pan   bread

8. mix   stir   pour   eat

Write the word with the correct meaning to complete each sentence below.

9. Who _____ that ball? (threw, through)

10. Connie tried _____ of the fresh bread. (sum, some)

11. Please _____ the milk now. (poor, pour)

12. Can you _____ ten and twelve? (add, ad)

13. Val _____ pizza in school today. (made, maid)

14. The _____ grew through a crack in the street. (flour, flower)

Reading and Thinking

1. Write three things that were needed to make banana bread. _____

   _____

   _____

2. How did Carlos know how to make bread? _____

   _____

3. What room do you think Carlos and Mosh were in? _____

Learning to Study

Use the table of contents below to answer the questions.

Robot Recipes

Table of Contents

1. What is the fourth chapter called?

   _____

2. On what page does the chapter about soups begin? _____

3. In what chapter could you find how to make nut bread? _____

   _____

Birthday Candles

What do you do with birthday candles?

1   Carlos and Mosh had some free time before dinner, so they watched TV. There was a show on about fire safety. Carlos and Mosh listened carefully to

what was being said. They learned how to prevent fires and what to do in case of fire. The show had just ended when Mrs. Garza said, "Go wash your hands, Carlos. It's time for dinner."

2   Carlos could hardly wait to surprise his dad with the bread he and Mosh had baked. As soon as dinner was over, Mosh, Carlos, and Marie stood up. "Excuse us," Carlos said. "We'll be right back. Mosh and I made something special for your birthday, Dad."

3   The three of them went into the kitchen. Carlos put lots of candles on the banana bread. After Marie lit the candles, Carlos proudly carried the bread to the table. He set it in front of his dad and said, "Happy birthday, Dad. Make a wish and blow out the candles."

4   Just then Mosh rolled into the room with a glass of water and poured it on the banana bread. The candles went out. Mr. Garza quickly started mopping up the puddle of water.

5   "Mosh, you spoiled Dad's bread," Carlos cried. "Fires on birthday candles are supposed to be blown out, not drowned."

6   "It will be all right," his mom said. "We'll just give it some time to dry out. I'm sure the bread will still taste delicious."

7   "I'm sorry Mosh ruined your surprise," Carlos said.

8   "Mosh gave me a bigger surprise," his dad said, laughing. "Maybe, since my candles went out so fast, my wish will come true sooner."

Knowing the Words

Write the words from the story that have the meanings below.

1. keep from happening _____
   (Par. 1)

2. forgive _____
   (Par. 2)

3. spoiled _____
   (Par. 7)

Synonyms are words that have the same or nearly the same meaning. Circle the pair of synonyms in each row.

4. ended   finished   begun   baked

5. wish   wash   clean   learn

6. laughing   crying   chuckling   sleeping

7. showed   cooked   baked   made

Learning to Study

Use the cookbook index below to answer the questions.

      baking, 6–10
      banana nut bread, 27
      biscuits, 38–40
      buns, 28, 31, 33

1. On what page would you look to find out about making banana nut

   bread? _____

2. On what pages would you find

   recipes for buns? _____

3. On what pages could you find out

   about how to bake? _____

4. On what pages could you find out

   how to make biscuits? _____

Reading and Thinking

1. Check the answer that tells what the story is mainly about.

   _____ surprising Mr. Garza

   _____ watching TV

   _____ mopping up water

2. Carlos said "Excuse us" when he left

   the table because _____

   _____.

3. Why did Mosh pour water on the

   candles? _____

   _____

4. Check three words that tell about Mr. Garza.

   _____ pleasant   _____ patient

   _____ frantic   _____ kind

5. What kind of person do you think Mrs. Garza is? Explain your answer.

   _____

   _____

Write the best word to complete each sentence below.

6. Sean tries to _____ accidents by being careful. (watch, prevent, surprise)

7. Joy got muddy when she stepped in

   the _____. (candle, pool, puddle)

Aunt Laura's Visit

Have relatives ever come to stay with you? What was it like?

1   Carlos crawled into his sleeping bag. "You know, Mosh," he said, "I like camping out in the den when Aunt Laura comes to stay. But I wish I could still go into my room anytime I want. I would get in a lot of trouble if I bothered Aunt Laura and her spoiled dog, Sweetie."

2   Carlos fluffed up his pillow. "I'm not tired," he complained. "I wish I had my book so I could read, but I left it in my room. I'm sure Aunt Laura is asleep already."

3   Carlos closed his eyes and tried to sleep. Suddenly, he heard a scream coming from his room. Sweetie was barking wildly. Carlos jumped out of his sleeping bag and rushed to his room.

4   "Help!" Aunt Laura yelled.

5   The whole family was there by the time Carlos arrived. Mrs. Garza turned on the light. Aunt Laura stood there looking quite scared. "In there," she whispered, pointing a shaky finger at the closet.

6   Mr. Garza held a baseball bat while he opened the closet door. Everyone gasped. There stood Mosh holding Carlos's book.

7   "I can't believe this," Aunt Laura said, angrily. "You let a machine run around breaking into rooms in the middle of the night?"

8   "I'm sorry," Carlos said quickly. "It won't happen again."

9   "I'll say it won't," his mother said firmly. "If it does, that robot will spend the rest of the week in the garage."

10   Carlos took Mosh back to the den. "Did you hear that, little buddy? You have to be careful while Aunt Laura is here, or you and the car will be sharing the garage." Mosh rolled into a corner and turned off its lights. Carlos felt sad because he knew his friend was upset.

Knowing the Words

Write the words from the story that have the meanings below.

1. upset _____
(Par. 1)

2. given too much _____
(Par. 1)

Working with Words

Circle the correct letters to complete each word and write them in the blank.

1. Did the elephants sc_____ you?

      ur   are   ear

2. I forgot to t_____n off the radio.

      ur   are   ear

3. Our dog b_____ked all night.

      er   or   ar

4. Jo cut her fing_____ on the broken glass.

      er   or   ar

5. My shoes are very d_____ty.

      or   ir   ar

The suffix **-ful** means "full of." *Careful* means "full of care." Add **-ful** to the words below. Use the new words to complete the sentences.

    help   joy   fear

6. The team members were _____ that they won the game.

7. I try to be _____ by cleaning up my room.

8. Stacy is _____ of loud noises.

Reading and Thinking

1. Number the sentences to show the order in which things happened.

_____ Mosh rolled into the corner and turned off its lights.

_____ Mr. Garza opened the closet door.

_____ Aunt Laura screamed.

_____ Carlos tried to go to sleep.

2. What was Mosh getting out of

Carlos's room? _____

3. Who is Sweetie? _____

4. What do you think Carlos did when he got back to the den after being in

Aunt Laura's room? _____

_____

5. What do you think Aunt Laura did

after everyone left her room? _____

_____

Mosh's Friend

Read to find out how a robot can become friends with a dog.

1   On the second day of Aunt Laura's visit, Carlos asked if she had seen Mosh. "Yes," Aunt Laura said. "Mosh is staying in the garage. My poor little Sweetie is afraid of that thing."

2   Carlos went to the garage. "This is just awful, Mosh," he said. "I bet if Sweetie knew what a nice robot you are, he wouldn't be afraid of you anymore. This is going to be a long week."

3   When Carlos went back inside, he saw Aunt Laura getting a leash. Carlos got an idea. "Aunt Laura, would you like me to take Sweetie for a walk?" he asked.

4   "Sure," Aunt Laura replied.

5   Carlos took Sweetie to the garage. "Mosh, this is your chance to prove to Sweetie that you won't hurt him. You can take him for a walk. Stay on the sidewalk and don't cross any streets."

6   About an hour later, Aunt Laura asked Carlos where Sweetie was. "I haven't seen him since his walk," she said.

7   Carlos had forgotten about the dog. He said, "I'll get him for you."

8   Carlos rushed outside and found Mosh standing in the driveway. Sweetie was standing with his front paws up on Mosh. He was licking Mosh's hand. Carlos called Aunt Laura outside to see what was going on.

9   "They're friends," she said, sounding surprised. "How did that happen?"

10   Carlos replied, "I thought if Mosh took Sweetie for a walk the dog would see there is no reason to be afraid of Mosh."

11   "That was a good idea," Aunt Laura said, smiling. "I guess it would be OK to let Mosh come back into the house now."

12   Mosh and Sweetie were together for the rest of the week. Mosh took the dog for a long walk each day. At night, Sweetie slept curled up next to the robot's wheels. Carlos was glad they were friends. Though, he had to admit he missed having Mosh all to himself.

Knowing the Words

Write the words from the story that have the meanings below.

1. chain or rope used to walk a dog _____ (Par. 3)

2. answered _____ (Par. 10)

Working with Words

Write the two words that were used to form each of these contractions.

1. wouldn't _____

2. haven't _____

3. didn't _____

Write a compound word using the underlined words in each sentence.

4. A book used to cook with is a

_____.

5. A ball made of snow is a

_____.

Circle the correct word in ( ) and write it in the blank.

6. The _____ balloon floated over the fairgrounds. (hug, huge)

7. The first _____ has a picture of a lion on it. (page, pig)

8. A robin's _____ is a beautiful color of blue. (egg, edge)

Reading and Thinking

Write **T** if the sentence is true.
Write **F** if the sentence is false.

1. _____ Carlos felt sad that Mosh had to stay in the garage.

2. _____ Mosh had hurt Sweetie.

3. _____ Sweetie was licking Mosh because he enjoyed the taste of metal.

4. _____ Mosh and Sweetie spent a lot of time together after the first walk.

5. Check the sentence that tells how Mosh and Sweetie are alike.

_____ They both had wheels.

_____ They both barked.

_____ They both belonged to people.

Circle the name or names that each underlined word stands for.

6. "I want that robot out of here," said Aunt Laura.

   Carlos   Mosh   Aunt Laura

7. "We can go for a walk," Carlos told Mosh.

   Mosh and Sweetie   Carlos and Mosh
   Carlos and Aunt Laura

8. "They are my friends," Carlos said, pointing to Susan and Mosh.

   Susan and Mosh   Susan and Carlos
   Carlos and Mosh

9. "You can ride along," Carlos said to Marie.

   Carlos   Marie   Mosh

69

Nurse Mosh

Read to find out what happens when Carlos gets sick and thinks Mosh can take care of him.

1   "Mom, I don't feel well," Carlos complained one morning. "My stomach hurts, and I feel hot all over."

2   Mrs. Garza took Carlos's temperature. "You have a fever," she said. "You need to stay home from school today, so I'll ask Mrs. Wilson to stay with you."

3   "You don't need to bother Mrs. Wilson," Carlos said. "Mosh can take care of me."

4   "I would feel better if Mrs. Wilson came over," Mrs. Garza said. "You never know when you might need extra help."

5   Carlos went back to sleep but soon woke up very thirsty. "Mosh, please bring me a glass of juice," he said.

6   Soon Mosh was back with a glass of water. "This isn't juice, but it will stop my thirst," Carlos said.

7   Then Carlos felt hungry. "I think I would like to eat some soup," he told Mosh. "I'm going to fix some now."

8   Carlos got a can of chicken soup and a pan. Suddenly he felt dizzy and thought he might fall. Mrs. Wilson saw Carlos in the kitchen and sent him back to bed. Mosh followed him.

9   Carlos asked Mosh to put the soup in the pan, add water, and bring it to him when it was hot. Soon Mosh came in carrying a hot pan. When Carlos looked in the pan, he saw the soup can in the hot water. "Nice try, Mosh," he said, "but you need to open the can first."

10   Just then Mrs. Wilson came in with a bowl of chicken soup for Carlos. "I saw Mosh fixing your soup," she said, smiling. "I thought you might like this."

11   "Thank you," Carlos said, feeling very hungry. Carlos held the bowl of soup out to Mosh and said, "This is what a bowl of soup should look like." Carlos ate and then lay back to rest some more.

12   Mrs. Garza called later. "How are you and Mosh getting along?" she asked.

13   "Well, I'm glad you asked Mrs. Wilson to come over," Carlos answered. "Mosh is a great friend but a terrible nurse."

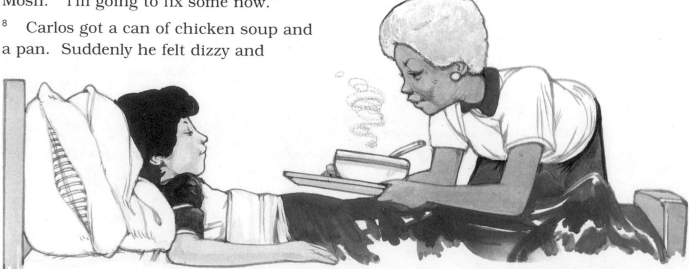

Knowing the Words

Write the word from the story that has the meaning below.

1. in good health _____
(Par. 1)

Check the meaning that fits the underlined word in each sentence.

2. Please fill my <u>glass</u> with milk.

_____ container for holding liquids

_____ a mirror

3. That is a <u>great</u> idea for a story.

_____ very large

_____ excellent

4. <u>Fall</u> begins in September.

_____ season

_____ to hit the ground

Working with Words

The ending **-er** sometimes means "more." It may be used to compare two things. The ending **-est** means "most." It is used to compare more than two things.

In each sentence below, add **-er** to the word before the blank if two things are being compared. Add **-est** if more than two things are being compared.

1. That was the great_____ movie I have ever seen.

2. An ant is small_____ than a bee.

3. Lynne is old_____ than I.

4. Heather is the quiet_____ person in our class.

5. An orange is sweet_____ than a lemon.

Reading and Thinking

1. Check the answer that tells what the story is mainly about.

_____ eating soup

_____ having a robot nurse

_____ staying home from school

2. Carlos had to stay home from school

because _____

_____.

3. What did Mosh bring instead of

juice? _____

4. Who was taking care of Carlos?

_____

Write the best word to complete each sentence below.

5. I have an _____ pen you may use. (extra, eager, ill)

6. I was so _____ I drank a large glass of cold milk. (hungry, thirsty, sleepy)

7. The _____ was made from fruit. (water, juice, milk)

71

Cleaning Up

Have you ever tried to think of an easy way to wash the dishes? Mosh did.

1 "The house needs to look good for our dinner party tonight," Mrs. Garza told Carlos one Saturday. "Marie is already doing her chores. I want you to clean your room, mop the kitchen floor, and wash the dishes this morning."

2 "OK, Mom," Carlos said. He got the mop and a pail of soapy water. "Guess what, Mosh. You get to clean the kitchen floor today."

3 Carlos taught the robot how to wash the floor. Then Carlos went to clean his messy room. After a little while, he checked up on Mosh.

4 "You're doing a great job, Mosh," Carlos said in surprise. "When you're finished, I'll show you how to wash the dishes." Carlos went back to work on his room.

5 About ten minutes later, Carlos heard Marie calling him, sounding amused. "Carlos, come to the kitchen right now," she sang. "Mosh has made another terrible mess."

6 Carlos sighed, "I knew the clean floor was too good to be true." When he got to the kitchen, he gasped. All the dishes were spread out on the floor, and Mosh was washing them with the mop. Soapy water was splashing everywhere.

7 "Stop!" Carlos cried. "Mosh, you can't wash dishes with a mop. Dishes need to be handled carefully. We're lucky you didn't break these."

8 Carlos put the dishes in the sink. Then he mopped up the water on the floor. Carlos was just finishing the dishes when his parents got home from the store.

9 "Oh, the floor looks marvelous," his mom said.

10 "Thanks to Mosh," Carlos grumbled.

11 "Mosh is getting better at cleaning. Maybe you should let your little friend do more," his dad said.

12 "Believe me, Mosh has done enough today," Carlos said, shaking his head.

Knowing the Words

Write the words from the story that have the meanings below.

1. lying around _____
   (Par. 6)

2. scattering water _____
   (Par. 6)

3. wonderful _____
   (Par. 9)

Circle the pair of antonyms (opposites) in each row.

4. morning   noon   night   late

5. soapy   clean   dirty   terrible

6. messy   lucky   careful   neat

Working with Words

The words below have been divided into syllables. Put a mark above the first vowel to show the sound it stands for. Mark the long vowels with ‾ over the letter. Mark the short vowels with ˘.

1. min/ute   5. rap/id   9. ro/bot

2. ba/by   6. fi/nal   10. man/age

3. o/ver   7. pa/per   11. sec/ond

4. la/ter   8. van/ish   12. fin/ish

Fill in each blank with the correct letters to make a word that completes each sentence below.

          mb   kn   wr

13. Did you see a _____en fly by the window?

14. The plu_____er fixed the leaky pipe.

15. The sharp _____ife cut through the meat.

Reading and Thinking

Write **T** if the sentence is true.
Write **F** if the sentence is false.

1. _____ Carlos had not expected Mosh to do such a good job mopping.

2. _____ Mosh tried to wash the dishes and the floor the same way.

3. _____ Marie thought it was funny that Mosh was making a mess.

4. Carlos did not stay to watch Mosh mop the floor because _____
   _____.

5. Do you think Mosh will ever be asked to wash the dishes again? Explain your answer. _____
   _____
   _____

6. What do you think Carlos did after he finished washing the dishes?
   _____
   _____

The Dinner Party

Do you think it would be a good idea to let Mosh help out at a dinner party?

1 "Mom, can Mosh help at the party?" Carlos asked. "I want Mrs. Chung to see how well Mosh works."

2 "Well, I suppose it wouldn't hurt to let Mosh put the guests' coats away," Mrs. Garza said as she sighed.

3 That evening Carlos took the guests' coats when they arrived. He gave them to Mosh. "Put these away in Mom and Dad's room," he ordered.

4 Mrs. Chung smiled when she saw Mosh. "I'm glad to see that the robot works," she said.

5 When dinner was almost ready, Carlos helped Marie light the candles on the table. Carlos liked the way it looked with the candles and flowers arranged in the middle. Just then Mosh came in with a box of baking soda. Before Carlos could stop the robot, it poured the baking soda on the candles. The flames went out. Carlos felt awful. Marie gasped.

6 "Mosh, you know you aren't supposed to put out candles," Carlos cried.

7 Carlos heard his mom tell the guests to come to the table. Quickly, he and Marie lit the candles before the guests sat down.

8 "The table looks lovely," Mrs. Chung said. "That powder gives the flowers a very soft look."

9 Mrs. Garza's eyes opened wide. "Carlos, what do you know about this?" she asked.

10 "Mosh thought the table was on fire. It put the candles out with baking soda," Carlos said.

11 All the guests laughed. "Now you see what life with a robot is like," Mrs. Garza said, chuckling. Then she whispered to Carlos, "Take Mosh out to the garage. We don't need any more mix-ups tonight."

12 "Mosh, if you don't learn how to behave, you'll never get invited to another dinner party," Carlos warned.

Knowing the Words

Write the words from the story that have the meanings below.

1. used for baking _____
(Par. 5)

2. mistakes _____
(Par. 11)

3. told of trouble
ahead of time _____
(Par. 12)

Working with Words

Circle the correct word in ( ) and write it in the blank.

1. Mosh is a robot and not a _____.
(toy, today)

2. The bath _____ made Joyce
sneeze. (pour, powder)

3. I forgot to wear my _____
to school today. (cat, coat)

4. Justin _____ his lunch.
(bought, boat)

To form the plural of a word that ends in f or fe, the f or fe is changed to v, and es is added. Form the plural of each word below.

5. life _____

6. calf _____

7. scarf _____

8. loaf _____

9. elf _____

Reading and Thinking

1. Number the sentences to show the order in which things happened.

_____ Mosh put out the candles.

_____ Carlos took the guests' coats.

_____ The guests came to the table.

_____ The guests arrived.

2. Write the name of one of the Garzas' guests. _____

3. What two things were in the middle of the dinner table? _____

_____

4. The flames on the candles went out because _____

_____.

Write the best word to complete each sentence below.

5. Sara _____ me to her birthday party. (laughed, poured, invited)

6. Last night we had potatoes for _____. (breakfast, dinner, lunch)

7. Alice _____ just when the bell rang. (arrived, liked, lit)

8. The loud horn _____ us that a tornado was coming. (heard, whispered, warned)

The Missing Coats

Do you remember what happened when Mosh was told to put clothes away?

1 "Carlos, would you please get our guests' coats?" Mr. Garza asked.

2 Carlos went to his parents' room. There were no coats on the bed. He searched the other rooms, but Carlos did not see the coats anywhere.

3 Carlos went to Marie. "I've got a problem," he whispered. "All the guests' coats are gone."

4 "What do you mean?" Marie asked, trying to stay calm. "Where did you tell Mosh to put them?"

5 "In Mom and Dad's room," Carlos answered, "but they aren't there."

6 Marie and Carlos searched for the coats again, but they couldn't find even one.

7 "Exactly what directions did you give Mosh?" Marie asked.

8 "I said to put them away in Mom and Dad's room," Carlos replied. Carlos thought for a few minutes. Then he got an idea. "When Mosh puts our clean clothes away, they go into the drawers. Maybe . . ."

9 Carlos opened a drawer. "Here's one," he said. He opened another drawer and found two more. Carlos had five coats by the time he finished looking in all the drawers.

10 Marie looked in another dresser. "I think I found the rest of the coats," she said. Marie and Carlos took all of the coats to the guests.

11 "Forgive us for taking so long," Marie said to the guests. "When Mosh helps, we never know what to expect. We found your coats in our drawers."

12 Everyone laughed. Mrs. Chung turned to Mrs. Garza and thanked her for a delightful evening. "Mosh made this a party we will never forget," she said, chuckling.

13 "We'll never forget this one either, will we, Carlos?" Mr. Garza said with a wink.

Knowing the Words

Write the words from the story that have the meanings below.

1. missing _____
   (Par. 3)

2. chest of drawers _____
   (Par. 10)

3. pleasant _____
   (Par. 12)

Synonyms are words that have the same or nearly the same meaning. Circle the pair of synonyms in each row.

4. look   find   discover   lose

5. idea   problem   thought   question

6. found   forget   gone   missing

Working with Words

Rewrite the following groups of words using 's or s' to show who owns something.

1. coats that belong to the guests

   _____

2. bedroom that belongs to Carlos

   _____

Circle the correct letters to complete each word and write them in the blank.

3. Where is your oth _____ glove?

   ar   er   or

4. Will you please f _____ give me?

   ar   er   or

5. Are you going to the p _____ ty?

   ar   er   or

Reading and Thinking

1. Check the answer that tells what the story is mainly about.

   _____ finding the lost coats

   _____ apologizing to the guests

   _____ forgetting the party

Write **T** if the sentence is true.
Write **F** if the sentence is false.

2. _____ Carlos did not want the guests to know their coats were lost.

3. _____ Marie thought it was funny that the coats were missing.

4. _____ Marie helped find the coats.

5. _____ Mrs. Chung is a polite person.

6. Where did Carlos and Marie find the coats? _____

7. What did it mean when Mr. Garza winked? _____

   _____

8. What do you think Carlos did after the guests left? _____

   _____

9. Do you think the Garzas will have another party? Explain your answer.

   _____

   _____

   _____

Nature Club Camping Trip

Have you ever camped out? What was it like?

1   Carlos's nature club went on a short camping trip. Carlos and Jake, his best friend in the club, were sharing a tent.

2   "Are you sure it was a good idea to bring Mosh?" Jake asked uneasily.

3   "Sure," Carlos answered. "Wasn't it good to have Mosh around when we put up our tent? Besides," he went on, "what could a robot hurt out here in the woods?"

4   "I guess you're right," Jake agreed. "Let's go to the pond till it's time for our five-mile hike."

5   Mosh and the boys went to the pond that was close to camp. The frogs were croaking loudly.

6   "I wonder what those frogs are saying to each other," Jake said.

7   Carlos replied, "They are probably complaining about the cold water."

8   "Mr. Jones is calling us. It must be time for our hike," Jake said.

9   "Stay here, Mosh. Hiking would be hard for you," Carlos said as he left.

10   Carlos was worn out when he got back to the tent after the hike. "I'm going to rest a while," he told Jake. Carlos stopped as soon as he looked inside the tent. "There must be a hundred frogs in here! Mosh!" Carlos screamed.

11   Jake asked, "Why would Mosh put frogs in there?"

12   Carlos thought for a minute before he remembered that he had said the frogs were complaining about the cold water. "Mosh is probably trying to keep them warm," he said. "Come on, let's get them out of here."

13   Jake held back the door of the tent while Carlos crawled around and waved his hands at the frogs to shoo them out toward the pond. "Did you finally get them all?" Jake asked.

14   "I think so," Carlos answered, lying down on his sleeping bag. Just then a frog hopped onto his stomach. Carlos was startled and jumped. "I know one thing about nature," he chuckled. "Frogs belong in ponds, not tents."

Knowing the Words

Write the words from the story that have the meanings below.

1. all things not
   made by humans _____
   (Par. 1)

2. not comfortably _____
   (Par. 2)

3. long walk _____
   (Par. 4)

4. chase away _____
   (Par. 13)

Write the words with the correct meaning to complete each sentence below.

5. Kathy lost a _____ down by the pond. (shoo, shoe)

6. I _____ where to find deer. (know, no)

7. There are _____ pears on the ground. (four, for)

8. I have _____ walk home after school. (too, to, two)

9. We will return in _____ hour. (won, one)

10. The children lost _____ balloons. (there, their)

Reading and Thinking

1. Carlos thought the frogs were croaking loudly because _____ _____.

2. Why wouldn't Carlos let Mosh go on the hike? _____ _____

3. How else might the boys have gotten the frogs out of the tent? _____ _____

Write the best word to complete each sentence below.

4. Roger was _____ at the people on the ship. (waving, complaining, hiking)

5. The _____ hopped off the rock and into the water. (snake, tent, frog)

Learning to Study

A dictionary entry shows the words divided into syllables. A space or a dot shows where the word can be divided at the end of a line of writing.

Read the words below. Next to each, write the number of syllables it has.

1. na ture _____   4. stom ach _____

2. un eas y _____   5. min ute _____

3. wa ter _____   6. grum ble _____

Creature in the Night

Are you ever afraid of the dark?

1   "Let's tell scary stories," Jake said from his sleeping bag.

2   "OK," Carlos agreed, "you go first."

3   "Once there was a group of kids camping out in the woods," Jake began. "At night, a creature with glowing eyes found them, but one of the campers woke up just in time and screamed. The scream scared the creature away. The creature has never been caught, and some say it still roams through the forest today."

4   After the story was finished, Carlos just lay there with his eyes opened wide.

5   "Come on, Carlos," Jake said. "It's your turn now."

6   "I've changed my mind," Carlos said. "One scary story is enough for me."

7   "OK," Jake said, laughing, "let's go to sleep."

8   Jake fell asleep quickly, but Carlos couldn't stop thinking about the story. He was getting jumpier by the minute. When Carlos heard an owl hoot, he almost jumped right out of his sleeping bag. Then he saw a shadow moving along the side of the tent. It had two glowing green spots.

9   "Wake up," Carlos whispered to Jake. "The creature is here."

10   "Go back to sleep," Jake mumbled. "That was only a story."

11   "There is a strange shadow outside our tent!" Carlos said.

12   Jake yelled, "Help, Mr. Jones!" The boys tried to escape, but they were so upset they couldn't even get out of their sleeping bags.

13   "What's going on in there?" Mr. Jones yelled from outside their tent.

14   "Watch out for the creature!" Jake warned Mr. Jones.

15   Mr. Jones laughed. "You mean this robot?" he said, holding the tent door open. There was Mosh with its green eyes glowing.

Knowing the Words

Write the words from the story that have the meanings below.

1. wanders _____
(Par. 3)

2. more nervous _____
(Par. 8)

Working with Words

When a word ends in a consonant followed by *y*, the *y* is changed to *i* before **-er** and **-est** is added. Change the *y* to *i* in each word in **( )**. Add **-er** or **-est** to make a word that completes the sentence. The first one is done for you.

Hope's tale was *scarier* than Jeff's. (scary)

1. I am _____ now than I was an hour ago. (hungry)

2. That is the _____ bug of all. (ugly)

3. A rose is the _____ flower I've ever seen. (pretty)

The suffix **-less** means "without." *Joyless* means "without joy." Add **-less** to the following words. Use the new words to complete the sentences.

sleep   care   home

4. The _____ kitten looked hungry and cold.

5. I had a _____ night because of a barking dog.

6. Because Donna was _____ , she got paint on her clothes.

Reading and Thinking

1. Number the sentences to show the order in which things happened.

_____ Carlos saw glowing green spots.

_____ Jake told a scary story.

_____ Jake fell asleep.

_____ The boys found out that the creature was Mosh.

2. Carlos was afraid because _____

_____ .

3. Who was camping with the boys?

_____

4. What did Carlos hear that frightened

him? _____

5. How did Carlos feel when he saw the shadow? Explain your answer.

_____

_____

6. How do you think Carlos felt when he found out that the creature was

Mosh? Explain your answer. _____

_____

A Mosh Special

What kind of sandwich might Mosh make?

1   "Wake up!" Carlos heard Marie say. "Your alarm clock didn't go off."

2   Carlos slowly opened his eyes. Usually, he was not happy about getting up early, but this morning was different. It was the last day of school, and his class was going on a field trip to the zoo. It was already eight o'clock, so he had only ten minutes to get dressed and pack a lunch. "I don't want to be late!" he said as he leapt out of bed. "I sure wish Mosh knew how to make a sandwich," Carlos said. Then he went to wash his face. He did not notice Mosh rolling out of the bedroom and into the kitchen.

3   By the time Carlos finished dressing, he only had five minutes to pack his lunch and get to school. When he walked into the kitchen, he stopped and smiled. There stood Mosh with a delicious-looking sandwich. "Thanks, Mosh," Carlos said. He quickly put the sandwich in a bag and grabbed a can of juice. Then he raced out the door.

4   For two hours, the children walked around the zoo looking at all kinds of animals from geese to lions. At last, the class sat down to eat lunch. Carlos was hungry. He was looking forward to the sandwich Mosh had fixed.

5   He eagerly took a large bite of the sandwich and started chewing. He stopped suddenly because it tasted a little odd. He looked between the two pieces of bread and started laughing.

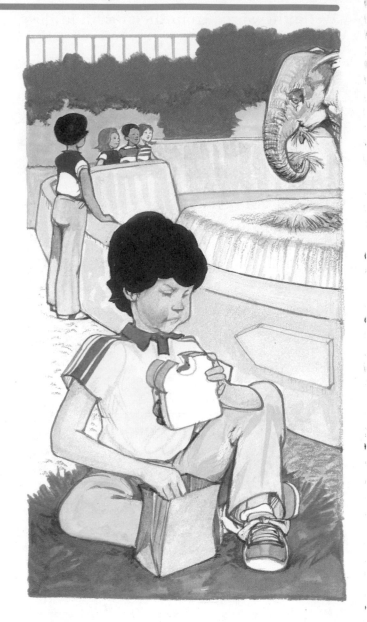

6   "What are you laughing about?" Susan asked.

7   Carlos showed her the sandwich. "Tuna fish, peanut butter, bananas, mustard, and pickles," Susan said, wrinkling up her nose. "What kind of a sandwich is that?"

8   "It is a Mosh special," Carlos said. "It's strange tasting, but I'm hungry." Susan laughed as Carlos took another big bite of the sandwich.

Knowing the Words

Write the words from the story that have the meanings below.

1. visit to someplace with a group _____ (Par. 2)

2. jumped _____ (Par. 2)

3. tasty _____ (Par. 3)

Working with Words

Sometimes the plural form of a word is made by changing the spelling of the word. The plural form of *goose* is *geese.*

Use the plural words below to complete the sentences.

    mice   women   feet   children

1. Two _____ live in a cage in our classroom.

2. These tennis shoes are too small for

    Kay's _____ .

3. Twenty _____ rode on a bus to the zoo.

4. My older sister and my mother are

    _____ .

Fill in each blank with the correct letters to make a word that completes each sentence below.

        ph   wr

5. There is a _____ inkle in my shirt.

6. Can you say the al_____ abet backwards?

Reading and Thinking

Write **T** if the sentence is true.
Write **F** if the sentence is false.

1. _____ Carlos had overslept.

2. _____ It took Carlos five minutes to get dressed.

3. _____ The class might have seen an ostrich at the zoo.

4. _____ Susan thought a Mosh special looked delicious.

5. _____ Carlos thought the sandwich would be tasty.

6. What did Mosh put in the sandwich?

    _____

    _____

7. What do you think the class did

    when they finished eating? _____

    _____

8. Do you think Mosh will be allowed to make another sandwich? Explain

    your answer. _____

    _____

    _____

Good-bye, Mosh?

How do you think it feels when you have to say good-bye to a good friend?

1 "Mrs. Chung was quite impressed with Mosh when she was here the other night," Mrs. Garza told Carlos. "She mentioned something about how nice it would be to buy the robot back."

2 "Mom, I don't want to sell Mosh," Carlos said, feeling sad. "Do I have to?"

3 "You have had Mosh for almost a year now," his mom said. "Don't you think you'll be getting tired of it soon?"

4 "No, Mosh is my best friend," Carlos answered. "But since Mrs. Chung is your boss, I'll think about it."

5 Carlos felt terrible. He could not imagine life without Mosh. The next day he went to Susan's house, hoping that his friend could cheer him up.

6 When Carlos got home, his house was dark and quiet. As soon as he opened the door, all the lights went on. "Surprise!" his parents and Marie yelled.

7 "What's going on?" Carlos asked, feeling confused.

8 "Did you forget Mosh's birthday?" Marie teased. "It was one year ago today that you brought that robot home."

9 Carlos tried to act happy as he and Mosh opened presents together. Marie gave Carlos some new lights for Mosh's eyes. His father's gift was a new can of oil.

10 "This one is from Mom," Carlos told Mosh. He opened the package and found a large battery. There was also a note that said "This will help Mosh give us another exciting year."

11 "But what about selling Mosh back to Mrs. Chung?" Carlos asked.

12 "Well, I told Mrs. Chung how important Mosh was to you," Mrs. Garza said. "She said she would never want you to sell your friend. But she did say she might like you and Mosh to be in an ad some day."

13 Carlos gave a cheer and hugged Mosh. Mosh's eyes lit up. Then the robot spun around in circles, which was its way of saying "Hooray!"

Knowing the Words

Write the word from the story that has the meaning below.

1. pleased _____
(Par. 1)

Synonyms are words that have the same or nearly the same meaning. Circle the pair of synonyms in each row.

2. box   gift   paper   present

3. terrible   awful   sad   brave

4. hope   imagine   tease   think

Working with Words

Write a compound word using the underlined words in each sentence.

1. The <u>day</u> of your <u>birth</u> is your

_____.

2. A <u>fish</u> the color of <u>gold</u> is a

_____.

3. <u>Paper</u> with <u>sand</u> on it is called

_____.

4. An <u>ache</u> in your <u>head</u> is a

_____.

5. <u>Light</u> from the <u>moon</u> is called

_____.

In each word below, draw a line to divide the word into syllables.

6. confuse   **9.** pillow

7. ribbon   **10.** journey

8. almost   **11.** lesson

Reading and Thinking

1. Check the answer that tells what the story is mainly about.

_____ saying good-bye to Mosh

_____ selling Mosh to Mrs. Chung

_____ having a party for Mosh

2. What did Marie give to Carlos for

Mosh? _____

3. What was Mrs. Garza's gift? _____

_____

4. What do you think Carlos and Mosh

did after the party? _____

_____

Write the best word to complete each sentence.

5. The crowd _____ loudly for the team. (teased, thought, cheered)

6. When I close my eyes, it is easy to

_____ I am a bird. (imagine, sell, mention)

7. A small _____ came in the mail today. (hug, cheer, package)

8. Can you _____ how to wrap a present? (explain, want, open)

9. After the long walk, Marge was very

_____. (nice, tired, brave)

Cat Bath

Why would a cat hide from its owner?

1   "Rick, how would you like to help your good friend give Herbie a bath?" Tracy said. "That dumb cat ran into a skunk, and he smells awful!"

2   "I'll be right there," Rick answered and hung up the phone.

3   When Rick arrived, Tracy said, "Use one hand to hold your nose. You can help me wash Herbie with the other one." Then she called, "Here, Herbie!" and a green-eyed cat came bounding out from the den.

4   "We'd better do this in the basement," Tracy said, "because Herbie just hates **W-A-T-E-R.**" She carried him down the steps and put him on the floor. Then she dumped some cat shampoo in the sink. As soon as Tracy turned the faucet handle, Herbie scrambled across the floor. He jumped into a pile of dirty clothes.

5   When Tracy reached in to get him, Herbie ran out the other side. He dashed up the stairs. "Help me catch him, Rick!" Tracy cried.

6   Rick whirled around and ran up the stairs behind Tracy. Rick and Tracy found Herbie hiding next to the refrigerator. Then they chased him into the broom closet.

7   "Gotcha!" Tracy said as she caught Herbie. They all headed for the basement.

8   "We won't forget to close the door this time," Rick said, pulling it shut behind him.

9   "Oh, no!" Tracy shouted as she started downstairs. "We forgot something even worse than that!"

10   There at the foot of the stairs was a huge soap puddle. A stream of water flowed over the sink.

11   "We forgot to turn off the water!" Rick cried, his eyes wide with surprise.

12   "We've got two messes to clean up now," Tracy moaned. "Let's get busy!"

Knowing the Words

Write the words from the story that have the meanings below.

1. jumping _____
(Par. 3)

2. pipe that water
comes out of _____
(Par. 4)

3. ran quickly _____
(Par. 4)

4. turned quickly _____
(Par. 6)

Some words sound alike but have different spellings and meanings. Write the word with the correct meaning to complete each sentence below.

5. Those _____
lead to the attic. (stares, stairs)

6. Please _____
the garage door. (close, clothes)

Working with Words

Circle the correct word in ( ) and write it in the blank.

1. Do not get _____ in your eyes when you wash. (soup, soap)

2. They _____
the butterfly in a net. (caught, cat)

3. I'll need a _____ to clean up this powder. (broom, brim)

4. Can you _____ that bottle of shampoo? (rich, reach)

Reading and Thinking

1. Check the answer that tells what the story is mainly about.

_____ a pile of dirty clothes

_____ a bath for Herbie

_____ two messes

2. Herbie ran away because

_____.

3. Put a check beside something that was probably in Tracy's basement.

_____ a car

_____ a washing machine

_____ a mailbox

4. Put a check beside the two answers that tell where Herbie hid.

_____ in the living room

_____ in the pile of dirty clothes

_____ beside the refrigerator

5. What did Tracy mean when she said that there were two messes to clean?

_____

_____

6. How do you think Rick and Tracy will clean the basement floor?

_____

_____

Ready to Roll

What could you do with a pair of roller skates that no longer fit?

1   One Saturday afternoon Tracy and her friend Elsa decided to roller skate to City Park. "Come in and put on your skates," Tracy said when Elsa arrived at her house. Elsa took off her sneakers and loosened the laces of her skates.

2   "Oof!" she grunted as she tried to squeeze her foot into a skate. "Either my skates have shrunk, or my feet have grown! What good is a pair of skates if they don't fit?"

3   "Hey, I've got an idea!" Tracy said. "If Mr. Levi will give us a board from his lumber pile, we can take your skate wheels off and . . ."

4   ". . . Build a skateboard!" Elsa broke in. "That's a great idea!"

5   Elsa put on her sneakers, and the two of them hurried down the street to explain their idea to Mr. Levi. Mr. Levi smiled and said, "I've got just what you need." He pulled a board from beneath a pile. "This was part of Skipper's old doghouse," he said.

6   "Thanks, Mr. Levi!" the girls said. Then they raced back to Tracy's house.

7   Elsa removed her skate wheels with a screwdriver. Tracy sanded some splinters off the board. Then they used nails to make holes for the screws. Once the wheels were attached, Elsa was ready to roll. "It fits perfectly," she said as she put one foot on the skateboard.

8   While Tracy put on her skates, Elsa set the skateboard on the sidewalk. Then she placed her left foot on top and pushed with her right. "It works!" Elsa yelled as she traveled down the street.

9   "Wait for me!" Tracy called.

10   "You know what I like best about this skateboard?" Elsa said when Tracy caught up. "It will always be a perfect fit, no matter how much my feet grow!"

Knowing the Words

Write the words from the story that have the meanings below.

1. tennis shoes _____
(Par. 1)

2. made less tight _____
(Par. 1)

3. strings used
for tying _____
(Par. 1)

4. tiny pieces
of wood _____
(Par. 7)

Check the meaning that fits the underlined word in each sentence.

5. <u>Roll</u> the ball across the floor.

_____ bread

_____ move by turning

6. Did you hurt your <u>foot</u>?

_____ part of the body

_____ twelve inches

7. I have <u>sand</u> in my shoe.

_____ to make smooth

_____ tiny bits of stone

Working with Words

An 's at the end of a word may be used to show that something belongs to someone. Add 's to each name below and write the new word in the correct blank.

Mr. Levi   Skipper   Elsa

1. _____ lumber

2. _____ skateboard

3. _____ doghouse

Reading and Thinking

1. Number the sentences to show the order in which things happened.

_____ Elsa rolled down the street on her skateboard.

_____ Mr. Levi gave the girls a piece of wood.

_____ Elsa discovered that her skates didn't fit.

_____ The girls attached the skate wheels to the board.

2. Check the sentence that tells why Elsa couldn't get her skates on.

_____ Her skates had shrunk.

_____ Her socks were too thick.

_____ Her feet had grown.

3. Check two words that tell about Mr. Levi.

_____ helpful   _____ selfish

_____ grouchy   _____ friendly

4. Check two sentences that tell how Elsa's skateboard and roller skates were alike.

_____ They both had laces.

_____ They both had screws.

_____ They both had wheels.

_____ They both were made of wood.

89

Leave It to Rags

Read to find out how Tracy meets her new neighbors.

1   Tracy watched the moving van turn the corner. "I wonder if the new family will have kids my age," she thought. Tracy sat down in a chair close to the window so she could watch the movers. Suddenly there was a loud crash in the alley. Tracy hurried outside to see what was making all the racket.

2   When she reached the alley, she found an empty garbage can lying on its side. Just then a scared puppy poked its head out from behind the can.

3   "Where'd you come from?" Tracy asked. She reached for the tags attached to the dog's collar. " 'My name is Rags,' " she read, " '10 South Street, Oak Hill.' That's nearly a hundred miles from here!" she exclaimed. "I'll get Mom and Dad to phone your owners," Tracy said. She picked up the garbage can.

Then she took the pup into her backyard and gave him a bowl of water.

4   Tracy and Rags were playing with a rubber ball when a boy and girl appeared at the fence. "Hi, my name's Lindsay, and this is my brother, Dale," the girl said. "We've just moved here from Oak Hill. It looks as if you found our dog."

5   "Is Rags your dog? That's great! Now we won't have to try to track down the owners in Oak Hill. I just found him out by the garbage can. He was really scared," Tracy said.

6   "He must have slipped out the door when the movers carried the furniture in, but nobody noticed," Lindsay said.

7   "I guess he couldn't wait to go exploring," Tracy chuckled. "My name is Tracy. I'm your new neighbor."

8   "Well, we had hoped to find some friends our age," Dale said. "Leave it to Rags to find one for us!"

Knowing the Words

Write the words from the story that have the meanings below.

1. large truck _____
   (Par. 1)

2. noise _____
   (Par. 1)

Abbreviations are shortened forms of words. The abbreviation for *inch* is *in.* Match each word from the first list with its abbreviation from the second list.

3. _____ street   **a.** mi.

4. _____ Mister   **b.** st.

5. _____ mile   **c.** Mr.

Learning to Study

A **table of contents** is on one of the first pages in a book. It shows the chapters that are in the book and on what page each one begins. Use the table of contents below to answer the questions.

All About Dogs

Table of Contents

1. How many chapters are in the book?

   _____

2. What is the first chapter called?

   _____

3. On what page does "Dogs as Pets" begin? _____

Reading and Thinking

1. Check the answer that tells what the story is mainly about.

   _____ meeting new neighbors

   _____ watching movers

   _____ noises in the alley

2. Check the two sentences that tell about Tracy.

   _____ She likes to meet people.

   _____ She is a good neighbor.

   _____ She does not like dogs.

Write **T** if the sentence is true.
Write **F** if the sentence is false.

3. _____ Dale knocked the garbage can over.

4. _____ Tracy could easily walk to Oak Hill.

5. _____ Tracy thought Rags was lost.

6. _____ Tracy wanted to keep Rags.

7. How far had Lindsay and Dale moved from their old home?

   _____

Write the best word to complete each sentence below.

8. The _____ in the kitchen is new. (barn, furniture, noise)

9. The _____ book is funny. (comic, metal, leftover)

10. We rode in the _____ to the game. (toast, pup, van)

Dinner for Rags

Have you ever worried about something and then found out things were not as bad as they seemed?

1   Since they had moved, Lindsay and Dale had been quite busy. They had unpacked all of their things and had made lots of new friends.

2   Lindsay and Dale were very happy in their new neighborhood. Only one thing troubled them. Even though he seemed to be healthy, Rags had not been eating the food they put out for him each day. Lindsay and Dale tried everything to get him to eat. They bought a different kind of food. They hid treats in the middle of the food. They even pretended they were going to eat his food if he didn't. But nothing worked.

3   Then Lindsay and Dale went to Tracy about their problem. She listened and thought for a minute. Then she snapped her fingers, smiled, and said, "Follow me. I think I know what is going on." Tracy led Lindsay and Dale to the house on the corner of the block. There, a few feet in front of them, stood a small tan dog and Rags sharing a bowl of dog food.

4   "That is Ruffy," Tracy said, pointing to the tan dog. "He belongs to Mr. and Mrs. Breen." Just then two people came to the back door and started talking to the dogs. Rags wagged his tail and barked as if he were talking to the Breens.

5   When Rags saw Lindsay and Dale, he ran over to them. "He just won't stay in our yard when we tell him to," Lindsay said to Mr. and Mrs. Breen. "I don't know how we'll ever get him to obey us."

6   Tracy said, "The Breens used to train dogs. Maybe they'll give you some helpful advice."

7   "We'll do better than that," Mr. Breen said. "We'll help you train this smart little pup. If you're interested, we can start Monday."

8   "That's great!" Lindsay and Dale said eagerly. "Thanks!" Then they took Rags home to tell their parents the good news.

Knowing the Words

Write the words from the story that have the meanings below.

1. worried _____
   (Par. 2)

2. special things _____
   (Par. 2)

3. teach _____
   (Par. 6)

Some words are spelled the same but have different meanings. For example, *yard* can mean "the land around a building" or "thirty-six inches."

Look at the list of words below. For each pair of sentences, one word from the list will correctly complete both. Choose the correct word to fill in the blank for each pair of sentences.

> bark   bowl   can

4. I like to _____ with my friends.

   I poured cereal and milk into

   my favorite _____.

5. Floppy doesn't _____ at people she knows.

   The tree _____ was bumpy.

6. Kevin _____ play the piano.

   The soup _____ was empty.

Match each word from the first list with its abbreviation from the second list.

7. ____ minute   **a.** ft.

8. ____ Monday   **b.** min.

9. ____ feet   **c.** Mon.

Reading and Thinking

Words such as *he, she, you, it, we,* and *they* are used in place of other words. Read these sentences. *Rags is a puppy. He is owned by Lindsay and Dale.* Instead of repeating the name *Rags* in the second sentence, *he* is used in the place of *Rags.*

Read each set of sentences below. Fill in each blank.

1. Lindsay told Rags to sit.
   She used a firm voice.

   She stands for _____.

2. Lindsay and Dale are training Rags.
   They enjoy the work.

   They stands for _____.

3. The collar wasn't very heavy.
   It was made for a puppy.

   It stands for _____.

4. Rags was not eating his food at home

   because _____.

Learning to Study

Number each list of words below in alphabetical order.

1. ____ problem   3. ____ treats
   ____ pretend   ____ tried
   ____ pride   ____ train

2. ____ happy   4. ____ ran
   ____ him   ____ Rags
   ____ house   ____ rain

Training Time

Read to find out about a lesson for Rags.

1 Rags seemed to know that something special was going to happen. He was more playful than usual. As the children walked down the block, they could barely hold on to Rags. One minute he tried to run between Dale's legs. The next minute he was trying to run up the steps of a new house.

2 The Breens were waiting for Lindsay and Dale when they arrived. They began to tell Lindsay and Dale how they could train Rags. The children listened carefully. "First you will give him a command," Mr. Breen told them. "When he obeys, you will reward him with praise and a pat on the head. When he doesn't obey, you must say *no* in a firm voice."

3 Mrs. Breen went on to explain that the first thing they taught the dogs was to sit.

4 "That sounds good," Dale said. "We'd like to start with something simple."

5 Lindsay and Dale found out quickly that no trick was going to be simple. They took turns telling Rags to sit. Every time they showed Rags how, he thought they wanted to play. He would jump up and start to lick them. Then he would bark as if to say "Let's have fun!"

6 The children were very patient and kept trying. After what seemed like hours, Rags finally caught on. Lindsay and Dale patted Rags on the head. They told him what a smart dog he was. By this time the children were very tired, but Rags was still lively. "What would you like to teach him next?" Mrs. Breen asked.

7 "Would it be all right if we went home and rested?" Dale said as he sat down, looking very tired. "I think we're going to need a lot more energy before we begin the next trick."

8 Everyone laughed when Rags jumped into Dale's lap as if begging to play some more.

Knowing the Words

Write the words from the story that have the meanings below.

1. something nice
   that is said _____
   (Par. 2)

2. strong _____
   (Par. 2)

3. waiting without
   getting upset _____
   (Par. 6)

Words that mean the same, or nearly the same, are called **synonyms.** Circle the pair of synonyms in each row.

4. command   ask   know   order

5. firm   bright   shy   smart

Learning to Study

At the top of each page in a dictionary are two words in dark print called **guide words.** They can help you find other words in the dictionary. The first guide word tells what the first word is on the page. The second guide word tells what the last word is on the page.

The words in a dictionary are listed in alphabetical order. To find a word, decide if it comes in alphabetical order between the guide words on the page. If it does, the word will be on that page. Check each word that could be found between these guide words.

scatter/scout

1. _____ science   5. _____ scissors

2. _____ scramble   6. _____ school

3. _____ scene   7. _____ scrub

4. _____ scratch   8. _____ scent

Reading and Thinking

1. Check the answer that tells what the story is mainly about.

   _____ getting tired

   _____ a long afternoon

   _____ how to train a dog

2. Did Rags mean to misbehave? _____

   Explain your answer. _____

   _____

3. What other things might Lindsay and

   Dale train Rags to do? _____

   _____

4. What did the children do when Rags

   obeyed their command? _____

   _____

5. Write **R** next to the two sentences that tell about real things.

   _____ Puppies can talk.

   _____ Puppies can bark.

   _____ Puppies can be trained.

6. Put a check next to the two answers that tell what a person needs to do when training a puppy.

   _____ praise the puppy

   _____ give up

   _____ give a command

   _____ yell loudly

Afternoon Adventure

What do you think Rick and Elsa might find in a cave?

1   Elsa and her family had brought a picnic lunch to Rocky Cave State Park. Carmen was still eating. "Hurry up, Carmen," Elsa said to her younger sister. "Rick and I want to see that cave." Elsa loved adventure and was always ready to go exploring.

2   Finally, Carmen was finished. Rick and Elsa grabbed their flashlights. Carmen and her father were close behind. They all started toward a huge opening in the side of the hill. Rick and Elsa went into the cave first and walked along a narrow pathway. It went deep into the cave. They reached a small opening that looked like a doorway. Rick and Elsa stooped down and went through the entrance. They found themselves in a damp, dark room.

3   "It looks like a secret hideout!" Rick exclaimed.

4   "Long ago, people used caves for shelter," Elsa replied.

5   "I hope nobody uses it now. I think this place is spooky!" Rick said as he glanced around.

6   "There's nothing to be scared of," Elsa told Rick. Then suddenly she stopped. "Look!" she said, her feet frozen to the ground and her body stiff with fear. A spot of light moved toward them, and they could hear footsteps.

7   Then in a low, deep voice someone said, "Elsa and Rick, are you in there?"

8   "I'd know that voice anywhere," Elsa said. "It's Dad with Carmen!"

9   Just then Carmen appeared at the entrance to the room and announced, "It's creepy in here!"

10   "You can say that again!" laughed Elsa and Rick.

Knowing the Words

Write the word from the story that has the meaning below.

1. place to go in _____
   (Par. 2)

Words with opposite meanings are called **antonyms.** Circle the pair of antonyms in each row.

2. narrow   small   wide   long

3. door   entrance   exit   tunnel

Working with Words

The endings **-y** or **-ly** can be added to some words. Write the correct word to complete each sentence below.

1. The mountain trail was _____ and difficult to climb. (rock, rocky)

2. This _____ is smooth, flat, and round. (rock, rocky)

3. I _____ grabbed my jacket and ran home. (quick, quickly)

4. _____ action kept the fire from spreading. (Quick, Quickly)

A word that means one of something is **singular.** A word that means more than one is **plural.** Most singular words are made plural by adding *s.* Most words that end in *s, ss, x, ch,* and *sh* are made plural by adding *es.* Form the plural of each word below by adding *s* or *es.*

5. hammer _____

6. porch _____

7. box _____

8. mess _____

9. bush _____

10. seed _____

Reading and Thinking

1. Check the answer that tells what the story is mainly about.

   _____ a picnic

   _____ frightened explorers

   _____ people who live in caves

Write **T** if the sentence is true.
Write **F** if the sentence is false.

2. _____ Rick was frightened in the cave.

3. _____ Elsa had a picnic in the cave.

4. _____ Someone was living in the cave.

5. Some things are real and some are make-believe. Write **M** next to the sentence that tells about a make-believe thing.

   _____ Caves are dark and damp.

   _____ Animals live in caves.

   _____ Monsters live in caves.

Write the best word to complete each sentence below.

6. I dropped the _____ and ran. (flashlight, shelter, tunnel)

7. I have a secret _____ in the attic. (hideout, shadow, cave)

8. We could not sleep outside because the ground was _____. (green, damp, soft)

9. Stay on the _____ so you don't get lost. (doorway, entrance, pathway)

Screamer

What would you do if you found a baby bird that had fallen from his nest?

1   Tracy and Dale were playing in Tracy's yard when they discovered a baby blue jay that had fallen from his nest. Tracy filled a shoe box with bits of yarn. Dale gently placed the bird in the box. They set it on the porch step.

2   Just then the baby bird opened his beak and let out a loud scream. "Feed me. I'm hungry!" he seemed to say. Tracy hurried inside to warm some milk while Dale found some birdseed in the garage. They put the seed in a bag. Then they crushed it with a hammer.

3   After mixing the crushed birdseed and milk, Tracy used an eyedropper to squeeze the mixture into the bird's mouth. The blue jay swallowed the food. Then he let out another noisy scream, asking for more. "I think we should name him Screamer," Dale said. Tracy agreed.

4   During the next few weeks, it seemed as if the young bird was hungry all the time. One morning Tracy and Dale fixed some baby cereal for Screamer. When they went outside to feed the bird, the box was empty.

5   They were sure something terrible had happened and that they would never see Screamer again. Heartbroken, they sat in silence beneath an oak tree.

6   Then something drifted down from above. It landed near Dale's foot. "Look!" he said, grabbing it. "It's a piece of yarn from Screamer's shoe box!"

7   Tracy looked high into the tree. Suddenly a loud scream rang out. A blue jay fluttered to the ground. "Hey, it's Screamer!" Dale cried with delight.

8   "We've been so busy taking care of Screamer we didn't notice how much he had grown!" Tracy exclaimed. "But now that Screamer has learned to fly, I guess he will be taking care of himself."

Knowing the Words

Write the words from the story that have the meanings below.

1. bird _____
   (Par.1)

2. broke into
   little pieces _____
   (Par. 2)

3. very sad _____
   (Par. 5)

4. flew gently _____
   (Par. 7)

In each row below, circle the three words that belong together.

5. beak   feather   shoe   wing

6. smash   flutter   crush   pound

Working with Words

A **contraction** is a short way to write two words. An apostrophe (') shows that one or more letters have been taken out. Write a contraction from the story for each pair of words below.

1. I am _____
   (Par. 2)

2. we have _____
   (Par. 8)

3. did not _____
   (Par. 8)

Most words that end in a consonant followed by *y* are made plural by changing *y* to *i* and adding *es*. Write the plural form of each word below.

4. grocery _____

5. library _____

6. city _____

Reading and Thinking

1. Number the sentences to show the order in which things happened.

   _____ Tracy and Dale fed Screamer.

   _____ Screamer flew to a tree.

   _____ Tracy and Dale found a blue jay.

   _____ Dale put the bird in a shoe box.

2. Tracy and Dale named the blue jay

   Screamer because _____

   _____.

3. Tracy and Dale mixed _____

   and _____ to feed
   to Screamer.

Write the best word to complete each sentence below.

4. This _____ will make warm socks. (cereal, yarn, seed)

5. Stir the _____ till it is smooth. (blue jay, mixture, scream)

6. The kids _____ that Screamer was young. (agreed, tugged, drifted)

99

Beginner's Luck

Read to find out how horseshoes is played.

1   One Friday, Tracy and Elsa were watching Mr. Levi trim bushes. "We can't think of anything to do, Mr. Levi," Tracy moaned. "Do you have any ideas?"

2   Mr. Levi stopped and thought for a few seconds. "When I was your age," he said, "I played horseshoes. You could use the ones in my basement if you'd like to learn how to play."

3   "That sounds like fun!" Elsa said. Mr. Levi went inside. He returned with some rusty horseshoes and two steel posts. He laid the posts thirty feet apart. Then he pounded them into the ground.

4   "Each player stands next to this post. Players pitch toward the other post twice," Mr. Levi explained. "A shoe that goes around the post is called a ringer.

It's worth three points. If a shoe leans against the post, it earns one point. You can also earn one point if the shoe lands within six inches of the post. The person with the highest score after twenty-five innings wins the game."

5   Tracy, Elsa, and Mr. Levi began playing. By the eighth inning, Mr. Levi and Elsa each had seven points. Tracy had scored only two. "I wish I had beginner's luck," she said as she stepped up to take her turn. She threw the horseshoe. It flew past the post. The shoe landed under the bushes.

6   Tracy looked under a bush for the shoe. After a moment she called, "Is this yours, Mr. Levi?" She dangled a gold chain with something shiny on the end.

7   "My pocket watch!" he exclaimed with surprise. "I lost that a week ago."

8   "Gee, I'm glad I threw that horseshoe crooked," Tracy said. "I guess I do have beginner's luck after all!"

Knowing the Words

Write the words from the story that have the meanings below.

1. covered with a reddish-brown coating _____
   (Par. 3)

2. turns to play _____
   (Par.4)

3. held something up so that it swung loosely _____
   (Par. 6)

4. not straight _____
   (Par. 8)

Match each word from the first list with its abbreviation from the second list.

5. ____ seconds   **a.** wk.

6. ____ Friday   **b.** sec.

7. ____ inch   **c.** Fri.

8. ____ week   **d.** in.

9. ____ feet   **e.** ft.

Learning to Study

Check each word that could be found between the dictionary guide words.

1. **colt/crooked**   3. **fiddle/flakes**

   ____ crash   ____ fly

   ____ crept   ____ finger

   ____ crisp   ____ flow

   ____ coconut   ____ fierce

2. **scare/shy**   4. **whole/write**

   ____ slept   ____ wrote

   ____ shore   ____ wink

   ____ sense   ____ won

   ____ scream   ____ wheat

Reading and Thinking

1. Check the answer that tells what the story is mainly about.

   ____ trimming the bushes

   ____ looking for a lost watch

   ____ learning to play horseshoes

Write **T** if the sentence is true.
Write **F** if the sentence is false.

2. ____ Mr. Levi's watch fell off his wrist.

3. ____ Horseshoes is a game that could be played indoors.

4. ____ Mr. Levi knew his watch was missing.

5. The number of innings in a game of horseshoes is _____.

6. Write two words from Paragraph 4 that are also used in the game of baseball. _____

   _____

Write the best word to complete each sentence below.

7. A _____ can be used to measure the door. (chain, yardstick, hammer)

8. Brad _____ about the rain. (pounded, whistled, complained)

9. The fence was _____ because it was old. (straight, tall, crooked)

Loud and Clear

How could you stretch a tin can phone between two second-story windows?

1 Soon after Lindsay moved in, she and Tracy discovered that their upstairs bedroom windows faced each other across the backyards. "Let's make a tin can telephone and stretch it between our windows," Lindsay said.

2 "Then we could have secret talks anytime we like," Tracy added. The girls found two empty soup cans. They washed the cans out. Then they put a hole in the bottom of each one. Finally Lindsay and Tracy threaded a long string through the cans and tied knots at each end.

3 "You take that end up to your room. I'll take this end up to mine," Tracy said with excitement. They each headed for their own houses. Suddenly they realized that it wouldn't work.

4 "If we run the string through our doors and up the stairs," Tracy said, "we won't be able to pull it tight and straight across the yards."

5 "You take both cans up to your room and throw one end over to me in my room," Lindsay suggested. It was a good idea, but every time Tracy tossed the can it landed in Lindsay's yard.

6 The girls met back in the yard. They were ready to give up when Tracy said, "I think I know how to fix it."

7 She grabbed the scissors and cut the string in half. "Take your end to your room. Leave the can on the windowsill. Drop the string out the window," Tracy

said. "I'll do the same with this end and meet you back here."

8 Before long a string hung out each window. The girls met outside. "We'll just tie a knot in the string," Tracy explained. Soon the string was connected. Both girls rushed to their rooms. They pulled the string tight.

9 "Can you hear me?" Lindsay asked hopefully.

10 "Loud and clear!" Tracy replied.

Knowing the Words

Write the words from the story that have the meanings below.

1. understood clearly _____
   (Par. 3)

2. gave an idea _____
   (Par. 5)

3. small shelf
   under a window _____
   (Par. 7)

4. wishing
   something
   might happen _____
   (Par. 9)

Check the meaning that fits the underlined word in each sentence.

5. The <u>back</u> door of the house is locked.

   _____ opposite of front

   _____ part of the body

6. I think I have a spot of gravy on my <u>tie</u>.

   _____ to fasten together

   _____ a piece of clothing

Learning to Study

Two pairs of dictionary guide words and their page numbers are shown in dark print. Beside each word below, write the number of the page on which it would be found.

thick/trim   p. 302
trouble/try   p. 310

1. _____ trumpet   5. _____ thread

2. _____ tremble   6. _____ trust

3. _____ truth   7. _____ tight

4. _____ truck   8. _____ trap

Reading and Thinking

1. Check the answer that tells what the story is mainly about.

   _____ old tin cans

   _____ the secret talk

   _____ making a telephone

2. How is a tin can phone different from a real telephone? _____

   _____

Write **T** if the sentence is true.
Write **F** if the sentence is false.

3. _____ Sounds can travel through a string.

4. _____ A tin can telephone will not work if the string goes around a corner.

5. _____ Tracy could make a long-distance call on the tin can telephone.

6. _____ A tin can telephone will not work with a knot in the string.

7. What had been in the cans before they were emptied? _____

Write the best word to complete each sentence below.

8. She _____ the yarn through the needle. (snatched, threaded, connected)

9. There is a _____ in this rope. (phone, string, knot)

The Seven-Flavor Favor

What problem did Elsa solve for her music project?

1 All month Elsa had looked forward to the music festival that was to be held at City Park. After much thought, she decided to do a project that would be both musical and colorful.

2 On the day of the festival, Elsa put seven glass jars of the same size into a wagon. She carried a folding table under her arm and pulled the wagon to the park.

3 At the park she set the table up next to a drinking fountain. Then Elsa began to fill a jar. Suddenly she realized she had not brought the dyes to color the water. "I don't have time to run home," she thought.

4 Then she looked across the park. She spied a sign that said "Fresh Fruit Juice." Elsa quickly made her way toward the stand, with the glass jars rattling in the wagon behind her.

5 "I'd like to buy one glass of each flavor you have," Elsa told the man behind the counter.

6 The man smiled as he said, "I've got seven different flavors. Are you sure you want that many glasses?"

7 Elsa explained that she'd planned to put colored water into seven jars. Then she would play a tune by tapping the jars with a wooden spoon. "But I left the dye to color the water at home," she said. "Each flavor of juice is a different color. I'll put juice in the jars in place of dye."

8 "You really know how to solve a problem," the man chuckled as he began to fill some cups with juice.

9 "How much do I owe you?" Elsa asked. The man set the last cup on the counter in front of her.

10 "Nothing," he said. "Anyone who can come up with a good idea like that deserves some help. Let's just call it a seven-flavor favor!"

Knowing the Words

Write the words from the story that have the meanings below.

1. something planned _____ (Par. 1)

2. a place to get water _____ (Par. 3)

3. where things are sold _____ (Par. 4)

4. large shelf _____ (Par. 5)

Synonyms are words that have the same or nearly the same meaning. Circle the pair of synonyms in each row.

5. dye   orange   coloring   water

6. radio   tune   song   piano

Working with Words

Use each group of words in a sentence that tells who owns something.

1. Elsa's glass jars _____

_____

2. man's fruit juice stand _____

_____

Some words are easier to read if they are divided into parts called **syllables.** Some words have two consonants between two vowels. These words can be divided into syllables between the consonants, as in *for/got.*

In each word below, draw a line to divide the word into syllables.

3. forward **5.** fountain **7.** carry

4. arrive   **6.** problem   **8.** enjoy

Reading and Thinking

1. Check the answer that tells what the story is mainly about.

_____ music in City Park

_____ solving a problem

_____ a fruit juice stand

2. Why didn't Elsa use plain water in

the jars? _____

_____

Write **T** if the sentence is true.
Write **F** if the sentence is false.

3. _____ The man thought Elsa's plan was a good one.

4. _____ Elsa could not pay for the fruit juice.

5. _____ Elsa could play eight different notes on the jars.

6. What do you think Elsa will do with the fruit juice after the music

festival is over? _____

_____

Write the best word to complete each sentence below.

7. The class _____ was finished. (flavor, dye, project)

8. A _____ rainbow appeared after the storm. (fresh, colorful, musical)

9. Would you like _____ with breakfast? (juice, cup, spoon)

Lemonade for Sale

Read to find out about a smart way to run a lemonade stand.

1   All the kids in the neighborhood seemed to be busy on Saturday afternoon except Heather and Michael. "Let's have a lemonade stand!" Michael said to his sister.

2   "Sure!" Heather said. They found some paper cups in the house, but they needed to go to the store on the corner to buy lemons.

3   The children raced back home and made the lemonade. Then they set up a table in the front yard. Michael taped a sign on it and waited for customers.

4   Heather and Michael sat there for thirty minutes. Not one person came by. "I'll bet we'd get some customers if we advertised," Heather said. That gave Michael an idea. He dashed inside to get something.

5   He came back with a pair of walkie-talkies. Michael announced, "I'll go out and find people who look thirsty. I'll let them know we're here! We'll keep in touch with the walkie-talkies."

6   After a few minutes he radioed, "Six kids on bikes should be arriving soon, Heather."

7   "OK, Michael," Heather replied. In the next half hour, Michael sent ten more people to the stand.

8   Soon Heather called to Michael. "I've just run out of cups," she said, "so don't send anybody else."

9   "I just sent a man who said he was awfully thirsty," Michael replied. "See if

he'll wait while I buy more cups."

10   "I'll do my best," Heather said, hoping she could convince the man to stay. In a few minutes, Michael came rushing down the street with a new package of cups.

11   "I guess I'm too late," he said when he did not see the man waiting.

12   "It's OK," Heather said, chuckling. "He was so thirsty he drank every last drop—right out of the pitcher!"

Knowing the Words

Write the words from the story that have the meanings below.

1. people who buy _____
   (Par. 3)

2. two-way radios _____
   (Par. 5)

3. make others believe _____
   (Par. 10)

4. a small bit of liquid _____
   (Par. 12)

Choose the correct word below to fill the blanks for each pair of sentences.

   pitcher   right

5. Is this the _____ answer?

   Stomp your _____ foot.

6. Pour milk into the _____.

   Who is the team _____?

Working with Words

Say *city*. Circle the words below that have the sound *c* stands for in *city*.

1. cave   cent   face   clown

2. center   dance   calm   twice

When a word ends with *e*, the *e* is usually dropped before adding **-ed** or **-ing**. Add **-ed** or **-ing** to the word in ( ) to make a word that completes each sentence.

3. Mom's plane is _____
   at three o'clock. (leave)

4. Tim _____
   the plants were dry. (notice)

Reading and Thinking

1. Check the answer that tells what the story is mainly about.

   _____ a thirsty man

   _____ Michael's walkie-talkies

   _____ selling lemonade

Write **T** if the sentence is true.
Write **F** if the sentence is false.

2. _____ Heather and Michael washed the used cups.

3. _____ Heather and Michael bought the lemonade at the store.

4. _____ Michael had money to buy more cups.

5. What did the children have to

   buy to get started? _____

6. Why did Michael go back to the

   store? _____

7. What do you think Heather and Michael will do now that the thirsty

   man has gone? _____

   _____

The Birthday Gift

Why do gifts that you make sometimes mean more than those you buy?

1   Tracy, Rick, and Elsa wanted to give Mr. Levi a special gift for his birthday. They counted their money. They had only two dollars among them. "I think he might like a handmade gift," Tracy said. The three of them tried to think of something they could make that would not cost too much money.

2   After a while, Rick said, "I've got it! In school last year, we made salt jars. We filled jars with green, blue, orange, and white salt to make a picture. All we would need to buy would be salt and colored chalk."

3   Tracy and Elsa agreed that Rick's idea was good. Rick told them what they needed to get started. "We will need a big box of salt, paper towels, chalk, newspapers, and three bowls. We each need a small jar with a lid, too."

4   After all the supplies had been gathered, Tracy covered a table with newspapers. Then Rick poured some salt on a paper towel. He rubbed a piece of blue chalk over the salt. As he rubbed and rubbed the salt turned darker and darker blue. Rick put the blue salt in a bowl. Next he made some orange salt. Finally Rick made some of the salt green.

5   The children took turns pouring the different colors of salt into their jars. They worked on making designs with the salt. Each jar was filled to the top. Then Tracy, Rick, and Elsa put the lids on them.

6   Elsa's jar looked like an orange desert with trees. Rick made a colorful rainbow. Tracy formed snow-covered mountains with a blue sky.

7   They set the jars in a shoe box and put the lid on it. The children wrapped the box carefully. The next morning they gave the gift to Mr. Levi.

8   "They're beautiful!" he exclaimed when he looked at the jars. "I'll put them on a windowsill and look at them every day. They'll remind me of you and how lucky I am to have such thoughtful and inventive friends!"

Knowing the Words

Write the words from the story that have the meanings below.

1. something used
for drying _____
(Par. 3)

2. things needed
for a project _____
(Par. 4)

3. able to
make things _____
(Par. 8)

Write the word with the correct meaning to complete each sentence below.

4. A _____ of chalk fell
to the floor. (peace, piece)

5. The _____ coat is my
favorite one. (blue, blew)

Working with Words

A **suffix** is a group of letters added to the end of a word that changes the meaning of the word. The suffixes **-ful** and **-ous** mean "full of." *Fearful* means "full of fear." *Joyous* means "full of joy."

Add **-ful** or **-ous** to the words below. Use the new words to complete the sentences.

power   humor   thought

1. It was very _____
of you to remember my birthday.

2. The _____ engine
pulled the train.

3. The _____ story made
us all laugh.

Reading and Thinking

1. Number the sentences in the order that tells how a salt jar can be made.

_____ Rub chalk over some salt.

_____ Pour the salt into the jar.

_____ Gather supplies.

_____ Put the lid on the jar.

2. Why did the children give Mr. Levi a

present? _____

3. Write one way in which the three

salt jars were alike. _____

_____

4. Write one way in which the three

salt jars were different. _____

_____

5. Check the word that tells how you think the children felt when Mr. Levi opened the box.

_____ proud _____ curious _____ sad

6. What did Mr. Levi do with the gifts?

_____

Hocus-Pocus

Read to find out about Rick's show.

1 Rick was making a sign one sunny day when Tracy and Elsa skated up to him. He was thinking so hard about what he was doing that he didn't even notice the girls at first. The girls said hello together.

2 Rick was startled. Then he smiled as he saw who it was. "Hi, I didn't hear you come up," Rick said.

3 "You look so busy. What are you making?" Elsa asked.

4 Rick held up a poster with the message "Magic show today. Bring a friend and be amazed. Show time is one o'clock."

5 Tracy and Elsa hurried off to tell their friends. As the girls skated away, they said, "See you at one, Rick."

6 People began arriving a few minutes before one o'clock. Rick had practiced. He knew his show would be a good one, but he was a little nervous anyway. He took a few deep breaths. Then he started the show.

7 "For my first trick," Rick said in a loud, clear voice, "I will pick up this ice cube without ever touching it with my hands." He put the ice cube in a glass of water and sprinkled salt on top of it. Then Rick laid a wet string over the ice. He waved a stick over the glass and slowly said, "Hocus-pocus, ice come up." When Rick picked up the ends of the string, the ice cube came up with it.

8 Then Rick said, "Now I would like a couple of volunteers." Dale and Michael each raised a hand. "Try to blow this ball of aluminum foil out of this funnel," Rick told them. Dale and Michael tried and tried, but neither one was successful. Then Rick took the funnel and said, "Hocus-pocus, ball come out." He blew into the funnel. The ball came out! Rick's audience was amazed. Tracy and Elsa wanted to know his secret. Rick just smiled. He knew that the children would soon learn these same tricks in their science classes.

Knowing the Words

Write the words from the story that have the meanings below.

1. a little frightened _____
   (Par. 6)

2. word said when a
   trick is being done _____
   (Par. 7)

3. helpers _____
   (Par. 8)

4. thin sheet
   of metal _____
   (Par. 8)

Working with Words

Say the word *show* and notice the sound *ow* stands for in the word. Circle the words below that have the sound *ow* stands for in *show*.

1. know   down   blow   cow
2. slow   arrow   town   throw
3. hollow   tower   how   glow

A **compound word** is made by combining two smaller words. Write a compound word using the underlined words in each sentence.

4. The yard in the <u>back</u> of a house is

   a _____.

5. The time of day <u>after</u> the <u>noon</u>

   hour is _____.

6. <u>Seed</u> given to a <u>bird</u> is _____

   _____.

7. A paper that reports the <u>news</u> is a

   _____.

Reading and Thinking

1. Number the sentences to show the order in which things happened.

   _____ Kids arrived for Rick's show.

   _____ Rick made a poster.

   _____ Rick did a trick with aluminum foil.

   _____ Rick did his first trick.

2. How were Rick's two tricks alike?

   _____

   _____

3. How were Rick's two tricks different?

   _____

   _____

Write **T** if the sentence is true.
Write **F** if the sentence is false.

4. ____ The word *hocus-pocus* made the tricks happen.

5. ____ The audience enjoyed Rick's performance.

6. ____ Rick's tricks were magic.

7. A **fact** is something that is known to be true. An **opinion** is what someone thinks or feels. Check two sentences that give facts.

   ____ Messages can be put on posters.

   ____ Lifting ice on a string is a good trick.

   ____ Tricks can be learned from books.

Stuck!

Read to find out what happens when Heather and Andy get stuck on a Ferris wheel.

1   Rick's family had planned a trip to the fair. Rick and his brother, Andy, had extra tickets. They invited Michael and Heather to go along. The fairgrounds weren't far from the neighborhood, but the bus ride seemed to take forever.

2   When they arrived, Heather and Andy wanted to go on the rides. Rick and Michael planned to explore the fairgrounds. Mr. and Mrs. Smith had to work at one of the stands. "Let's split into pairs. We'll meet at the bus stop at three o'clock," Mrs. Smith said.

3   The others agreed. They set their watches on the same time. Then each pair hurried off in a different direction. At 2:45, Heather and Andy each had a ticket for one more ride. They chose the Ferris wheel. They were at the top of the first turn when it quit moving.

4   "I'll bet there's something wrong with the motor," Heather guessed.

5   Suddenly Andy pointed in the distance. He cried, "Look, the others are waiting at the bus stop! Somehow we've got to let them know what has happened!"

6   Heather thought a moment. Then she leaned forward to explain the problem to a man in the next car. He told the couple in front of him. They passed the word to the people ahead of them. Before long the message reached a man on the ground. He rushed off to tell Rick, Rick's parents, and Michael not to leave.

7   Finally the Ferris wheel was fixed. Rick and Michael were waiting at the bottom.

8   "What a great way to see the fair!" Heather exclaimed when she got off.

9   "Well, I hope it never happens again," Andy sighed with relief.

10   "I thought you weren't afraid of heights," Rick teased.

11   "I'm not," Andy replied, "but you have my bus fare!"

Knowing the Words

Write the words from the story that have the meanings below.

1. a ride at a fair _____
   (Par. 3)

2. feeling better _____
   (Par. 9)

3. high places _____
   (Par. 10)

4. money that people pay
   to ride somewhere _____
   (Par. 11)

Write the word with the correct meaning to complete each sentence below.

5. The city bus _____
   is sixty cents. (fair, fare)

6. I'll _____ you downtown
   this evening. (meet, meat)

7. I had _____ tickets
   for rides. (for, four)

Learning to Study

The word you look up in a dictionary is called an **entry word.** Many words with endings are not listed as entry words. To find these words, look up the word to which the ending was added. To find the word *teased*, look up *tease*.

Write the word you would look under to find each of these words in a dictionary.

1. tickets _____

2. arrived _____

3. waiting _____

4. completely _____

Reading and Thinking

1. Check the answer that tells what the story is mainly about.

   _____ a long bus ride

   _____ a visit to the fair

   _____ how a Ferris wheel works

2. Andy didn't want Rick to leave

   the fair without him because _____

   _____.

3. How were Heather and Andy alike?

   _____

Write **F** if the sentence gives a fact.
Write **O** if the sentence gives an opinion.

4. _____ Riding a bus is one way to travel.

5. _____ It is scary at the top of a Ferris wheel.

6. _____ Ferris wheels are fun to ride.

7. _____ Ferris wheels have seats.

8. If Heather and Andy had been left behind, how might they have gotten

   home? _____

   _____

Confusion

What kinds of things do you need a good memory for?

1   Tracy and Elsa were fixing lunch when Rick came over to introduce his new friends. "This is Lin," he said, motioning to the dark-haired girl. "She will be in our class at school." Then he nodded toward the boy in the striped shirt. "This is her brother, Tat," he said. "They've just taught me a great game. It's called *Confusion.*"

2   "Why don't you explain it? We'll make ham and cheese sandwiches for everyone," Tracy said to Lin.

3   "In this game, each player has a sign," Lin began. "I'll scratch my ear, and that will be my sign. Then I'll wiggle my thumbs, and that could be Rick's sign. Rick must repeat what I've done and add another player's sign. That person repeats the entire thing and adds someone else's sign."

4   "It goes on and on till someone gets confused and forgets the order of the signs," Tat added. "Any questions?"

5   No one had any questions, so Elsa said, "OK, let's play." She set the sandwiches on the table. Each child chose a sign. Soon they were all wiggling, scratching, waving, and giggling. Then Tracy's third turn came. She tried to repeat eleven signs, but she got very confused. Tracy started to laugh. Then she patted her stomach and pointed to her mouth.

6   "Hey, that isn't anybody's sign," Rick broke in.

7   "Yeah, what's that supposed to mean?" asked Tat.

8   "It means," Tracy explained with a chuckle, "that my stomach is growling. That's a sign that it's time for me to eat! Would anyone care to join me?"

9   "Sure," they all answered.

10   "After lunch we can start the game over. We'll use all new signs," Tat suggested. Everyone groaned, but Tat could tell by the smiles on their faces that they thought it was a good idea.

Knowing the Words

Write the words from the story that have the meanings below.

1. mistaking one
   thing for another _____
   (Par. 1)

2. parts of your hands _____
   (Par. 3)

3. whole _____
   (Par. 3)

In each row below, circle the three words that belong together.

4. thumb   stomach   ear   shirt

5. wave   stripe   pat   wiggle

6. ham   cheese   plate   bread

Working with Words

Write the two words that were used to form each of these contractions.

1. they've _____

2. I'll _____

3. that's _____

Say *children.* Circle the words below that have the sound *ch* stands for in *children.*

4. chose   handkerchief   ache

5. sandwich   chuckle   stomach

Reading and Thinking

1. Check the answer that tells what the story is mainly about.

   _____ meeting new neighbors

   _____ playing a game

   _____ making sandwiches

2. What was Lin's sign? _____

   _____

3. What were the children having for

   lunch? _____

   _____

4. Rick came over to Tracy's house

   because _____

   _____.

5. What do you think the children did after Tracy explained why she

   pointed to her mouth? _____

   _____

Write the best word to complete each sentence below.

6. The zebra is a _____
   animal. (confused, striped, tiny)

7. Please _____
   this word. (repeat, motion, scratch)

8. Don fixed a _____
   for lunch. (sign, shirt, sandwich)

9. The bear was _____.
   (chuckling, reading, growling)

The Contest

Read to find out what happens when Tat and Lin enter the Crunchy Munchies contest.

1   Tat and Lin loved to enter contests. It did not matter what the prize was. Once they wrote a poem for a magazine contest. They won free copies of the magazine for a year. Another time they guessed how many marbles were in a glass jar. They won all the marbles.

2   One morning Tat was reading the Crunchy Munchies cereal box as he ate breakfast. "Lin," he said, "here's another contest to enter. The first-place winner gets a bike. Second prize is a tent."

3   "Those are great prizes," Lin said. "How do we enter?"

4   "Just print our names and address on the back of a Crunchy Munchies box top. Then we send it to the company for a drawing. We've got four weeks to collect all the box tops we can."

5   Starting right then, they ate Crunchy Munchies for breakfast every day. They also asked everyone they knew to save the box tops for them. By the end of the four weeks, Tat and Lin had sixteen box tops to send to the company. "I'm glad that's over," Tat laughed. "I'm tired of eating Crunchy Munchies!"

6   "If I have to look at another box of that stuff, I don't know what I'll do," Lin added.

7   A few weeks passed. One day the mail carrier brought a letter and a large package. "We've won third prize in the Crunchy Munchies contest!" Lin exclaimed as she read the letter.

8   "I didn't even know there was a third-place prize," Tat said as he ripped the carton open. Then Tat and Lin got a surprise. There were two dozen boxes of Crunchy Munchies cereal in the carton.

Knowing the Words

Write the words from the story that have the meanings below.

1. gather _____
   (Par. 4)

2. person who
   delivers mail _____
   (Par. 7)

3. cardboard box _____
   (Par. 8)

Synonyms are words that have the same or nearly the same meaning. Circle the pair of synonyms in each row.

4. delivered   came   brought   went

5. win   collect   buy   gather

6. eleven   some   dozen   twelve

7. frown   chuckle   sneeze   laugh

Working with Words

The ending **-er** sometimes means "more." It may be used to compare two things. The ending **-est** means "most." It is used to compare more than two things.

In each sentence below, add **-er** to the word before the blank if two things are being compared. Add **-est** if more than two things are being compared.

1. Apple juice is sweet _____ than lemonade.

2. Ken is the young _____ of three sons.

3. The lamp is bright _____ than the flashlight.

4. Kay is the fast _____ swimmer on the team.

Reading and Thinking

1. Write **O** next to two sentences that give opinions.

   _____ Cereal tastes best for breakfast.

   _____ Cereal is in the bread food group.

   _____ A ten-speed bicycle is a good prize.

2. Why did Tat and Lin eat so much cereal? _____

   _____

3. How many box tops did Tat and Lin send in? _____

4. How many boxes of cereal did Tat and Lin win? _____

5. How do you think the children felt when they saw what they had won?

   _____

Write **T** if the sentence is true.
Write **F** if the sentence is false.

6. _____ Tat and Lin won even more cereal than they had eaten.

7. _____ Crunchy Munchies was like oatmeal.

8. What do you think Lin and Tat will do with the cereal they won?

   _____

   _____

Wee Willie Goes Walking

Look at the picture. Is Michael walking the dog? Or is the dog walking Michael?

1   Michael wanted to earn some money. He had started a dog-walking business. So far that day he had walked a bulldog, a poodle, and a beagle. Now he was going to walk Ms. Silva's dog, Wee Willie.

2   Wee Willie was a Saint Bernard puppy who already weighed more than Michael. "Willie is very friendly, but he has lots of spirit. He gets excited easily," Ms. Silva warned. "If you can handle him, I'll let you walk him every day."

3   "I could use the extra money," said Michael. He fastened a chain to Willie's collar. He opened the screen door. Wee Willie scrambled for the sidewalk. He was dragging Michael behind him.

4   Suddenly a robin flew down from a treetop. It landed in their path. Before Michael could say, "No, Willie," the dog had jerked the chain out of Michael's hand. Wee Willie went speeding after the bird.

5   Michael dashed down the alley after Willie, but soon he ran out of breath. He stopped near City Park. He wondered how he'd explain this to Ms. Silva. Just then he heard splashing and barking. It seemed to be coming from the park.

6   Michael ran through the park to the fountain. There he found Wee Willie jumping and biting at the water. Michael leaped into the fountain. The excited dog gave him a messy, wet kiss. Michael coaxed Wee Willie out of the fountain with a soggy dog biscuit.

7   "Ms. Silva," Michael began when he finally got the dog home, "you may not believe this, but . . ."

8   "How thoughtful of you to give Willie a bath as well as a walk!" Ms. Silva said in a pleased voice. "You're hired to walk Wee Willie *every* day!"

Knowing the Words

Write the words from the story that have the meanings below.

1. kind of dog _____
   (Par. 2)

2. gently talked into doing something _____
   (Par. 6)

3. very wet _____
   (Par. 6)

4. gave a job for pay _____
   (Par. 8)

Check the meaning that fits the underlined word in each sentence.

5. The collar was too big for the poodle.

   _____ part of a shirt

   _____ something a dog wears

6. Park the car in that empty space.

   _____ stop for a time

   _____ a place to play

7. Bootsie hid my brother's block under the couch.

   _____ a toy

   _____ area bordered by four streets

Learning to Study

Write the word you would look under to find each of these words in a dictionary.

1. spending _____

2. businesses _____

3. weighed _____

4. copies _____

Reading and Thinking

1. Check the answer that tells what the story is mainly about.

   _____ jumping in a fountain

   _____ walking a Saint Bernard

   _____ seeing a robin

Write **T** if the sentence is true.
Write **F** if the sentence is false.

2. _____ Wee Willie is a lazy dog.

3. _____ Wee Willie likes water.

4. _____ Michael could carry Wee Willie in his arms.

5. What three kinds of dogs did Michael walk before he walked Wee Willie?

   _____

6. What do you think Michael said when Ms. Silva offered to hire him to walk Willie every day?

   _____

   _____

Write the best word to complete each sentence below.

7. Ann has a _____ named Puff. (collar, screen, poodle)

8. Ms. Kay _____ a gift shop in town. (spends, hires, manages)

9. A bird was _____ in the birdbath. (splashing, leaping, laughing)

119

Heather's Quarters

Heather loses something and finds something. Read to find what happened.

1 "Hi, Heather!" Mr. Taylor said as Heather entered the store. "What can I do for you today?"

2 "I have two quarters to spend. I'd like to look around awhile before I decide," Heather said.

3 "Take your time," Mr. Taylor said. Heather was heading for the comic books when she bumped into a rack of birthday cards. She dropped one of her quarters. As she stooped to look for it, she heard another coin drop. A man wearing a green sweatshirt kneeled near her. He looked under a toy shelf.

4 Just as Heather spied her quarter beneath the shelf, the man snatched it. He thought it was his. The man dropped the quarter into his pocket and left.

5 Upset and disappointed, Heather began searching again when suddenly a flash of gold caught her eye. "Look, Mr. Taylor! I'll bet this belongs to the man who found my quarter," she said as she held up a shiny coin.

6 Mr. Taylor looked at the coin. He said in surprise, "That's a twenty-dollar gold piece!"

7 Just then the door flew open. The man in the green sweatshirt burst in. "I've lost my lucky gold piece!" he shouted.

8 "This little girl just found an unusual coin," Mr. Taylor said pointing to the coin in Heather's hand. "Perhaps she'd trade it for the quarter you found."

9 "Make it two quarters!" the man offered quickly and he dropped two quarters into Heather's palm. "I'm sorry. I didn't notice which coin I'd dropped when I picked up your quarter. Thank you so much. I've had that lucky gold piece for years."

10 Heather jingled her three coins. She grinned from ear to ear. "Mr. Taylor," she chuckled, "I think it'll take me even longer to make up my mind now."

Knowing the Words

Write the words from the story that have the meanings below.

1. a piece of clothing _____
    (Par. 3)

2. rushed in suddenly _____
    (Par. 7)

Circle the pair of antonyms (opposites) in each row.

3. buy   spend   sell   trade

4. door   enter   agree   exit

5. open   drop   loose   close

6. found   rolled   lost   heard

7. now   near   later   gold

Working with Words

Some words that have one consonant between two vowels are divided into syllables after the first vowel. The first vowel sound in these words is most often long, as in *tī/ger.*

Other words that have one consonant between two vowels are divided after the consonant. In these words, the first vowel sound is most often short, as in *trăv/el.*

The words below have been divided into syllables. Put a mark above the first vowel in each word to show if the vowel stands for a long or short sound. Mark the long vowels with ‾ over the letter. Mark the short vowels with ˇ.

1. lem/on   4. si/lence   7. clos/et

2. wag/on   5. fro/zen   8. sto/len

3. mo/tor   6. cop/y   9. cab/in

Reading and Thinking

1. Number the sentences to show the order in which things happened.

    _____ Heather dropped a quarter.

    _____ The man dropped a coin.

    _____ The man grabbed the quarter.

    _____ The man returned the quarter.

Write **T** if the sentence is true.
Write **F** if the sentence is false.

2. _____ Heather had been in Mr. Taylor's store before.

3. _____ Heather had one dollar to spend in Mr. Taylor's store.

4. _____ Mr. Taylor had never seen a gold piece before.

5. How much was the gold piece worth?

    _____

6. What might Heather buy with her

    money? _____

7. How do you think Heather felt when the man gave her two quarters?

    _____

Write the best word to complete each sentence below.

8. Jim found a _____ in his pocket. (shirt, shelf, coin)

9. Three _____ equal seventy-five cents. (quarters, pieces, cards)

Down the Middle

What is the quickest way to get a difficult job done?

1   Rick and Andy shared a bedroom. Each Saturday they were responsible for cleaning it. Most of the time this was not a problem, but they had been especially careless during one week. The room was an awful mess. Clothes and toys were all over the floor. Books and papers were stacked high on the desk. Notes were falling off the overcrowded bulletin board.

2   The boys spent quite a bit of time arguing about who would clean what. Finally they agreed that each of them would take care of his own bed, but the desk, the floor, and the bulletin board would be divided in half. They could tape them down the middle so each boy could see his part.

3   "We can't even see the top of the desk to put tape on it yet," Rick said. "I'll put these books on the shelf. You put those papers in the drawers." With that done, they were able to tape the desk down the middle.

4   They decided to divide the floor next. Once again, they had to move things. They put clothes in the dirty laundry and toys in the toy box before they could even begin to divide the floor.

5   Last, they did the bulletin board. "Here, these are yours, so put them on that side," Andy said to Rick. "These are mine, so I'll put them over here. These notes are old, so I'll throw them away." Now they could see the bulletin board to put tape on it.

6   After they had the room divided they stood back. They looked to see what still needed to be done. Both boys were amazed by what they saw. The room was completely cleaned! Rick and Andy started laughing. Andy said, "I guess we make a pretty good team after all. Next week, let's not waste all this time arguing and taping."

7   "Good idea," Rick said. "Think of the things we can do with the time we'll save."

Knowing the Words

Write the words from the story that have the meanings below.

1. in charge of _____
   (Par. 1)

2. more than usually _____
   (Par. 1)

3. holding too much _____
   (Par. 1)

In each row, circle the three words that belong together.

4. desk   clothes   bed   chair

5. stood   said   stooped   bent

6. laugh   agree   argue   talk

Working with Words

Circle the correct word in ( ) and write it in the blank.

1. The _____ talked for a long time. (buys, boys)

2. Did you _____ out the garage alone? (clean, clothes)

3. Rick _____ in line for thirty minutes. (stand, stood)

4. When Andy went _____, Rick was lonely. (away, awake)

Reading and Thinking

1. Check the answer that tells what the story is mainly about.

   _____ clothes on the floor

   _____ a divided room

   _____ cleaning a room together

2. Rick and Andy divided the room

   because _____

   _____.

3. Check three words that tell what Rick and Andy divided in half.

   _____ desk   _____ bulletin board

   _____ floor   _____ toy box

Write **F** if the sentence gives a fact.
Write **O** if the sentence gives an opinion.

4. _____ Cleaning is difficult work.

5. _____ Vacuum cleaners can be used to sweep rugs.

6. _____ A bed is a piece of furniture.

7. _____ Cleaning should be done once a week.

8. Were Rick and Andy still arguing at the end of the story? Explain your

   answer. _____

   _____

9. What might Rick and Andy do after

   they clean their room? _____

   _____

Where's Herbie?

Why do you think Herbie is hiding, and where do you think he is?

1 Tracy was so thrilled she could hardly sit still long enough to eat her cereal and toast. Today was Monday, and she was leaving to spend a few weeks with Aunt Ruth and Uncle Stan. She would stay at their home in the country. "I'll be ready in a few minutes, Dad," she said, gulping down the rest of her orange juice. She brushed her teeth. Then she finished packing a few things in her blue canvas bag.

2 Tracy set the bag in the kitchen and went to say good-bye to Herbie. The cat usually napped beneath the couch, but when Tracy glanced under it he was not there. She looked behind the drapes and under the rocking chair, but Herbie was nowhere in sight.

3 "We have to leave in ten minutes, Tracy," her father called. "We've got to get to the bus station in time to pick up your ticket."

4 "I can't find Herbie to say good-bye," Tracy said. "Have you seen him, Dad?"

5 "No, I haven't. Why don't you look in your bedroom?" he suggested. Tracy raced upstairs. She expected to find Herbie asleep on her pillow. He wasn't there either.

6 "Herbie must not care that I'm going away," Tracy said as she came downstairs. She was wearing a long, sad face.

7 "He just doesn't understand that you're leaving," her father said. "I wish there were more time to search for him, but we really need to leave soon."

8 Tracy's sadness now turned to anger. "If Herbie doesn't care, then neither do I!" she grumbled.

9 "Don't forget this," her father said. He handed her a jacket. Tracy unzipped her bag. She was stuffing her jacket inside when she felt something soft and furry. Then two gray ears poked out of the bag.

10 "That's why Herbie didn't say good-bye," she laughed. "He packed himself to come along with me!"

Knowing the Words

Write the words from the story that have the meanings below.

1. a strong cloth _____
   (Par. 1)

2. a long seat
   with cushions _____
   (Par. 2)

3. said unhappily _____
   (Par. 8)

4. covered with hair _____
   (Par. 9)

Synonyms are words that have the same or nearly the same meaning. Circle the pair of synonyms in each row.

5. shades   curtains   windows   drapes

6. swallow   chew   lick   gulp

Learning to Study

Some words have more than one meaning. In a dictionary, the different meanings of a word are numbered.

Read each word in dark print and the dictionary meanings that follow. Then read each sentence below and decide the meaning of the underlined words. Write the number of the correct meaning in the blank.

coun try 1 nation **2** land outside a city

1. _____ Dave works on a farm in the country.

2. _____ Each country has its own flag.

room 1 area with walls inside a building **2** space

3. _____ We have room for one more.

4. _____ The girls gave the room a new coat of paint.

Reading and Thinking

1. Check the answer that tells what the story is mainly about.

   _____ looking for a pet

   _____ a visit to the country

   _____ the blue canvas bag

2. Do you think Tracy meant it when she said she did not care about Herbie? Explain your answer.

   _____

   _____

   _____

Write **T** if the sentence is true.
Write **F** if the sentence is false.

3. _____ Tracy's aunt and uncle live down the street from her.

4. _____ Tracy knew she would miss Herbie while she was gone.

5. _____ Aunt Ruth and Uncle Stan probably met Tracy at the airport.

6. What do you think Tracy did with

   Herbie after she found him? _____

   _____

The Fall

What is sometimes the best way to get over being afraid of something?

1   Tracy and Aunt Ruth had saddled up their horses. They were ready to ride when Aunt Ruth said, "Tracy, would you like to ride Big Gabe today?"

2   Tracy had dreamed of the day she would be allowed to ride Big Gabe. He was a huge, tan horse. Tracy was

thrilled. Her knees started shaking, and she nearly shouted, "I'd love to!"

3   Tracy managed to get up on Big Gabe. She sat there for a minute feeling proud and tall as she held the reins. Then she gave the horse a gentle kick. Big Gabe started off at an easy trot. Tracy was just beginning to relax when something ran in front of Big Gabe. It frightened him so that he reared up on his hind legs.

4   Tracy was thrown to the ground. Although she was not hurt, she was scared. "I hate that horse. I'm never going to ride him again!" she cried in anger as Aunt Ruth helped her up.

5   "I once knew a girl your age who had been thrown from her horse," Aunt Ruth said. "Afterwards, she was terribly afraid to ride. She wouldn't even go near the horse. But one day there was an emergency at home. A doctor was needed. The girl had to ride the horse into town to get a doctor.

6   "After that," Aunt Ruth went on, "the girl realized that her bravery had helped save someone's life. She made up her mind to practice riding again. After a while she wasn't afraid any more. That girl went on to become a fine rider. She's now grown and sitting next to you."

7   "You, Aunt Ruth?" Tracy inquired, looking surprised.

8   "That's right," she replied. "Now let's walk the horses back to the stalls."

9   "You can walk Ginger if you like," Tracy said as she climbed onto her horse. "I'll ride Big Gabe back home!"

Knowing the Words

Write the words from the story that have the meanings below.

1. something used to
control a horse _____
(Par. 3)

2. awfully _____
(Par. 5)

Write the word with the correct meaning to complete each sentence below.

3. Spring _____ help flowers to grow. (reins, rains)

4. _____ are horses out in the pasture. (Their, There)

5. Who _____ the race? (one, won)

Working with Words

Write a compound word using the underlined words in each sentence.

1. A <u>bowl</u> in which a <u>fish</u> lives is

a _____.

2. A <u>knob</u> used to close a <u>door</u> is

a _____.

The words below have been divided into syllables. Put a mark above the first vowel in each word to show if the vowel stands for a long or short sound. Mark the long vowels with ‾ over the letter. Mark the short vowels with ˘.

3. na/tion   **6.** min/ute   **9.** nev/er

4. re/cess   **7.** fin/ish   **10.** sta/tion

5. vis/it   **8.** pi/lot   **11.** fi/nal

Reading and Thinking

1. Check the answer that tells what the story is mainly about.

_____ riding to town on a horse

_____ a riding accident

_____ how to ride a horse

2. Check three answers that tell about both Tracy and Aunt Ruth.

_____ had a scary accident

_____ lives in the city

_____ rides horses

_____ is no longer afraid of horses

_____ is an adult

3. Check two words that tell how Tracy felt when Big Gabe threw her.

_____ scared   _____ pretty

_____ hungry   _____ angry

_____ sleepy   _____ proud

4. Do you think Tracy will ride Big Gabe after today? Explain your answer.

_____

_____

Write the best word to complete each sentence below.

5. Pull the _____ to make the horse stop. (saddle, reins, rider)

6. Because of her _____, the woman was given a medal. (fear, bravery, stable)

127

The Bean Thief

How do you think Tracy will catch whoever is stealing beans from the garden?

1   Tracy liked to work in her aunt and uncle's garden. Each morning she hooked the hose up to the faucet in the stable. Then she watered the young plants. If she saw a weed popping up, she would pull it out by the roots. Tracy was proud of the results of her daily care.

2   One morning she noticed that a row of bean sprouts had been chewed off. She did not think much about it. But more sprouts were missing the following day. It was then she decided to catch the thief. That night Tracy planned to sit on the porch. She thought she would watch the garden all night, but she fell asleep. She didn't wake up till the sun rose. Tracy felt awful when she saw more beans were missing.

3   Then Tracy had a great idea. She put a stake at each corner of the garden. She tied string from one corner to the next until the garden was surrounded. Then she hung aluminum pie pans from the string. "When the thief bumps the string, the pans will rattle. I'll wake up and catch whoever is responsible," she said to herself proudly.

4   Tracy hadn't been asleep long that night when she was awakened by the sound of the pans clattering. She grabbed her flashlight and shined it toward the garden. Sure enough, there was the thief. He was chewing a tasty bean sprout!

5   "Clyde, you naughty goat!" Tracy shouted as she ran toward the garden. "How did you get out of your pen?"

6   Tracy took Clyde back to the pen. She was walking away when Clyde came up to her. She realized that the goat had learned to jump over the side of the pen. "Well, Clyde, I guess you'll just have to be tied up at night. I promise that I will share the beans with you when they are ready," Tracy said, patting Clyde on the head.

Knowing the Words

Write the words from the story that have the meanings below.

1. something that happens because of something else _____ (Par. 1)

2. a post _____ (Par. 3)

3. closed in on all sides _____ (Par. 3)

Circle the pair of antonyms (opposites) in each row.

4. pull   push   drop   fall

5. month   night   year   day

6. race   watch   asleep   awake

7. found   planned   missed   lost

Choose the correct word to fill in the blank for each pair of sentences.

rose   felt   row

8. David's costume was made from

yellow and purple _____.

The sidewalk _____ hot under my feet.

9. Ty helped _____ the boat yesterday.

The _____ of beans is straight.

10. The sun _____ in the East.

Kevin found a _____ near the edge of the garden.

Reading and Thinking

1. Number the sentences to show the order in which things happened.

_____ Tracy hung aluminum pans around the garden.

_____ The thief was caught.

_____ Tracy noticed that some beans were missing.

_____ Clyde rattled the pie pans.

2. Why did Tracy hang aluminum pans from a string? _____

_____

3. How do you think Tracy felt when she saw who the thief was? _____

_____

4. Why did Tracy say she would share the ripe beans with Clyde?

_____

5. What do you think will happen to Clyde now? _____

_____

Learning to Study

Number each list of words below in alphabetical order.

1. _____ flavor   2. _____ caught

_____ fresh   _____ catch

_____ friend   _____ corner

129

A Helping Hand

Read to find out what Tracy did when she got bored.

1   It was raining for the third day in a row. Tracy was getting bored. She had already read two books. She had finished a paint-by-number picture. She had also written a letter to her parents.

2   She wandered out to the garage where Uncle Stan was busy at the workbench. Tracy gazed out the window and murmured, "Will this rain ever stop?"

3   Just then she saw a little wren sitting on the windowsill. It was trying to stay dry. "I wonder if it is hard for birds to find food in all this rain," Tracy said.

4   Then the idea came to Tracy that she could help this wren and other birds, too. She asked Uncle Stan if he would help her build a bird feeder out of wood. She found some plans in one of her uncle's books. Uncle Stan cut out the pieces she needed. Tracy nailed them together. She sanded the bird feeder to make it smooth. Then she painted it white. As she finished the project, the rain stopped, and the sun came out from behind the clouds. Tracy was happy because she could hang her feeder outside. She would fill it with seeds and wait for her feathered friends to visit.

5   For the rest of her visit, Tracy spent some time each day watching the birds at the bird feeder. They would sit on the fence after they ate. They sang songs for her. Tracy imagined they were saying thank you.

6   Uncle Stan and Aunt Ruth suggested that Tracy take the bird feeder home with her. They said the birds in the city might need help to find food during the winter. Tracy knew she would always remember this vacation. She would have the bird feeder to remind her.

Knowing the Words

Write the words from the story that have the meanings below.

1. a high table
used for work _____
(Par. 2)

2. said in a
low voice _____
(Par. 2)

Synonyms are words that have the same or nearly the same meaning. Circle the pair of synonyms in each row.

3. gazed laughed cried stared

4. called finished completed tripped

5. wrote murmured read said

6. garage city town window

Working with Words

A **prefix** is a group of letters added to the beginning of a word that changes the meaning of the word. The prefixes **un-** and **dis-** mean "not" or "the opposite of." *Distrust* means "the opposite of trust." *Unfair* means "not fair."

Complete each sentence by writing **un-** or **dis-** in the blank.

1. It is _____ safe to climb on that rock.

2. Sean's wool socks were causing him

some _____ comfort.

3. Dan and I _____ agree.

4. I was _____ able to go to the movies because I was sick.

Reading and Thinking

1. Check the answer that tells what the story is mainly about.

_____ how birds fly

_____ Tracy's project

_____ talking with Uncle Stan

Write **T** if the sentence is true.
Write **F** if the sentence is false.

2. _____ Uncle Stan has no hobbies.

3. _____ Tracy likes to help.

4. _____ Tracy is tired of the rain.

5. Write three things Tracy had done to

keep herself busy. _____

_____

6. Write **R** next to two sentences that tell about real things.

_____ A girl could fly in a plane.

_____ A boy could fly like a bird.

_____ A bird could fly through the clouds.

Write the best word to complete each sentence below.

7. Bob _____ he was on a ship. (pleased, imagined, sang)

8. The _____ is big enough for two cars. (skate, garage, workbench)

9. The plant on the _____ gets lots of sunshine. (closet, river, windowsill)

Vegetable Soup

Look at the picture. Can you tell where this story takes place?

1   Rick's father was a cook. One day when Rick didn't have to go to school, he went to work with his father. They had to get up very early. Rick and his father were on the job before it was light outside. They had to get the food prepared by noon.

2   Rick filled a large pot with water. He set it on the stove. Rick's father cleaned and chopped carrots, potatoes,

tomatoes, and green beans. He was cutting some beef into small chunks when someone came to the back door.

3   "You're a little earlier than usual this morning, Mr. Hastings," Rick's father said. "If you will stop by after your rounds, I'll have some beef scraps for your dog."

4   "Great," Mr. Hastings said. "Just leave them in the refrigerator." Then he emptied the trash bins onto his truck.

5   Rick's father finished cutting up the meat. He added all the vegetables and pieces of beef to the boiling water. He put the beef scraps into a white plastic jar. Then he set the jar inside the refrigerator.

6   When the soup was done cooking, Rick's father poured it into jars. They looked just like the one with the beef scraps. After he put the jars inside the refrigerator, Rick's dad began to fix some salads.

7   By twelve o'clock all the food was prepared, and it was time to go home. "Take some of this soup home for lunch," the chef said. He handed Rick a jar from the refrigerator.

8   "I can't wait to taste your soup, Dad," Rick said when they got home. But when Rick took the lid off of the jar, he could not believe his eyes. "Dad," he cried with amazement, "we've got the jar with the beef scraps!"

9   "Oh, they must have got mixed up in the refrigerator," his father moaned. "Well, I sure hope Mr. Hastings's dog likes my vegetable soup!"

Knowing the Words

Write the words from the story that have the meanings below.

1. leftover pieces _____
   (Par. 3)

2. cook who is in charge _____
   (Par. 7)

Synonyms are words that have the same or nearly the same meaning. Circle the pair of synonyms in each row.

3. garbage   collect   trash   truck

4. jar   bucket   water   pail

5. hope   ready   prepared   leave

6. begin   clean   stay   start

Working with Words

Write a compound word using the underlined words in each sentence.

1. A <u>room</u> with a <u>bed</u> in it is a

   _____.

2. A <u>bench</u> at which to <u>work</u> is a

   _____.

The suffix **-ment** means "the act of." *Enjoyment* means "the act of enjoying." Add **-ment** to the following words. Use the new words to complete the sentences.

amuse   agree

3. Joel has an _____
   with his brother about sharing toys.

4. The joke was told for our

   _____.

Reading and Thinking

1. Check the answer that tells what the story is mainly about.

   _____ making vegetable soup

   _____ Mr. Hastings's dog

   _____ eating in a restaurant

2. The soup and beef scraps got mixed

   up because _____

   _____.

3. What did Mr. Hastings plan to do

   with the beef scraps? _____

   _____

Write **T** if the sentence is true.
Write **F** if the sentence is false.

4. _____ Mr. Hastings is a cab driver.

5. _____ It was evening when Rick went to work with his father.

6. _____ Rick's dad made a lot of soup.

7. What was in the soup besides

   vegetables? _____

8. Number the sentences in the order that tells how the soup was made.

   _____ The mixture was cooked.

   _____ Water was boiled.

   _____ Vegetables and beef were put in the pot.

   _____ Vegetables and beef were cut up.

   _____ The soup was put into jars. 133

It's Alive!

Look closely at the picture. Do you see anything strange that gives a hint about what will "come alive" in the story?

1   Andy liked to play harmless tricks on Rick. Usually Rick didn't mind. But then Andy hid in the bedroom closet and scared Rick. That was just too much. "I guess you'd be scared of just about anything!" Andy had teased.

2   The next day Rick thought of a plan and explained it to Heather. She agreed to help. They gathered leafy twigs and branches from the yard and put them in the basement.

3   That evening Rick quietly crept downstairs. He tied branches to his legs and arms. He stuffed his pockets with twigs and taped leaves to his forehead.

4   It was getting dark outside when the phone rang. Rick knew it was Heather calling for Andy. While Andy talked to her, Rick tiptoed upstairs. He sneaked out the front door. Then he hid next to some bushes.

5   Heather said she was coming over and asked Andy to wait for her outside. He was sitting on the porch step when a strange noise startled him. "Is that you, Heather?" Andy called nervously. There was no reply. "It's just my imagination," he thought. Then he heard the noise again. Andy was glad when he saw Heather coming across the front lawn.

6   "There's something spooky going on, Heather," he whispered. Suddenly something brushed against Andy's arm. He jumped back, shouting, "What was that?" Then a bush began to shake and moan. "It's alive!" Andy yelled. His whole body was shaking with fear.

7   All at once the bush reached out. It gently tapped Andy on the shoulder. The bush, with a voice exactly like Rick's, laughed. Then it said, "Would you like to make a deal with your brother?"

Knowing the Words

Write the words from the story that have the meanings below.

1. having many leaves _____
    (Par. 2)

2. moved slowly
    and quietly _____
    (Par. 3)

3. moved without
    anyone knowing _____
    (Par. 4)

4. picturing in
    one's mind _____
    (Par. 5)

In each row below, circle the three words that belong together.

5. forehead   closet   elbow   shoulder

6. sneaked   crept   tiptoed   stuffed

7. tease   moan   shout   whisper

Working with Words

To write the plural of a word that ends in *f* or *fe*, the *f* or *fe* is changed to *v*, and *es* is added. Write the plural form of each word below.

1. leaf _____

2. wife _____

3. half _____

4. shelf _____

Say *large.* Circle the words below that have the same sound *g* stands for in *large.*

5. danger   gathered   grab   engine

6. sponge   ginger   giant   dragon

Reading and Thinking

1. Number the sentences to show the order in which things happened.

    _____ Andy waited for Heather.

    _____ Heather telephoned Andy.

    _____ Rick hid beside some bushes.

    _____ Rick scared Andy.

    _____ Rick tied branches to himself.

2. Check the sentence that tells about Rick.

    _____ He was always mean to Andy.

    _____ He wanted to hurt Andy.

    _____ He wanted to teach Andy a lesson.

3. Do you think Rick and Andy will

    make a deal? What kind? _____

    _____

4. Write **R** next to two sentences that tell about real things.

    _____ Bushes can talk and moan.

    _____ Fear can make people tremble.

    _____ People can imagine scary things.

Camping Out

What sort of noises would you expect to hear if you camped out?

1   Andy and Michael got permission to camp out in Andy's yard one night. They used an old blanket for a tent. "Hey, this is great!" Michael said. He sat inside the homemade tent and shined his flashlight on the ceiling. He made a shadow with his hands. The shadow looked like a dog. He asked Andy to guess what it was.

2   Then Andy formed a shadow of a giraffe, but Michael couldn't guess what it was supposed to be. "Giraffes have long necks, but your shadow doesn't have a long neck," Michael said.

3   "It's a baby giraffe," Andy chuckled. Then he unzipped his sleeping bag and snuggled inside. The boys talked for a long time. They told each other their favorite jokes and funniest stories.

4   Just then there was a howling noise from somewhere nearby. Michael sat up, saying, "What's that?"

5   "It's probably a dog," Andy said. "There's no reason to be scared." Soon there was another noise. It sounded like someone tapping on the windows of the house. "It's just the acorns falling off the oak tree. They're hitting the roof of the house," Andy said. "Stop worrying about the noises. Go to sleep," he said as he yawned and turned over. Before long, Andy was sleeping soundly. Michael still wasn't the least bit tired.

6   The next morning Andy woke up early. Michael was gone. Later that day Andy teased Michael, "I didn't think you'd let those noises scare you away."

7   "Did you know you sound like a bulldozer when you're sleeping?" Michael said. "I went home because your snoring was keeping me awake!"

Knowing the Words

Write the words from the story that have the meanings below.

1. the OK to
do something _____
(Par. 1)

2. got comfortable _____
(Par. 3)

3. breathing loudly
while sleeping _____
(Par. 7)

Synonyms are words that have the same or nearly the same meaning. Write **S** after each pair of synonyms. Write **A** after each pair of antonyms (opposites).

4. zip-unzip ____   7. tired-sleepy ____

5. old-new ____   8. better-worse ____

6. early-late ____   9. nearby-close ____

Learning to Study

A dictionary shows words divided into syllables. A space or a dot shows where the word can be divided at the end of a line of writing.

Read the words below. Next to each write the number of syllables it has.

1. let ter ____   5. gi raffe ____

2. ac ci dent ____   6. morn ing ____

3. an oth er ____   7. ceil ing ____

4. chuck le ____   8. prob a bly ____

Reading and Thinking

1. Check the answer that tells what the story is mainly about.

_____ shadows on the roof

_____ the howling dog

_____ camping out

2. Andy thought Michael's reason for

going home was _____

_____.

3. Did Andy own a real tent? Explain

your answer. _____

_____

4. Was Michael used to sleeping outdoors? Explain your answer.

_____

5. Write two things Andy and Michael did before they went to sleep.

_____

_____

Write the best word to complete each sentence below.

6. A _____
was used to clear the land.
(alligator, bulldozer, yawn)

7. The _____
ate leaves. (beagle, giraffe, shadow)

8. You will need a _____
on your bed. (tent, blanket, story)

Accidents Will Happen

Read to find out how Herbie makes Tracy pay.

1   Tracy had saved her allowance for a long time. She bought a radio-controlled model car. Tracy was outdoors showing all of her friends how it worked. They were excited, but after a while they got bored just watching.

2   Tat suggested that they all play a game of tag. Rick was fast and liked to run, so he volunteered to be "it" first.

3   Tracy yelled, "Hey, wait for me. I need to put my car in the house. I'll just take a minute." She rushed inside and put the car on a table. This was a careless mistake because Herbie was inside the house.

4   Herbie was a very curious cat. It was not long before he saw the new toy. He circled the car. Then he walked around the control box. Soon he batted at the strange-looking machine. When he stepped on top of the control box, the toy came to life and started to roll. Herbie was afraid, so he stepped back. Then the car started coming straight at him. This frightened poor Herbie so much that he jumped from the table onto a rocking chair. The chair started moving back and forth. It bumped against a lamp table. With a loud crash, the lamp fell over and broke.

5   Tracy and the others heard the noise. They scrambled inside to see what had happened. First Tracy noticed the broken lamp. Then she saw Herbie in the rocking chair. Finally she saw that the car was on the floor.

6   "Oh, no," Tracy moaned. "Well, maybe I won't be in trouble if I tell my mom and dad how this happened. Next time, I think I'll put my toys away. Then there will be one curious cat that will not be able to get to them."

Knowing the Words

Write the words from the story that have the meanings below.

1. part where power is _____
(Par. 4)

2. moving back and forth _____
(Par. 4)

Circle the pair of antonyms (opposites) in each row.

3. long   large   short   huge

4. whispered   yelled   laughed   sang

5. new   tall   fast   slow

Working with Words

Write the two words that were used to form each of these contractions.

1. wasn't _____

2. you're _____

3. it'll _____

4. it's _____

The suffix **-less** means "without." *Hopeless* means "without hope." Add **-less** to the following words. Use the new words to complete the sentences.

     breath   cloud   spot

5. The windows were _____ after Jeff washed them.

6. The _____ sky was a beautiful color of blue.

7. Adam was _____ after running the race.

Reading and Thinking

1. Check the answer that tells what the story is mainly about.

_____ a pet cat

_____ playing tag

_____ a result of carelessness

2. Why didn't Tracy put the car in a

safe place? _____

_____

3. How did Herbie make the car move?

_____

4. Check two words that tell how Tracy might have felt when she saw the broken lamp.

_____ angry   _____ tired

_____ sorry   _____ thrilled

Write **T** if the sentence is true.
Write **F** if the sentence is false.

5. _____ Tracy bought the car with her allowance money.

6. _____ Herbie broke the car.

7. _____ Tracy didn't know how the lamp got broken.

8. Write **O** next to three sentences that give opinions.

_____ Cats are too curious.

_____ A toy car could be put on a table.

_____ Toys should always be put in a toy box.

_____ Cats should not be left alone.

Carmen's Penny

Elsa isn't very happy about taking Carmen to the store with her. Read to find out why she changes her mind.

1   Elsa's dad was folding clothes. He asked Elsa to run an errand for him. He gave her a list and some money. As Elsa was leaving, Carmen ran up to her. She begged to join Elsa. Elsa had planned to ride her bike, but she couldn't if Carmen was tagging along. Since Carmen loved to go to the store, Elsa agreed to take her.

2   Elsa muttered all the way to the store about not being able to ride her bike. Carmen asked Elsa to give her a piggyback ride. Elsa replied unkindly, "No, you wanted to come along, so you can just walk." They walked the rest of the way in silence.

3   At the store the girls gathered all of the items on the list. They stood in the checkout line for a long time because the store was quite busy. Finally, their turn came. When Elsa saw the total she nearly panicked. It was three cents more than she had! Elsa felt nervous. Her mind started racing as she tried to think of a solution to her problem. She checked all of her pockets twice. When she didn't find any more money, she told the clerk, "I'm sorry, but I don't have enough money. Could we put something back on the shelf?"

4   Just then Carmen reached into her pocket and calmly pulled out a coin. "Do you want this penny?" Carmen asked Elsa, holding a nickel out to her. Elsa glanced down at the money. She smiled in relief. Then she handed the money to the clerk.

5   After the girls left the store, Elsa gave Carmen a big hug. Elsa said, "Do you know you saved the day? Dad will be so proud when I tell him how you helped me out. How would you like it if we spent some time doing what you want to do?"

Knowing the Words

Write the words from the story that have the meanings below.

1. following closely _____
(Par. 1)

2. said in a low voice _____
(Par. 2)

3. things _____
(Par. 3)

4. answer _____
(Par. 3)

Working with Words

When a word ends in a consonant followed by *y*, the *y* is changed to *i* before an ending is added. Change the *y* to *i* in each word in ( ). Add **-ly** to make a word that completes the sentence.

1. Mark spoke _____
to the naughty pup. (angry)

2. Max _____ won
the race. (easy)

3. Jan walked _____
through the field. (lazy)

Rewrite the following groups of words using 's or s' to show who owns something. The first one is done for you.

the nickel that Carmen owns

Carmen's nickel
_____

4. the coins that belong to the girls

_____

5. the vacuum cleaner that Bill owns

_____

Reading and Thinking

1. Number the sentences to show the order in which things happened.

_____ Elsa realized she didn't have enough money.

_____ Carmen asked to go to the store.

_____ Carmen gave Elsa a coin.

_____ The girls stood in line.

_____ Elsa gave Carmen a hug.

2. Why did Carmen say she had a penny when she really had a nickel?

_____

_____

_____

Write **T** if the sentence is true.
Write **F** if the sentence is false.

3. _____ The store the girls went to was close by.

4. _____ The girls were both upset when they left the house.

5. _____ Elsa was angry with Carmen on the way home.

Write the best word to complete each sentence below.

6. The _____ was twelve cents. (errand, clerk, total)

7. Mark _____ to the bank. (laughed, skipped, stopped)

The Clubhouse

What would you put inside a clubhouse to make it seem cozy?

1   Tracy, Rick, and Elsa thought their clubhouse was the finest ever built. "We need some stuff to make it feel cozy inside," Elsa suggested. Rick brought some wooden crates for stools. Elsa hung a poster on the wall. Tracy wanted to do something special for the clubhouse, too. But she couldn't think of anything to add.

2   Then one Saturday while she was doing her chores, she thought of what the clubhouse needed. She told the plan to her dad. Together they went to work. They carried some things to the club. Tracy taped a sign on the door that said "Keep Out—Working in Clubhouse!"

3   When Rick and Elsa came over, Tracy would not allow them in the clubhouse. "You'll have to wait till we're through working," she said. Rick and Elsa tried to peek through the windows, but Tracy had covered each one.

4   As Rick and Elsa sat patiently waiting, they heard the pounding of nails. They were so curious that they could hardly wait to go inside.

5   At last the clubhouse door opened. Tracy announced, "Welcome to the best clubhouse in town!" When Rick and Elsa stepped inside, their feet touched something soft. Pieces of red, blue, and green carpet covered the floor. It made a colorful design. "We've made a patchwork rug!" Tracy said proudly.

6   "I knew these old carpet scraps would be useful sometime," Tracy's father said, smiling.

7   "This is wonderful!" Elsa said. She ran her palms across the soft, shaggy floor.

8   "Now our clubhouse really feels like home!" Rick added.

Knowing the Words

Write the words from the story that have the meanings below.

1. boxes _____
(Par. 1)

2. small jobs _____
(Par. 2)

3. without
making trouble _____
(Par. 4)

In each row, circle the three words that belong together.

4. finger   thumb   arm   palm

5. job   stool   chore   work

6. wall   rug   carpet   mat

7. scraps   chunks   pieces   chores

Learning to Study

Write the word you would look under to find each of these words in a dictionary.

1. patiently _____

2. smiling _____

3. stepped _____

4. finest _____

Number each list of words below in alphabetical order.

5. ____ blue

____ club

____ angry

____ crate

____ animal

6. ____ cat

____ door

____ floor

____ can

____ camp

Reading and Thinking

1. Check the answer that tells what the story is mainly about.

____ Tracy's chores

____ Tracy's idea

____ a sign that said "Keep Out!"

2. Why had Tracy's dad saved the carpet scraps? _____

_____

3. Check the answer that tells what Tracy was probably doing when she thought of making a patchwork rug.

____ washing the dishes

____ making her bed

____ sweeping the carpet

4. Tracy put up a sign and covered the windows because _____

_____

_____.

5. Check two sentences that tell how the clubhouse was like a house.

____ A poster hung on the wall.

____ The floor was carpeted.

____ The sign on the door said "Keep Out!"

Vote for Tat

Have you ever run for class president? Read to find out how Tat ran his campaign.

1   At the end of the week, Tat's class would vote for class president. Tat was running for president even though he had tried last year and lost. He was certain he could do a good job. His task was to convince the rest of his classmates. That would take a bit of work.

2   To begin his campaign, Tat spent three hours making a poster. It showed his picture and a list of promises that he would keep if elected. Tat got permission first thing Monday morning to put the poster near the door of his classroom. That way the students would see it each time they left the room.

3   Next, Tat made a campaign shirt out of one of his father's old T-shirts. He painted "Vote for Tat" on it. All day Tuesday he wore the shirt.

4   The next day Tat used his whole recess to talk to every student from his class. He told them why he would make a good president. Then Tat asked for their votes on Friday.

5   He spent all of Thursday evening writing a speech for election day. After two tries, Tat had a speech that he liked. Tat forgot part of his speech when he practiced it in front of Lin, his parents, and his stuffed animals. He was so worried that he would forget the speech the next day that he practiced it two more times. When he finished, his family praised him for a fine speech.

6   On Friday morning, Tat felt a little nervous as he dressed for school. He put on his favorite shirt, his lucky socks, and a new pair of pants. "Well, what do you think, Lin?" Tat said.

7   "You look like a winner to me," Lin replied. "Good luck today."

8   "Thanks," Tat said as he left for school.

9   Tat's speech had gone well, but he held his breath as the name of the new president was read. It took Tat a minute to realize that his hard work had finally paid off. He had won!

Knowing the Words

Write the words from the story that have the meanings below.

1. the project of getting votes _____
   (Par. 2)

2. filled with something _____
   (Par. 5)

Write the word with the correct meaning to complete each sentence below.

3. _____ poster is the most colorful. (Hour, Our)

4. Jake has a _____ of tickets for the movie. (pair, pear)

5. Dan has a _____ red wagon. (new, knew)

6. Jo gets a letter in the mail every _____. (weak, week)

Working with Words

Fill in each blank with the correct pair of letters to make a word.

        wr   kn   mb   ph

1. co _____   3. _____ ote

2. _____ ob   4. ele _____ ant

Circle the correct word in ( ) and write it in the blank.

5. She _____ for the scarf with quarters. (pad, paid)

6. Will you _____ me for lunch? (join, junk)

Reading and Thinking

1. Check the answer that tells what the story is mainly about.

   _____ being president

   _____ making a poster

   _____ running for president

2. Tell two things Tat did to get votes.

   _____

   _____

3. Write **O** next to the sentence that gives an opinion.

   _____ There are usually five days in a school week.

   _____ A poster is important to a campaign.

Learning to Study

Use the table of contents below to answer the questions.

How to Win an Election

Table of Contents

1. How many chapters are in this book?

   _____

2. On what page does "Nearing Elections" begin? _____

3. What chapter tells how to give a speech? _____

Superskater

Have you ever dreamed of being famous?
Could such a dream come true?

1 When Rick awoke, his nose was stopped up, and his throat felt scratchy. "You'll have to stay indoors today," his mother said. Rick had planned to go ice skating at City Park. Now, though, he didn't really feel like going. He just felt like resting. Rick lay his head back on the pillow and fell asleep again.

2 Rick dreamed he was a famous skater who performed all over the world. He would glide smoothly across the ice. Then he would spin so fast his skate blades would flash in the spotlight. After his performance, the audience would clap and cheer until he came back to do one more act. Later, people would crowd around him to take pictures. They would ask for his autograph. They would say nice things about his skating.

3 Rick had not been sleeping long when his father knocked on the bedroom door. "Come in," Rick said sleepily. He rolled over and sat up in bed.

4 "I picked up something for you at the store," his father said. He handed him a brown paper bag.

5 "Orange juice!" Rick exclaimed as he looked inside the package. "Thanks, Dad!"

6 "I've also been to the library," his father said. He handed Rick a book. "Since you're stuck indoors, I thought you'd enjoy reading this story. It's about a champion ice skater who won a gold medal at the Olympics."

7 "Dad," Rick exclaimed with surprise, "I was just dreaming that I was a famous skater! Do you suppose it means something special?"

8 "Who knows?" his father replied with a wink and a smile. "Perhaps it means that someday your dream will come true."

Knowing the Words

Write the words from the story that have the meanings below.

1. a bright light _____
   (Par. 2)

2. best at something _____
   (Par. 6)

3. a reward _____
   (Par. 6)

4. world sports contests _____
   (Par. 6)

Working with Words

Circle the prefix or suffix in each word. Then use the words to complete the sentences.

reread	useful
unzip	sleepless

1. Old rags are _____ for cleaning dirty windows.

2. _____ your coat and hang it on a hanger.

3. Les will _____ the book because he likes it.

4. Tom had a _____ night because a storm kept him awake.

Write the singular form of each word.

5. patches _____

6. cities _____

7. shelves _____

8. boxes _____

9. blueberries _____

Reading and Thinking

1. Check the answer that tells what the story is mainly about.

   _____ a famous Olympic ice skater

   _____ a trip to the library

   _____ a dream that could come true

2. Write two places Rick's father went.

   _____

3. Why do you think Rick's dad brought Rick a book about a skater?

   _____

   _____

4. Dreams are not real, but sometimes they can come true. Check two sentences that tell about dreams that could come true.

   _____ Jim dreamed he was a famous artist.

   _____ Jeff dreamed he lived in a pumpkin.

   _____ Kate dreamed she was an astronaut.

Write the best word to complete each sentence below.

5. The knife _____ is sharp. (handle, blade, cover)

6. "May I have your _____ on this card?" the man asked the singer. (pillow, medal, autograph)

7. The small _____ was on the desk. (package, smile, ice)

147

Tracy's Storm Delights

Do you like to cook? Read to find out what happens when Tracy makes muffins.

1 Even though it was Saturday, Tracy rolled out of bed early. She looked out the window. A thick blanket of snow covered the ground.

2 "It's a good day for a warm breakfast," Tracy thought. "I'll surprise Mom and Dad with some muffins." She found the recipe in a cookbook. Then she measured the things she needed:

1 egg
2 tablespoons sugar
3/4 cup milk
2 cups baking mix
1/2 cup brown sugar
1 1/2 teaspoons cinnamon

3 She set the oven at 400°F so it would have time to heat. Then she put twelve paper baking cups into a muffin pan. She mixed the egg, sugar, milk, and baking mix in a large bowl. She poured the lumpy batter into the baking cups so each was about two-thirds full. Next she stirred the brown sugar and cinnamon together. Last, she sprinkled the mixture on the muffins.

4 Tracy put the muffins into the oven to bake for fifteen minutes. After ten minutes she checked on the muffins because she hadn't smelled them. They were still a soupy batter. She felt the oven door with her hand. It was not even warm.

5 As she leaned against the wall to think about the problem, her arm bumped the light switch. The light did not come on. "So that's the trouble!" she said. "The storm last night must have knocked a power line down, so there is no electricity."

6 Tracy read a book while she waited for the lines to be fixed. A half hour later, the light flickered. The oven began to heat. As soon as the muffins were done, she sat down to eat. "Mmm, these were worth waiting for," she said as she bit into a warm buttered muffin. "From now on, I think I'll call these Tracy's Storm Delights!"

Knowing the Words

Write the words from the story that have the meanings below.

1. cooking directions _____
   (Par. 2)

2. a spice _____
   (Par. 3)

3. covered lightly
   with drops _____
   (Par. 3)

4. flashed off and on _____
   (Par. 6)

Match each word in the first list with its abbreviation from the second list.

5. _____ minutes   **a.** tsp.

6. _____ teaspoon   **b.** Sat.

7. _____ Saturday   **c.** min.

Working with Words

Use the following words to form compound words. Then use the compound to complete the sentences.

snow   cook   flake   book

1. This _____
   has a recipe for bean soup.

2. A _____
   landed on my mitten and melted.

Circle the correct word in ( ) and write it in the blank.

3. Add _____ to the brown
   sugar. (campaign, cinnamon)

4. The fruit _____ spilled.
   (juice, jack)

Reading and Thinking

1. Number the sentences in the order that shows how Tracy's muffins are made.

   _____ Pour the batter into baking cups.

   _____ Combine brown sugar and cinnamon.

   _____ Mix the egg, sugar, milk, and baking mix.

   _____ Put the topping on the muffins.

   _____ Bake the muffins for fifteen minutes.

2. Why didn't the muffins bake?

   _____

Write **T** if the sentence is true.
Write **F** if the sentence is false.

3. _____ Tracy made twelve muffins.

4. _____ Tracy baked the muffins in a gas oven.

5. _____ Tracy would need two eggs to make two dozen muffins.

6. _____ Tracy made the muffins for Tat.

7. _____ The muffins had fruit in them.

Write the best word to complete each sentence below.

8. The blue flame _____
   in the breeze. (flickered, bumped, leaned)

9. They _____
   the muffins turn brown. (watched, decorated, baked)

149

Crazy Sleds

If you wanted to go sledding but had no sled, what might you use instead?

1 Neither Tracy, Rick, nor Elsa owned a sled, but that didn't stop them from entering the sled races at City Park. They searched their homes for things that would glide on snow. Then they met at the park to practice.

2 Tracy arrived first. She was carrying a blown-up inner tube. Soon Rick came trudging through the snow. He had a garbage can lid that was missing its handle. Finally Elsa appeared. She was dragging a rope with a plastic laundry basket attached.

3 "These are the craziest looking sleds I've ever seen!" Tracy laughed.

4 "Do you think they'll really work?" Rick asked, sounding doubtful.

5 "There's only one way to find out," Elsa said as she climbed into her laundry basket. She grabbed the handles and asked Rick to give her a shove. "It's sort of hard to steer, but it works!" Elsa shouted when she reached the bottom of the hill.

6 Tracy sat on her rubber inner tube and said, "I hope I don't get a flat!" She kicked off with her foot and slid down the slope. "It's not bad except for a few bumps and bounces!" she called.

7 "Here comes the trash can racer!" Rick shouted. He sat cross-legged on the metal lid. Then he gave himself a spin. "I'm a little dizzy, but it got me where I wanted to go!" Rick said when he stopped whirling.

8 "I'm not sure we'll win any races with these," Elsa said as they climbed back to the top of the hill.

9 "Yeah, the kids with regular sleds will probably have the most speed," Rick agreed.

10 "But," Tracy added, "the kids with the crazy sleds will probably have the most fun!"

Knowing the Words

Write the words from the story that have the meanings below.

1. filled with air _____
   <small>(Par. 2)</small>

2. walking heavily _____
   <small>(Par. 2)</small>

3. not sure _____
   <small>(Par. 4)</small>

Circle the pair of antonyms (opposites) in each row.

4. tube   inner   rubber   outer

5. doubtful   answer   certain   guess

6. beside   top   bottom   near

Working with Words

Use each group of words in a sentence that tells who owns something.

1. children's ideas _____

   _____

2. Elsa's basket _____

   _____

3. friend's sled _____

   _____

4. kids' races _____

   _____

In each word below, draw a line to divide the word into syllables.

5. dizzy   7. minus   9. pencil

6. metal   8. garbage   10. crazy

Reading and Thinking

1. Check the answer that tells what the story is mainly about.

   _____ winning a race

   _____ building a sled

   _____ practicing for a race

2. Where were the sled races to be held?

   _____

3. Tracy, Rick, and Elsa had crazy sleds

   because _____

   _____.

4. Do you think the kids with the crazy sleds will win the race? Explain

   your answer. _____

   _____

5. Check the answer that tells what Tracy thinks is most important about sledding.

   _____ being the first-place winner

   _____ having a good time

   _____ having the best-looking sleds

In each sentence below, a word is underlined. Circle the name or names that the underlined words stand for.

6. "I will go first," said Elsa to Tracy.
   Tracy   Rick   Elsa

7. "You look cold," Tracy said to Rick.
   Rick   Elsa   Tracy

8. "We should leave," Rick said to Tracy.
   Rick   Rick and Tracy   Tracy

Secret Codes

Have you ever shared a secret code with someone?

1   Heather and Michael had a favorite game. They played it quite often. They made up mysteries for each other to solve. One day when it was just too cold to go outdoors, Heather thought that a mystery was needed.

2   She got a small piece of paper. On it she wrote RM GSV UILMG XOLHVG. Then she quietly dropped it on the floor near the chair where Michael was reading a book. Soon afterwards, Michael got up to get a glass of milk. He found the note.

3   When he first looked at it, he was quite confused. Then he remembered a code he and Heather had used once. They used a backward alphabet so that *a* was written as *z*, *b* as *y*, *c* as *x*, and so on. Michael decoded the message. It said "In the front closet."

4   He didn't know what that meant, but when he looked in the front closet he found another note. This one said LM BLFI WVHP. When he got to his desk, he found a third note! He saw that note number three said "In the den." Michael hurried to the den where he thought he'd find another note. Sure enough he did. But this one looked a little different from the rest. This is what it looked like:

In the kitchen you will see the answer to this mystery.

5   When Michael held this note up to a mirror, he could read it with no trouble at all. He followed the instructions on the note and found Heather sitting in the kitchen. "What's up?" he asked.

6   Heather said, "Well, I thought you might like some hot cider on a chilly day. I just wanted to make you curious first."

Knowing the Words

Write the words from the story that have the meanings below.

1. special way
   of writing _____
   (Par. 3)

2. figured out a
   secret code _____
   (Par. 3)

3. directions _____
   (Par. 5)

In each row, circle the three words that belong together.

4. message   note   drop   code

5. paper   read   pen   pencil

6. yard   den   kitchen   bedroom

7. chair   lamp   coat   table

8. read   fold   solve   think

Learning to Study

Read each word in dark print and the dictionary meanings that follow. Then read the sentences below and decide the meaning of each underlined word. Write the number of the correct meaning in the blank.

den **1** small room in a house
      2 an animal's home

1. _____ The fox was asleep in its <u>den</u>.

2. _____ Is the TV in the <u>den</u>?

glass **1** something that holds liquid
        2 material that can break

3. _____ I spilled the <u>glass</u> of water.

4. _____ A piece of <u>glass</u> was in the tire.

Reading and Thinking

1. Number the sentences to show the order in which things happened.

   _____ Heather dropped a note near Michael's chair.

   _____ Michael decoded the message.

   _____ Michael met Heather in the kitchen.

   _____ Michael went to the den.

   _____ Michael found the first note.

Write **T** if the sentence is true.
Write **F** if the sentence is false.

2. _____ Michael had never seen this code before.

3. _____ It was the middle of summer.

4. _____ All of the notes were inside the house.

5. How many notes did Heather write

   in all? _____

6. How were all the notes alike?

   _____

7. How was one note different from the

   others? _____

   _____

Cocoon Surprise

Have you ever felt sure of something but then found out you were wrong?

1   A white rat, a turtle, and three goldfish all lived in Tracy's classroom. The class took turns caring for the pets. Tracy was glad her teacher, Ms. Carr, liked animals because Tracy did, too.

2   Tracy had a cocoon in a jar that she kept in the garage. She had found the cocoon on a bush. When her dad cleaned the garage on Saturday, he asked her if she still wanted the cocoon.

"Yes, may I take it to school?" Tracy asked. "I don't think Ms. Carr would mind."

3   "OK," her father answered. "Just make sure you take it on Monday."

4   Tracy took the cocoon to school that Monday. She asked her teacher if she could put it beside the pets. Ms. Carr said that was fine with her. "Great!" Tracy said, smiling. "The class will get to see the butterfly come out."

5   "Are you certain that a butterfly will come out of the cocoon, Tracy?" asked Ms. Carr.

6   "Oh, yes, I'm sure," Tracy answered. "And I think it will hatch any day now."

7   "We'll see," Ms. Carr told Tracy.

8   Tracy did not have to wait long to find out what was in the cocoon. Two days later she got quite a surprise. She was the first child in the room that day. As she walked into the room, Ms. Carr pointed toward the corner where the pets were kept. "Look, Tracy!" she said.

9   Tracy saw a large insect in the jar. "What is it?" she asked, wrinkling up her nose.

10   "It's a moth," her teacher told her. "See how its wings are open while it is resting."

11   "Gee, its body looks furry," Tracy said as she pressed her face against the jar.

12   Ms. Carr laughed and said, "Now let's get your moth outside where it can try its wings."

Knowing the Words

Write the words from the story that have the meanings below.

1. a place where
   some insects grow _____
   (Par. 2)

2. insect _____
   (Par. 10)

Choose the correct word below to fill the blanks for each pair of sentences.

rest   fine

3. That is _____ with me.

   The thread was too _____
   to see.

4. Roger needs to _____.

   Did you get the _____
   of the programs?

Working with Words

Fill in each blank with the correct pair of letters to make a word. Then use each of the words in a sentence below.

sh   ch   wr   ph

1. bu _____   3. hand _____ iting

2. stoma _____   4. autogra _____

5. My _____ hurts.

6. Leo has beautiful _____.

7. May I have your _____?

8. Look at the cocoon on that _____.

Reading and Thinking

Write **F** if the sentence gives a fact.
Write **O** if the sentence gives an opinion.

1. ____ A moth is a pretty insect.

2. ____ The body of a moth looks furry.

3. ____ Some insects come out of cocoons.

4. ____ A moth is an insect.

5. Why do you think Tracy and Ms. Carr took the moth outside?

   _____

   _____

6. What kind of person do you think Ms. Carr is? Explain your answer.

   _____

Learning to Study

You can look in an **encyclopedia** to find facts about different topics. You may need to look under more than one topic to find the facts you need. To learn more about cocoons, Tracy could have looked under *cocoon*. Also, she could have looked under *moth* or *insect*.

Read each sentence below. Write the names of two topics you might look under.

1. You want to know about blue

   jays. _____

2. You want to learn about forest

   animals. _____

A Trip into the Past

What will Michael learn on his class trip?

1 "All right," Michael said to himself, "I've got my lunch. I have my permission note. I guess I'm ready to go."

2 Michael's class was taking a short trip. They were going to Castle Dugan. Michael's grandparents told him he'd have fun. "History is interesting," they said. Michael was not so sure.

3 At the castle, the class was met by a tour guide. "Welcome to Castle Dugan," he said. "This castle was built in the early 1800's. Here, you won't find some of the things you have in your homes. For example, you will not see electric lights. You will not see any closets. Please come this way."

4 The guide led them through several huge rooms. Michael did not see what was so special about the castle. Then the class went into the library. The guide said, "Here's something I think you'll like." He pressed a button on the wall. A hidden door opened, and a secret stairway appeared. The guide explained why the stairway was built. Michael started to pay attention.

5 The guide led the class down the steps to an underground pathway. The only light was from candles. Just as they reached the bottom, the candle closest to them went out. They stopped for a minute to let their eyes get used to the dark. The pathway was cold and damp. When Michael talked, the sound echoed. "I wonder if children used to

play here," he thought. The guide led them forward.

6 The pathway led to the stables on the other side of the street. Six old carriages were kept there. Michael dreamed of what it would have been like to drive one of them.

7 As the class ate lunch in the garden, Michael gazed at the castle. His grandparents had been right. History can be interesting.

Knowing the Words

Write the word from the story that has the meaning below.

1. a trip to see
   something special _____
   (Par. 3)

Check the meaning that fits the underlined word in each sentence.

2. My new shirt is <u>light</u> blue.

   _____ pale

   _____ not heavy

3. We are planning a <u>trip</u> to England.

   _____ vacation

   _____ to stumble

4. I left a <u>note</u> on the table.

   _____ a musical sound

   _____ a short letter

Working with Words

Write the contraction for each pair of words below.

1. you have _____

2. would not _____

3. what is _____

4. you will _____

5. we are _____

6. I will _____

7. do not _____

8. I have _____

Reading and Thinking

1. Check the answer that tells what the story is mainly about.

   _____ cold, damp walls

   _____ a secret stairway

   _____ visiting a castle

2. Write **R** next to two sentences that tell about real things.

   _____ A person can drive to a castle.

   _____ A person can drive into the past.

   _____ Castles have walls.

   _____ Castles have dragons.

Learning to Study

Each book of an encyclopedia is called a **volume.** Write the number of the volume you could use to find the topics below.

1. castles _____   6. carriages _____

2. bicycle _____   7. gardening _____

3. history _____   8. horses _____

4. cotton _____   9. dolls _____

5. fish _____   10. England _____

157

WTLR News

Read to learn about a special kind of report.

1 Rick, Tracy, and Lindsay were painting letters on a large box in Tracy's garage. Elsa came by and asked what they were doing.

2 "You'll see," Rick said, smiling.

3 "I think I know," Elsa bragged. "I saw you in the library. Are you working on your project for Monday?"

4 Tracy said, "You'll see."

5 On Monday, Elsa told all the kids in their class that Tracy, Rick, and Lindsay had a surprise for their report. The whole class was eager to see what the three of them had done. When it was time for the reports, Rick, Tracy, and Lindsay were asked to go first.

6 Tracy dragged the box to the front of the room. She and Lindsay sat behind it. Rick stood off to the side and told the class, "You will need to pretend the year is 1903. If there had been TVs then, this interview might have been on the news."

7 Tracy began by saying, "Good evening. This is WTLR news. Tonight we will talk with Mary Anderson about her recent invention. It is a device for wiping rain and snow off of a windshield." Tracy turned to Lindsay. She said, "Hello, Mary. Tell us about your invention."

8 "Well," Lindsay began, "the purpose of this device is to keep the windshield clear on the outside. It helps people drive safely."

9 Then Rick stepped up to the news desk. Tracy turned to him and said, "You have used this device. Can you tell us what you think of it?"

10 "Yes, it has helped my driving quite a bit. I used to have to stop every once in a while to clean off my windshield. But now Mary's invention does it for me."

11 "So, there you have it, folks," Tracy concluded. "Someday we may wonder how we ever got along without this device."

12 The class applauded. They had been surprised.

Knowing the Words

Write the words from the story that have the meanings below.

1. invention _____
(Par. 7)

2. ended _____
(Par. 11)

Choose the correct word to fill in the blank for each pair of sentences.

drive   saw

3. Ed is too young to _____.

_____ the nail into the wood.

4. We _____ you at the game.

Where did you put the _____?

Learning to Study

Names of people are listed in an encyclopedia by the person's last name. Write the number of the volume you could use to find the topics below.

1. invention _____

2. computers _____

3. Mary Anderson _____

4. Thomas Edison _____

Reading and Thinking

Write **T** if the sentence is true.
Write **F** if the sentence is false.

1. _____ Tracy, Lindsay, and Rick had been to the library.

2. _____ Tracy pretended she was a news reporter.

3. _____ The class was not interested in the project.

4. Did Tracy really talk to Mary Anderson? Explain your answer.

_____

5. Why did Mary Anderson make a device for cleaning a windshield?

_____

_____

Read each set of sentences below. Fill in each blank.

6. Lindsay pretended she was Mary Anderson.

She stands for _____.

7. Rick said he liked the new invention.

He stands for _____.

8. The inventor thought she had a good idea.

She stands for _____.

9. The class was surprised when it saw the report.

It stands for _____.

Elephant Disappearance

How do you feel when you lose something you need?

1 "Now where is that stuffed elephant?" Dale muttered as he searched through the toy box. "I know it was here yesterday because I was playing with it."

2 Dale was getting upset. A few of his friends in the neighborhood were going to put on a puppet show, and they asked Dale to join them. Dale told them he'd like to, but he didn't have a puppet. Tracy said, "That's OK. Just bring a stuffed animal." So that is just what Dale planned to do.

3 "Lindsay, have you seen my stuffed elephant?" Dale asked hopefully.

4 "No, I haven't, Dale. When and where did you have it last?" Lindsay asked. "It might help to think about that."

5 "Rags and I played with it in my room yesterday. It couldn't have walked out on its own," Dale grumbled. "And I think I've looked everywhere in my room."

6 Dale went on searching. He asked his parents if they had seen the toy. Neither one had. He even talked to Rags about his problem.

7 Finally, Dale began to cry. He was so disappointed and angry! He petted Rags as he said, "Without that elephant, I won't be able to help put on the show."

8 Dale went to his room and lay on his bed. He was not at all happy. After thinking, he said to himself, "Well, I guess I could make a sock puppet." He began to gather everything he needed. Just as he sat down to make the puppet, Rags came into the room. The dog had something in his mouth. He was growling and shaking it. When Dale looked down, he realized that Rags had the lost elephant. Dale was so excited! He raced right outside to find his friends.

9 Lindsay had seen Rags go into Dale's room with the toy. As she watched Dale rush out, she just shook her head. "I don't think he even stopped to wonder why Rags had that elephant or how he got it," she said to herself.

Knowing the Words

Write the word from the story that has the meaning below.

1. moved from side to side _____
   (Par. 9)

Circle the pair of antonyms (opposites) in each row.

2. sing   cry   laugh   applaud

3. lost   helped   looked   won

4. answered   said   inquired   grumbled

Working with Words

The suffix **-ly** helps tell how something was done. *Smoothly* means "done in a smooth way."

Add **-ly** to the words below. Use the new words to complete the sentences.

silent   friend   loose   clear

1. When he was in the library, Robert

   read a book _____.

2. Amy tied the knot _____.

3. Pat was happy to see the

   _____ puppy.

4. The announcer spoke _____.

Say *gather.* Circle the words below that have the sound *g* stands for in *gather.*

5. began   edge   giant   against

6. get   goldfish   message   charge

7. forget   eager   magic   bridge

8. cage   goose   give   together

Reading and Thinking

Write **T** if the sentence is true.
Write **F** if the sentence is false.

1. _____ Dale wanted to help with the puppet show.

2. _____ Dale did not try very hard to find his stuffed elephant.

3. _____ Dale thought of a new way to solve his problem.

4. _____ Dale finally found the toy himself.

5. Dale was going to make a sock

   puppet because _____

   _____.

6. What do you think Dale will do now that his elephant has been found?

   _____

   _____

Write the best word to complete each sentence below.

7. James _____ why the tire was flat. (wondered, jumped, searched)

8. The _____ was bigger than a car. (mouse, robin, elephant)

161

Just for Carmen

How could you cheer up a friend who is ill?

1   Andy and Elsa were already at Tracy's house when Dale arrived. "Sorry it took me so long," he apologized. "I could not find my elephant for a while."

2   "Why are we doing this show anyway?" Dale asked.

3   Elsa answered, "Well, Carmen has a bad cold, so she had to stay inside today. Tracy and I thought a puppet show would cheer her up."

4   "What can we have our puppets do?" Andy asked.

5   "Let's act as if our puppets are circus performers," Elsa suggested. The others agreed that Elsa had a good idea. They began to practice.

6   After practicing several acts, they were ready to perform. They gathered their things and took off running towards Elsa's house. In no time they were inside, making a stage curtain.

7   The children stood behind the curtain. Carmen sat up in bed. The show was about to start. "Attention, please, Carmen!" Tracy said. "You are about to see the best circus show ever! For our first act, the trapeze artists will perform amazing stunts with no net. As a matter of fact, the stunts will be done with no trapeze!"

8   Elsa and Andy made the puppets look as if they were swinging back and forth on a make-believe trapeze. Then they made their puppets look as though they were flipping from one trapeze to another. Carmen giggled and clapped.

9   "Great!" Tracy broke in. "Now sit back and enjoy our elephant act."

10   Dale made his elephant stand on its head. Then he made it walk on its hind legs. Carmen was pleased.

11   Carmen watched the rest of the acts eagerly. She clapped loudly after each one. Tracy, Elsa, Dale, and Andy felt good. They enjoyed helping Carmen forget about her cold.

Knowing the Words

Write the words from the story that have the meanings below.

1. asked forgiveness _____
   (Par. 1)

2. common sickness _____
   (Par. 3)

Check the meaning that fits the underlined word in each sentence.

3. It is very <u>cold</u> outside.

   _____ low temperature

   _____ sickness

4. This is the third <u>act</u>.

   _____ to behave in a certain way

   _____ part of a show

Learning to Study

An **index** is a part of a book. It lists a book's topics in alphabetical order. It also lists page numbers so you can find those topics. An index is usually at the back of a book. Use the index below to answer the questions.

> performances, 1–5
> plays, 4, 21
> puppets, 4, 8–10
> stages, 11–15

1. What topic would you find on pages

   1–5? _____

2. What could you learn from pages 11–15?

   _____

3. On what pages would you look if you

   wanted to make a puppet? _____

Reading and Thinking

1. Number the sentences to show the order in which things happened.

   _____ The puppets did a trapeze act.

   _____ The elephant performed.

   _____ Tracy announced the first act.

   _____ The children went to Elsa's house.

   _____ Dale went to Tracy's house.

Write **F** if the sentence gives a fact.
Write **O** if the sentence gives an opinion.

2. _____ An elephant's skin has wrinkles.

3. _____ The trapeze acts are the most thrilling to watch.

4. _____ An elephant can be trained to stand on its hind legs.

5. _____ Many circuses have elephants.

6. _____ A circus isn't exciting.

Read each sentence below. Fill in the blank.

7. The children knew they had made Carmen happy.

   They stands for _____.

8. Dale believed he had done a good job.

   He stands for _____.

9. Carmen applauded as she watched the performance.

   She stands for _____.

Spring Concert

How much do you believe in yourself?

1 Elsa and Rick were going to sing a song together at the spring concert. They had practiced hard for weeks.

2 The day before the concert Rick told Mr. Barnes, the music teacher, that he did not think he could perform. "Let me ask you a few questions," Mr. Barnes said. "Do you feel as if you know the song?"

3 "Yes, I have it memorized," Rick said.

4 Then Mr. Barnes asked, "Do you like to sing?"

5 "Very much," replied Rick.

6 "Are you nervous?" Mr. Barnes said, going on with his questions.

7 "Well, maybe a little," Rick admitted.

8 Then Mr. Barnes said, "Do you believe me when I say you are a very good singer?"

9 Rick answered, "Sure."

10 Mr. Barnes smiled and said, "Well, now all you have to do is believe in yourself. If you believe in yourself, you won't get so nervous."

11 "OK, I'll try," Rick said as he shrugged his shoulders.

12 Rick was quite nervous on the night of the concert. He said to Elsa, "What if I don't start singing at the right time? What if I forget the words? What if. . ."

13 "Relax," Elsa said, "you'll do fine."

14 Finally, Rick heard Mr. Barnes introduce them to the audience. Elsa walked onto the stage with Rick close behind her. The piano started to play. When Rick started to sing, his voice came out a squeak. Then he quickly thought, "Mr. Barnes thinks I can do it. Elsa thinks I can do it. I must think I can do it." Soon he was singing the song just the way he had practiced it. Before he knew it, the song was over.

15 The crowd applauded, and Rick spotted his parents. He could see by their smiles that they were really proud of him. Rick said to himself, "After I thought I could do it, I did it!"

Write the words from the story that have the meanings below.

1. a season _____
   (Par. 1)

2. said something
   was true _____
   (Par. 7)

3. moved up
   and down _____
   (Par. 11)

4. saw _____
   (Par. 15)

Choose the correct word below to fill the blank for each pair of sentences.

close   spring

5. _____ begins in March.

   The _____ in my pen
   is broken.

6. Please _____ the window.

   Do not stand too _____ to
   the fire.

Learning to Study

Number each list of words below in alphabetical order.

1. ____ shrug   2. ____ crowd

   ____ sing   ____ cry

   ____ shoulders   ____ cute

   ____ piano   ____ concert

   ____ smile   ____ crawl

   ____ memorize   ____ believe

   ____ question   ____ beg

Reading and Thinking

Write **T** if the sentence is true.
Write **F** if the sentence is false.

1. ____ Elsa was very nervous.

2. ____ Rick and Elsa had practiced
   the song more than once.

3. ____ The concert took place at the
   beginning of the school year.

4. Rick did not want to sing in the

   concert because _____

   _____.

5. Who was Mr. Barnes? _____

   _____

6. Why did Mr. Barnes tell Rick he
   needed to believe in himself?

   _____

7. How do you think Rick felt about
   himself after he sang the song?

   _____

8. Do you think Rick will ever sing in
   a concert again? Explain your

   answer. _____

   _____

Tracy's First Job

Read to find out what Tracy learned.

1   Tracy told Rick about the bike she had seen for sale down the street. "It needs a new seat and some paint, but I think it's a bargain for twenty dollars," she said. "It will probably be sold before I can save that much money though."

2   "I'm giving up my paper route," Rick said. "You could have that twenty dollars in no time if you took my route. Why don't we talk to Mr. Wise and see if it's OK?"

3   "Great!" Tracy said. "I can almost feel myself riding that bike now."

4   Mr. Wise said it would be fine with him if Tracy took Rick's route. Then he asked Rick to show Tracy the route and explain the job.

5   That afternoon Rick showed Tracy how to fold papers. He gave her hints about how to throw a paper so it landed right in front of the door. As they went through the route, Rick told her the name of each customer as he pointed out the houses on the route. "Maybe you should write down these names and addresses, Tracy," Rick said.

6   "No, I don't need to. I have a good memory," Tracy said.

7   The next day Tracy did the paper route alone. She started at three o'clock. At 3:30 she was at the last house. "That was easy," she thought. "And I still have time to play before supper." But when she looked in her bag there was one more paper. Tracy had no idea where it belonged. How could she find out? Finally, she decided to call Rick to get addresses of all the customers. This time she wrote them down.

8   Tracy found that she had forgotten to give a paper to the Blair family. After the paper was delivered, she looked at her watch. It was time for supper.

9   "Well, I learned two things today," Tracy thought. "One, my memory is not as good as I thought. Two, I will save time if I do my route right the first time."

166

Knowing the Words

Write the words from the story that have the meanings below.

1. good price _____
   (Par. 1)

2. might be _____
   (Par. 1)

Check the meaning that fits the underlined word in each sentence.

3. Did you see the <u>play</u> Michael was in?

   _____ a show

   _____ to have fun

4. Did Ken <u>watch</u> TV yesterday?

   _____ something that keeps time

   _____ to look at

Working with Words

Circle the correct word in ( ) and write it in the blank.

1. I hope I _____ two inches this year. (group, grow)

2. The _____ of his scream frightened me. (sound, sand)

3. Has Sam _____ of a name for his kitten? (thought, that)

4. The _____ begins at 8:30. (shoe, show)

5. Did you write _____ the correct address? (dawn, down)

6. Jenny _____ us how to tie a knot. (should, showed)

Reading and Thinking

1. Why was Tracy saving money?

   _____

2. Tracy had to call Rick because

   _____

   _____.

3. How do you think Tracy felt about asking Rick for the addresses?

   _____

4. What do you think Tracy did after she delivered her last paper?

   _____

Learning to Study

Read each question below. Write **dictionary** or **encyclopedia** to answer each one.

1. Where would you find the meaning of the word *newspaper*?

   _____

2. Where could you find the history of newspapers?

   _____

3. Where could you find facts on how newspapers are made?

   _____

4. Where could you find the word *newspaper* divided into syllables?

   _____

Knowing the Words

Write the words from the story that have the meanings below.

1. announcements of something for sale ___ads___ (Par. 3)

2. equipment ___devices___ (Par. 3)

3. machine that obeys commands ___robot___ (Par. 4)

In each row below, circle the three words that belong together.

4. (run) (walk) sleep (wander)
5. (machine) snack (robot) (device)
6. (fingers) (arms) dust (chest)

Working with Words

A word that means one of something is **singular.** A word that means more than one is **plural.** Most singular words are made plural by adding s. Most words that end in s, ss, x, ch, and sh are made plural by adding es. Form the plural of each word below by adding s or es.

1. button _s_   4. robot _s_
2. boss _es_   5. clock _s_
3. wish _es_   6. circus _es_

Reading and Thinking

1. Check the answer that tells what the story is mainly about.
   - _✓_ finding a robot
   - ___ going to the office
   - ___ fixing a clock

2. What day of the week is it in this story? ___Saturday___

3. What do you think will happen when Carlos saves up ten dollars? ___He will buy the robot.___

4. Some things are real, and some are make-believe. Write **M** next to the two sentences that tell about make-believe things.
   - ___ Robots are machines.
   - _M_ Robots can think for themselves.
   - _M_ Robots have feelings.
   - ___ Robots can obey commands.

Write the best word to complete each sentence below.

5. Andrea had six square ___buttons___ on her good coat, but one fell off. (zippers, buttons, dollars)

6. There was a typewriter in each ___office___. (office, automobile, meadow)

7. The bike was ___hidden___ by some bushes. (written, wanted, hidden)

3

Knowing the Words

Write the words from the story that have the meanings below.

1. said in a low voice ___grumbled___ (Par. 6)

2. say something is true ___admit___ (Par. 8)

Working with Words

A **contraction** is a short way to write two words. An apostrophe (') shows that one or more letters have been taken out. Write a contraction from the story for each pair of words below.

1. it is ___it's___ (Par. 3)
2. I will ___I'll___ (Par. 3)
3. would not ___wouldn't___ (Par. 5)
4. is not ___isn't___ (Par. 7)
5. do not ___don't___ (Par. 8)

Circle the correct letters to complete each word and write them in the blank.

6. Get into the c_ar_ and put on your seat belt.
   or   ir   (ar)

7. Did you f_or_ get to sweep the floor?
   (or)   ir   ar

8. Meet us at the corn_er_ after the show.
   or   ar   (er)

Reading and Thinking

1. Number the sentences to show the order in which things happened.
   - _4_ Carlos made the robot wave.
   - _1_ Carlos and his dad went to the storeroom.
   - _3_ Carlos and his dad took the robot to the van.
   - _2_ Carlos tried to roll the robot.

2. How big was the robot? ___It was almost as big as Carlos.___

3. Carlos and his dad had to carry the robot because ___it would not roll___

4. Tell two ways that a robot is different from a child. ___
   ___(Answers will vary.)___
   ___

5. What do you think Carlos will do as soon as he gets the robot home? ___
   ___(Answers will vary.)___

5

Knowing the Words

Write the words from the story that have the meanings below.

1. something being worked on ___project___ (Par. 1)

2. try out ___test___ (Par. 4)

3. very upset ___frantic___ (Par. 7)

Check the meaning that fits the underlined word in each sentence.

4. Jane passed her math test.
   - _✓_ something to measure what a person knows
   - ___ try out

5. The dog walked through the bed of daisies.
   - ___ piece of furniture
   - _✓_ place for flowers

6. I forgot to wear my watch.
   - _✓_ something that keeps time
   - ___ look for

Reading and Thinking

1. Check the answer that tells what the story is mainly about.
   - ___ bringing the robot home
   - ___ stopping the robot
   - _✓_ getting the robot to work

2. How do you think Carlos felt when he tried to get the robot to move? ___
   ___(Answers will vary.)___

3. How do you think fixing a robot might be like fixing a radio? ___
   ___(Answers will vary.)___

4. Carlos pressed buttons on the robot's chest because ___he wanted the robot to move___

Learning to Study

Number each list of words below in alphabetical order.

1. _3_ dusted   3. _4_ smile
   _4_ friend   _1_ fix
   _2_ camping   _2_ mouth
   _1_ battery   _3_ removed

2. _3_ wires   4. _4_ yard
   _1_ lights   _3_ watch
   _2_ robot   _2_ stop
   _4_ yell   _1_ pressed

7

Knowing the Words

Write the words from the story that have the meanings below.

1. showed by example ___demonstrated___ (Par. 2)

2. commands ___orders___ (Par. 3)

3. small jobs ___chores___ (Par. 3)

Words with opposite meanings are called **antonyms.** Match each word from the first list with its antonym from the second list.

4. _b_ moved   a. full
5. _a_ empty   b. stopped
6. _c_ outside   c. inside

Working with Words

Circle the correct word in ( ) and write it in the blank.

1. Chris ___took___ a beach ball to the lake. (tank, (took))

2. Nan lives in a ___house___ down the street. (hose, (house))

3. ___Maybe___ we will see a full moon tonight. (Merry, (Maybe))

Form the plural of each word below by adding s or es.

4. grass _es_   7. dish _es_
5. hand _s_   8. back _s_
6. lid _s_   9. ax _es_

Reading and Thinking

1. Number the sentences to show the order in which things happened.
   - _1_ Carlos showed his family what the robot could do.
   - _3_ The robot dumped the trash on the ground.
   - _2_ Carlos showed the robot how to empty the trash.
   - _4_ The robot dumped the trash on the lid of the trash can.

Write **T** if the sentence is true.
Write **F** if the sentence is false.

2. _T_ Carlos was excited because his robot followed orders.

3. _F_ Carlos kept his robot's tricks a secret.

4. _T_ Carlos had to be careful when he gave orders to the robot.

5. _F_ The robot could not hear well.

Words such as he, she, you, it, we, and they are used in place of other words. Read these sentences. The robot was made of metal. It had green eyes. In the second sentence, it is used in place of the robot.

Read each set of sentences below. Fill in each blank.

6. Carlos yelled to his family. He wanted them to see the robot.
   He stands for ___Carlos___

7. Marie liked the robot. She liked to see Carlos having fun.
   She stands for ___Marie___

9

Knowing the Words

Write the words from the story that have the meanings below.

1. wonderful __terrific__ (Par. 5)

2. things such as happiness, sadness, and anger __feelings__ (Par. 7)

3. said with a quiet voice __whispered__ (Par. 8)

Some words sound alike but have different spellings and meanings. Write the word with the correct meaning to complete each sentence below.

4. Ann can hardly __wait__ for the show to begin. (wait, weight)

5. Please don't __write__ on that paper. (right, write)

6. __I__ will go to the playground. (Eye, I)

Working with Words

Circle the correct word in ( ) and write it in the blank.

1. Phyllis __taught__ her puppy a trick. (**taught**, that)

2. Please __wait__ for me while I get my jacket. (want, **wait**)

3. Do you know where Muffy has hidden her __bowl__? (boil, **bowl**)

Reading and Thinking

1. Check the answer that tells what the story is mainly about.
   ___ fixing supper
   ___ talking to Marie
   _✓_ naming the robot

2. What name was given to the robot? __Mosh__ Why was it given that name? __It stands for *my own special helper.*__

3. What other commands do you think the robot could be taught? _____
   (Answers will vary.)

Write **T** if the sentence is true.
Write **F** if the sentence is false.

4. _T_ The robot did exactly what it was told to do.

5. _F_ The robot could talk.

6. _T_ The robot knocked the ice out of Marie's hand.

7. _T_ Carlos thinks Mosh has feelings.

Write the best word to complete each sentence below.

8. Gilda was __fixing__ a flat tire on her bike. (bumping, **fixing**, preparing)

9. Please __shake__ off that sand before you come inside. (wait, **shake**, whisper)

11

Knowing the Words

Write the words from the story that have the meanings below.

1. sad __blue__ (Par. 1)

2. for a reason __intentionally__ (Par. 13)

In each row below, circle the three words that belong together.

3. (girl) robot (boy) (child)
4. (street) (sidewalk) yard (driveway)
5. (chase) (run) ask (roll)
6. start (down) (behind) (beside)
7. (sat) (yell) look (cry)

Working with Words

A **compound word** is made by combining two smaller words. Write a compound word using the underlined words in each sentence.

1. A <u>house</u> for a <u>dog</u> is a __doghouse__.

2. A <u>yard</u> in <u>back</u> of a house is a __backyard__.

3. A <u>room</u> where you can <u>store</u> things is a __storeroom__.

4. Days at the <u>end</u> of the <u>week</u> are called the __weekend__.

5. A <u>cup</u> used for <u>tea</u> is a __teacup__.

Reading and Thinking

1. Number the sentences to show the order in which things happened.
   _2_ Mrs. Wilson picked flowers.
   _1_ Mosh learned to play tag.
   _4_ Carlos met Susan.
   _3_ Mosh chased a girl.

2. Who is Mrs. Wilson? __Carlos's neighbor__

Write **T** if the sentence is true.
Write **F** if the sentence is false.

3. _F_ Mrs. Wilson was angry.

4. _F_ Mosh chased the girl away.

5. _T_ Carlos was glad Mosh chased the girl.

6. What do you think it meant when Mosh winked at the end of the story? _____
   (Answers will vary.)

7. Write **R** next to the two sentences that tell about real things.
   ___ Flowers can fly by themselves.
   _R_ Robots can roll.
   _R_ Children can meet new friends.

8. What do you think Carlos and Mosh did after they got home? _____
   (Answers will vary.)

13

Knowing the Words

Write the words from the story that have the meanings below.

1. edge of the street __curb__ (Par. 1)

2. mistake __fault__ (Par. 6)

3. looked at closely __examined__ (Par. 7)

Words that mean the same, or nearly the same, are called **synonyms**. Circle the pair of synonyms in each row.

4. (hurried) whispered (dashed) picked
5. guess sorry (halt) (stop)
6. busy (mad) happy (angry)
7. (big) small (large) quick

Write the word with the correct meaning to complete each sentence below.

8. Have you seen __our__ trash can? (hour, **our**)

9. I did not __hear__ the phone ring, did you? (here, **hear**)

Working with Words

An 's at the end of a word may be used to show that something belongs to someone. Add 's to each name in ( ) and write the new word in the blank.

1. __Dad's__ clock (Dad)

2. __Mosh's__ lights (Mosh)

3. __Marie's__ room (Marie)

Reading and Thinking

1. Check the answer that tells what the story is mainly about.
   ___ fixing a clock
   _✓_ moving trash cans
   ___ getting angry

2. Mosh moved all of the neighbors' trash cans because __no one told it to stop__

3. Why do you think Mosh turned off its lights and would not move? __Carlos yelled at Mosh. (Answers may vary.)__

4. Was Carlos still angry at the end of the story? Explain your answer. __No. Carlos said he was sorry.__
   (Answers may vary.)

5. What do you think Mosh did after Carlos said he was sorry? _____
   (Answers will vary.)

15

Knowing the Words

Write the words from the story that have the meanings below.

1. women's shirts __blouses__ (Par. 4)

2. sparkle __twinkle__ (Par. 4)

3. set of clothes __outfit__ (Par. 6)

4. walked heavily __stomped__ (Par. 7)

Write the word with the correct meaning to complete each sentence below.

5. We rode our bicycles __for__ an hour this morning. (**for**, four)

6. Please __close__ the screen door. (clothes, **close**)

7. This dark __wood__ came from a cherry tree. (would, **wood**)

8. Gina has __two__ sharpened pencils. (**two**, to)

Working with Words

Say *city.* Circle the words below that have the sound *c* stands for in *city*.

1. (fancy) can (since) clothes
2. (center) expect (except) (force)

A word without any ending is a base word. The base word of *asked* is *ask*. Circle each base word below.

3. (mix)ed   6. (laugh)ing
4. (wear)ing   7. (go)ing
5. (frown)s   8. (look)ed

Reading and Thinking

Write **T** if the sentence is true.
Write **F** if the sentence is false.

1. _T_ Carlos's chore was to put away the clean clothes.

2. _T_ Mr. Garza was too big for Marie's blouse.

3. _F_ Mr. Garza was very angry.

4. _T_ Carlos was not happy at the end of the story.

5. Whose shirt was Mrs. Garza wearing? __Carlos's__

6. Marie stomped into Carlos's room because __she was angry about having the wrong clothes__

7. What do you think Carlos might do after he puts the clothes away? ___
   (Answers will vary.)

17

Knowing the Words

Write the words from the story that have the meanings below.

1. right away _____instantly_____
   (Par. 6)

2. shook _____trembled_____
   (Par. 6)

Some words are spelled the same but have different meanings. For example, *can* might mean "something that food comes in" or "able to do something." Look at the list of words below. For each pair of sentences, one word from the list will correctly complete both. Choose the correct word to fill in the blanks for each pair of sentences.

        fly   left   like

3. That kite looks just __like__ mine.

   I really __like__ to watch circus performers.

4. Do you have any money __left__?

   Do you write with your __left__ hand?

5. How do you think birds __fly__?

   The __fly__ walked on the table.

Working with Words

Fill in each blank with the correct letters to make a word.

        kn   igh   wr   ph

1. __wr__ong   3. __kn__ee

2. r__igh__t   4. micro__ph__one

Reading and Thinking

1. Number the sentences to show the order in which things happened.

   _3_ Susan removed Mosh's battery.

   _2_ Carlos taught Mosh to push a swing.

   _1_ Mosh was knocked down by a baseball.

   _4_ Carlos fixed Mosh's wires.

2. Check two words that tell how Carlos probably felt when Mosh wouldn't obey him.

   _✓_ frightened   ___ amused

   ___ bored   _✓_ confused

3. Mosh wouldn't stop pushing the swing because __the robot was broken__ _____

4. What did Susan do to get Mosh to stop? __took out the battery__

5. Check two sentences that tell how Carlos and Susan are alike.

   ___ They both own a robot.

   _✓_ They are both children.

   _✓_ They had trouble with Mosh.

Write the best word to complete each sentence below.

6. Do you __tremble__ when you are scared? (command, tremble, push)

7. Barb felt __dizzy__ when she got off the ride. (ready, new, dizzy)

19

Knowing the Words

Write the words from the story that have the meanings below.

1. not done on purpose __accidentally__
   (Par. 5)

2. bother __worry__
   (Par. 9)

Choose the correct word below to fill in the blanks for each pair of sentences.

        can   yard

3. This __can__ does not have a label on it.

   I __can__ finish my homework in fifteen minutes.

4. A deer is in the __yard__.

   Joan bought a __yard__ of ribbon.

Working with Words

A **suffix** is a group of letters added to the end of a word that changes the meaning of the word. The suffix **-ly** helps tell how something was done. *Shyly* means "done in a shy way."

Add **-ly** to the words below. Use the new words to complete the sentences.

        accidental   sad   loud

1. Gretchen watched __sadly__ as her friend rode away.

2. Steve __accidentally__ spilled his apple juice.

3. Agnes laughed __loudly__.

Reading and Thinking

1. Check the answer that tells what the story is mainly about.

   _✓_ digging for worms

   ___ going fishing

   ___ talking to Mrs. Wilson

2. Mosh dug up Mrs. Wilson's garden because __the robot was looking for worms__

3. What kind of person do you think Carlos is? Explain your answer.

   _____

   (Answers will vary.)

Read each set of sentences below. Fill in each blank.

4. The seeds were planted yesterday. They haven't started growing yet.

   They stands for __the seeds__

5. Lucy and I are the same age. We go to school together.

   We stands for __Lucy and I__

21

Knowing the Words

Write the words from the story that have the meanings below.

1. breathed in quickly __gasped__
   (Par. 5)

2. said you were sorry __apologized__
   (Par. 7)

Choose the correct word to fill in the blanks for each pair of sentences.

        spoke   second

3. The alarm clock will ring any __second__ now.

   Tracy sits in the __second__ seat in the first row.

4. Donna __spoke__ in a whisper.

   The wheel on Ann's bike has a broken __spoke__.

Working with Words

Words are sometimes easier to read if they are divided into parts called **syllables**. Some words have two consonants between two vowels. These words can be divided into syllables between the consonants, as in *ex/pect*. In each word below, draw a line to divide the word into syllables.

1. wel|come   5. tem|per

2. per|haps   6. blos|som

3. for|give   7. traf|fic

4. aw|ful   8. bor|row

Reading and Thinking

Write **T** if the sentence is true.
Write **F** if the sentence is false.

1. _T_ Mosh put the worms in Marie's suitcase.

2. _T_ Marie was upset when she saw the worms.

3. _T_ Susan thought it was funny to see the worms in the suitcase.

4. What two things did Mosh do while Carlos put the fishing poles in the car? __put the worms in the suitcase, gave the suitcase to Marie__

5. Why do you think Marie called Mosh a pile of bolts? _____

   (Answers will vary.)

6. What do you think Carlos will do after he cleans out the suitcase?

   _____

   (Answers will vary.)

Write the best word to complete each sentence below.

7. The baby was __crawling__ through the grass. (putting, finding, crawling)

8. Jenny __opened__ the can of soup. (opened, grumbled, stayed)

9. Rose wore a __pale__ blue blouse. (round, pale, plenty)

23

Knowing the Words

Write the word from the story that has the meaning below.

1. high sounding __high-pitched__
   (Par. 3)

Circle the pair of antonyms (opposites) in each row.

2. (pushing) crying (pulling) whistling

3. soon (bent) side (straight)

4. later other (right) (wrong)

5. (started) winked (finished) cried

Working with Words

Write a contraction from the story for each pair of words below.

1. you have __you've__
   (Par. 4)

2. I am __I'm__
   (Par. 6)

3. I have __I've__
   (Par. 8)

4. had not __hadn't__
   (Par. 9)

5. could have __could've__
   (Par. 10)

Circle the correct letters to complete each word and write them in the blank.

6. Did Jennifer or Mary go f__ir__st?

   or (ir) ar

7. Will you __or__ der spaghetti?

   (or) ir ar

8. Let's go ov__er__ to my house.

   (er) ar or

9. Do you h__ear__ any strange noises?

   are (ear) ore

Reading and Thinking

1. Number the sentences to show the order in which things happened.

   _3_ Mrs. Wilson caught a fish.

   _1_ Carlos showed Mosh how to fish.

   _2_ Carlos and Susan traded places with Carlos's dad.

   _4_ Mr. Garza sat next to Mosh.

2. Write **R** next to the two sentences that tell about real things.

   _R_ Worms are used to catch fish.

   ___ Rainbows can be used to catch fish.

   _R_ Fish can be on one side of a dock and not the other.

3. The fish were biting because __Mosh was making a noise__

4. What do you think will happen when Carlos's dad is sitting next to Mosh?

   _____

   (Answers will vary.)

   _____

Write the best word to complete each sentence below.

5. The fish on Lin's __hook__ was a foot long. (water, hook, lake)

6. Pat put the boat next to the __dock__. (dock, noise, rainbow)

25

Top-left quadrant

Write the words from the story that have the meanings below.

1. said in a
   mean way _____ snapped
   (Par. 6)

2. without fault _____ innocently
   (Par. 8)

3. looks like _____ appears
   (Par. 10)

Synonyms are words that have the same or nearly the same meaning. Circle the pair of synonyms in each row.

4. paper   stuff   (garbage)   (trash)
5. cleaned   (served)   put   (gave)

Working with Words

When a word ends with a vowel and a consonant, the consonant is usually doubled before adding **-ed** or **-ing**. For example, *snap + ed = snapped*.

Double the last consonant in the word in ( ). Then add **-ed** or **-ing** to the word to make a word that completes each sentence.

1. Are you _____ putting _____ that book on the shelf? (put)

2. Joan _____ slipped _____ on the ice. (slip)

3. Lou is always _____ dragging _____ that toy around. (drag)

Fill in each blank with the correct letters to make a word.

    wr   igh   mb

4. du_mb_   5. _wr_ite   6. h_igh_

Top-second quadrant

Reading and Thinking

1. Check the answer that tells what the story is mainly about.
   _____ drinking lemonade
   _✓_ learning a lesson
   _____ going to Mrs. Wilson's

2. What did Mrs. Wilson serve to the kids? _____ lemonade

3. Why did Mosh throw Sara and Bill's cups away as soon as they were finished? _Mosh knew that papers belong in the trash._
   (Answers may vary.)

4. What do you think Carlos meant when he called Mosh a "one-of-a-kind friend"? _Mosh is Carlos's special friend._
   (Answers may vary.)

5. Why do you think Mosh dumped the papers in Sara's lap? _____
   (Answers will vary.)

27

Top-third quadrant

Write the words from the story that have the meanings below.

1. talk about things
   that are wrong _____ complain
   (Par. 3)

2. confused _____ puzzled
   (Par. 4)

3. said in a
   low voice _____ mumbled
   (Par. 6)

4. calm _____ patient
   (Par. 8)

In each row below, circle the three words that belong together.

5. (taught) (learned) (remembered) have
6. hour (deliver) (newspaper) (route)
7. (phone) (ring) trash (talk)

Choose the correct word below to fill in the blanks for each pair of sentences.

    ring   saw

8. I _____ saw _____ Jill at school.
   This _____ saw _____ is too dull.

9. We hear the bell _____ ring _____ every day at noon.
   This _____ ring _____ does not fit my finger.

Top-fourth quadrant

Reading and Thinking

1. Where did Carlos find the newspapers? _in the trash can_

2. The papers had to be delivered twice because _Mosh picked them up and threw them away_

Write **T** if the sentence is true.
Write **F** if the sentence is false.

3. _F_ Mosh helped deliver the papers.
4. _T_ Carlos had not been delivering papers for very long.
5. _F_ Susan told Carlos where he could find the newspapers.

6. What do you think Carlos did after he delivered the papers again? _____
   (Answers will vary.)

Learning to Study

Number each list of words below in alphabetical order.

1. _4_ rush   3. _1_ finish
   _1_ remember   _2_ flash
   _3_ robot   _4_ friend
   _2_ ring   _3_ found

2. _4_ trash   4. _4_ mumble
   _1_ tell   _1_ many
   _3_ too   _3_ Mosh
   _2_ that   _2_ meant

29

Bottom-left quadrant

Write the word from the story that has the meaning below.

1. stopped for
   a moment _____ paused
   (Par. 2)

Check the meaning that fits the underlined word in each sentence.

2. Sue tried to <u>fix</u> the clock.
   _____ prepare
   _✓_ repair

3. The <u>wash</u> was hung on the fence.
   _____ clean with water
   _✓_ clothes being cleaned

Working with Words

Write a compound word using the underlined words in each sentence.

1. A place where a <u>bird</u> can take a <u>bath</u> is a _____ birdbath _____.

2. The <u>time</u> when you eat <u>lunch</u> is called _____ lunchtime _____.

An **'s** at the end of a word is used to show that something belongs to one person or thing. To show that something belongs to more than one person or thing, an apostrophe (**'**) is added to the end of a plural word that ends in s.

Circle each group of words below that shows that more than one person or thing owns something.

3. book's pages   5. (kids' games)
4. (cars' wheels)   6. Sara's chair

Bottom-second quadrant

Reading and Thinking

1. Number the sentences to show the order in which things happened.
   _3_ Carlos was sprayed with water.
   _1_ Marie and Carlos agreed to baby-sit.
   _2_ Marie started to fix lunch.
   _4_ Sara apologized.

2. What kind of a person do you think Sara is? Explain your answer. _____
   (Answers will vary.)

3. Write two ways in which Sara and Bill's car wash was different from a real car wash. _There was just one hose. The cars were pretend._
   (Answers may vary.)

4. Who turned the water on when Carlos got sprayed? _____ Sara

5. Did Carlos stay mad at Sara? _No_
   How do you know? _He said the water cooled him off. (Answers may vary.)_

Write the best word to complete each sentence below.

6. Jane _____ soaked _____ the sponge in the sink. (asked, soaked, pretended)

7. Ruth _____ cried _____ when the bee stung her. (cried, chuckled, ate)

31

Bottom-third quadrant

Write the words from the story that have the meanings below.

1. look into _____ investigate
   (Par. 2)

2. wanting something that
   someone else has _____ jealous
   (Par. 5)

3. a little bit _____ slightly
   (Par. 6)

4. cloths used
   for drying _____ towels
   (Par. 7)

Working with Words

Some words that have one consonant between two vowels are divided into syllables after the first vowel. The first vowel sound in these words is most often long, as in *bā/by*.

Other words that have one consonant between two vowels are divided after the consonant. In these words, the first vowel is most often short, as in *wăg/on*.

The words below have been divided into syllables. Put a mark above the first vowel in each word to show if the vowel stands for a long or short sound. Mark the long vowels with ¯ over the letter. Mark the short vowels with ˘.

1. něv/er   4. clŏs/et   7. sī/lent
2. cō/zy   5. sĕv/en   8. pō/ny
3. păl/ace   6. pī/lot   9. lā/dy

Say *gentle*. Circle the words below that have the sound *g* stands for in *gentle*.

10. (cage) get (page) (hedge)
11. (giant) (age) agree gum
12. gift (edge) (engine) garden

Bottom-fourth quadrant

Reading and Thinking

1. Check the answer that tells what the story is mainly about.
   _____ playing with Mosh
   _____ camping out
   _✓_ taking care of Fluffy

2. Why did Fluffy sit in the corner of her cage and shake? _because Mosh scared her_

3. Mosh put the rabbit in the closet because _Mosh was jealous of Fluffy_

4. Did Mosh hurt the rabbit? _No_
   How do you know? _The story said she was safely asleep._

5. What do you think Carlos and Mosh did after they put Fluffy back in her cage? _____
   (Answers will vary.)

33

Knowing the Words

Write the words from the story that have the meanings below.

1. covered with hair _____ furry _____
   (Par. 1)

2. dressed up so you
   can't be recognized _____ disguised _____
   (Par. 8)

Circle the pair of antonyms (opposites) in each row.

3. neighbor (friend) beast (enemy)
4. (quickly) loudly (slowly) sadly
5. shaggy (soft) (hard) gentle
6. (great) huge (terrible) old

Learning to Study

The word you look up in a dictionary is called an **entry word.** Many words that have endings are not listed as entry words. To find these words, look up the base word to which the ending is added. To find the word *sighed,* look up *sigh.* Write the word under which each of these words would be listed in a dictionary.

1. wheels _____ wheel _____
2. reading _____ read _____
3. rolled _____ roll _____
4. wanted _____ want _____
5. screaming _____ scream _____
6. suddenly _____ sudden _____
7. directions _____ direction _____

Reading and Thinking

1. How was Mosh like a pet when Carlos finished dressing it up?
   _____ Mosh was brown and furry. _____

2. What did Marie say Mosh looked like? _____ a monster _____

3. Mosh rolled out the door because
   _____ Carlos said *move* _____.

Write **T** if the sentence is true.
Write **F** if the sentence is false.

4. _T_ Mosh was dressed up to look like an animal.
5. _T_ Carlos missed his friend.
6. _F_ Carlos watched Mosh roll out of the house.
7. _F_ The kids were afraid of Mosh's wheels.

35

Knowing the Words

Write the word from the story that has the meaning below.

1. things used to
   do a job _____ supplies _____
   (Par. 4)

Synonyms are words that have the same or nearly the same meaning. Circle the pair of synonyms in each row.

2. spill (rush) start (hurry)
3. (stare) hide (look) push
4. suggest like (stay) (remain)

Learning to Study

At the top of each page in a dictionary are two words in dark print called **guide words.** They can help you find other words in the dictionary. The first guide word tells what the first word is on the page. The second guide word tells what the last word is on the page.

The words in a dictionary are listed in alphabetical order. To find a word, decide if it comes in alphabetical order between the guide words on the page. If it does, the word will be on that page. Check two words that could be found on each page that has these guide words.

1. **mop/nobody**   3. **closet/door**
   ___ push   ✓ cried
   ✓ named   ✓ did
   ✓ nervous   ___ back

2. **paint/robot**   4. **school/teacher**
   ✓ push   ✓ surprise
   ___ sound   ✓ stare
   ✓ principal   ___ thanks

Reading and Thinking

1. Number the sentences to show the order in which things happened.
   _2_ Mrs. Bell spilled some paint.
   _4_ Carlos showed the class some of the things Mosh could do.
   _1_ Mosh followed Carlos and Susan to school.
   _3_ Chad found Mosh.

2. Where did Carlos and Susan hide Mosh? _____ in a closet with cleaning supplies _____

3. The children hid Mosh because _____ there wasn't time to take Mosh home _____

Write the best word to complete each sentence below.

4. Alice hung her winter coat in the
   _____ closet _____. (sink, tent, closet)

5. Do you know the name of the
   _____ principal _____ at our school? (command, trouble, principal)

37

Knowing the Words

Write the words from the story that have the meanings below.

1. investigate _____ check _____
   (Par. 3)

2. looked angry _____ scowled _____
   (Par. 4)

Choose the correct word below to fill in the blanks for each pair of sentences.

top   check

3. Leah watched the _____ top _____ spin.
   My paper is on _____ top _____.

4. Did you _____ check _____ the spelling of the words in that story?
   Brenda wrote a _____ check _____ to pay for the movie tickets.

Learning to Study

The meanings of words can be found in the dictionary. Some words have more than one meaning. Look at the words and their meanings below. Answer the questions.

trip **1** to fall **2** journey
try   to work at
tub   container for water

1. Which word means "container for water"? _____ tub _____

2. What does the word *try* mean?
   _____ to work at _____

3. What is the first meaning of *trip*?
   _____ to fall _____

Reading and Thinking

Write **T** if the sentence is true.
Write **F** if the sentence is false.

1. _T_ Marie was baby-sitting for Carlos.

2. _F_ Carlos was happy with the water in the bathtub.

3. _T_ Carlos is much shorter than his dad.

4. _F_ Carlos's parents were angry with him.

5. What was Carlos doing when Marie told him to go take a bath? _____
   _____ reading a book _____

6. What do you think Carlos did after he spoke to his parents? _____
   _____ (Answers will vary.) _____

Write the best word to complete each sentence below.

7. Vickie wrote a funny _____ story _____ about a robot. (menu, story, word)

8. Put the shirt in the _____ drawer _____ when you take it off. (drawer, bathtub, garage)

9. I can't understand you when you
   _____ mumble _____. (laugh, mumble, ask)

10. I think I should _____ wear _____ my brown pants today. (hurry, hear, wear)

39

Knowing the Words

Write the words from the story that have the meanings below.

1. a special way
   things are arranged _____ order _____
   (Par. 2)

2. doing with others _____ sharing _____
   (Par. 3)

3. small sack _____ pouch _____
   (Par. 7)

Working with Words

A **prefix** is a group of letters added to the beginning of a word that changes the meaning of the word. The prefix **re-** means "again." *Rewire* means "wire again."

Read the words below. Write the correct word next to its meaning.

reread   reorder   reteach   rewrap

1. teach again _____ reteach _____
2. order again _____ reorder _____
3. read again _____ reread _____
4. wrap again _____ rewrap _____

Most words that end in a consonant followed by *y* are made plural by changing the *y* to *i* and adding *es.* The plural of *city* is *cities.* Write the plural form of each word below.

5. baby _____ babies _____
6. company _____ companies _____
7. penny _____ pennies _____

Reading and Thinking

1. Check the answer that tells what the story is mainly about.
   ✓ trying to fool the class
   ___ teaching Mosh to speak
   ___ dropping the question cards

Write **T** if the sentence is true.
Write **F** if the sentence is false.

2. _T_ Carlos was trying to teach Lizzy Wood a lesson.

3. _T_ When Carlos picked up his cards, they were not in the right order.

4. _F_ Something was wrong with the tape player inside Mosh.

5. _T_ Carlos's trick taught him a lesson.

Write the best word to complete each sentence below.

6. During the show, Pat made a penny
   _____ vanish _____. (sing, vanish, wish)

7. Elsa _____ dropped _____ her books on the way to school. (dropped, played, roared)

8. Please write one _____ question _____ to ask our guest. (card, answer, question)

9. Jamie gave a _____ clever _____ answer. (honor, hollow, clever)

10. The children's _____ laughter _____ filled the room. (laughter, book, tape)

41

Knowing the Words

Write the words from the story that have the meanings below.

1. worried ___nervous___
   (Par. 1)

2. what a person in a play says and does ___part___
   (Par. 2)

3. let down; unhappy ___disappointed___
   (Par. 6)

Check the meaning that fits the underlined word in each sentence.

4. Carrie went to the park to play.
   - ✓ have fun
   - _____ a show on stage

5. Did Janice eat part of this apple?
   - _____ in a play
   - ✓ a small piece of something

6. Did you hear the limb snap?
   - ✓ break suddenly
   - _____ speak angrily

Working with Words

Write the two words that were used to form each of these contractions.

1. I'm ___I am___

2. you're ___you are___

3. we'll ___we will or we shall___

4. isn't ___is not___

5. don't ___do not___

6. doesn't ___does not___

Reading and Thinking

1. Check the answer that tells what the story is mainly about.
   - ✓ getting a part in the school play
   - _____ Lizzy's part in the play
   - _____ walking to school

2. Write two words to describe Lizzy.
   ___(Answers will vary.)___

3. Carlos wasn't sure he would get to be the captain in the play because ___Lizzy tried out, too, and she was very good___

4. What part was Lizzy asked to play?
   ___first officer___

5. Why was Lizzy unhappy? ___She wanted to be the captain.___

43

Knowing the Words

Write the words from the story that have the meanings below.

1. awfully ___terribly___
   (Par. 3)

2. earned ___deserved___
   (Par. 8)

3. in an excited way ___dramatically___
   (Par. 8)

In each row below, circle the three words that belong together.

4. (stage) (curtain) sky (play)

5. (blast-off) sick (spaceship) (maps)

6. (friends) (Mosh) (Carlos) stage

Working with Words

Write a compound word using the underlined words in each sentence.

1. A ship used to travel in space is a ___spaceship___

2. Corn that will pop when it is heated is ___popcorn___.

3. A game in which a ball is kicked with the foot is ___football___.

Circle the correct word in ( ) and write it in the blank.

4. Jeanne drew a ___circle___ on the card. (circle, correct)

5. The ___ice___ in my glass melted. (act, ice)

Reading and Thinking

1. Number the sentences to show the order in which things happened.
   - _1_ Mosh chased Lizzy around the stage.
   - _3_ Carlos pulled out Mosh's battery.
   - _2_ Lizzy yelled for help.
   - _4_ Lizzy apologized.

Write **T** if the sentence is true.
Write **F** if the sentence is false.

2. _F_ Mosh was disobeying on purpose.

3. _T_ Lizzy was frightened when Mosh chased her around the stage.

4. _T_ Carlos rescued Lizzy.

5. _F_ Carlos planned to take Mosh's battery out during the play.

6. _T_ Carlos forgave Lizzy.

7. Write **R** next to the two sentences that tell about real things.
   - _____ Robots get sick.
   - _R_ Robots can be in plays.
   - _R_ Robots can run on batteries.

Read each sentence and fill in the blank.

8. The people laughed because they enjoyed the play.
   They stands for ___people___

9. Lizzy screamed when she needed help.
   She stands for ___Lizzy___.

45

Knowing the Words

Write the words from the story that have the meanings below.

1. part of the body where legs begin ___hips___
   (Par. 4)

2. pulling toward something ___attracting___
   (Par. 6)

3. wishing for something ___hopefully___
   (Par. 7)

Check the meaning that fits the underlined word in each sentence.

4. Pam ate an orange for lunch.
   - _____ a color
   - ✓ fruit

5. Please point to the problem you are working on.
   - ✓ show with a finger
   - _____ a dot

6. We bought bread at the store.
   - ✓ place to buy food
   - _____ save for later

Reading and Thinking

1. Check the answer that tells what the story is mainly about.
   - _____ hundreds of oranges
   - _____ an angry woman
   - ✓ trouble in the grocery store

2. The woman screamed because ___Mosh was scaring her___

3. What did Carlos put on the crackers?
   ___cheese___

4. How might this story have ended if Mosh had been left at home? _____
   ___(Answers will vary.)___

5. Was Mr. Johnson angry at the end of the story? Explain your answer.
   _____
   _____
   ___(Answers will vary.)___
   _____

Learning to Study

Number each list of words below in alphabetical order.

1. _5_ attract   2. _3_ hundred
   _3_ ask   _1_ hand
   _1_ again   _2_ hip
   _2_ angry   _4_ hurt
   _4_ ate   _5_ hush

47

Knowing the Words

Write the words from the story that have the meanings below.

1. two-way radios ___walkie-talkies___
   (Par. 1)

2. very dirty ___filthy___
   (Par. 7)

Synonyms are words that have the same or nearly the same meaning. Write **S** after each pair of synonyms. Write **A** after each pair of antonyms (opposites).

3. bought—sold _A_

4. yell—whisper _A_

5. tiny—little _S_

6. glad—happy _S_

7. back—front _A_

8. filthy—dirty _S_

9. loud—soft _A_

10. dirt—soil _S_

Working with Words

Write the two words that were used to form each of these contractions.

1. it's ___it is or it has___

2. he's ___he is or he has___

3. I'll ___I will or I shall___

4. doesn't ___does not___

5. there's ___there is or there has___

6. I've ___I have___

7. let's ___let us___

Reading and Thinking

1. Number the sentences to show the order in which things happened.
   - _2_ Mosh swept up the screws to the walkie-talkies.
   - _3_ Carlos searched through the dirt for the screws.
   - _4_ Mrs. Garza came home.
   - _1_ Carlos showed Mosh how to clean the carpet.

2. Where was Mrs. Garza when the story began? ___at the office___
   _____

3. Check one answer that tells how Mrs. Garza probably got to work.
   - ✓ in a car
   - _____ on a bus

4. What chore was Carlos doing? _____
   ___washing the dishes___

Write the best word to complete each sentence below.

5. Adam could not find a broom to ___sweep___ the sidewalk. (empty, feel, sweep)

6. There is a blue ___carpet___ in the living room. (dirt, carpet, noise)

7. You cannot ___vacuum___ the rug with a broom. (vacuum, find, help)

49

Knowing the Words

Write the word from the story that has the meaning below.

1. saw _____spotted_____
   (Par. 3)

Write the word with the correct meaning to complete each sentence below.

2. Did you ___see___ tigers and elephants at the zoo? (sea, see)

3. Jeannette has a ___new___ notebook. (new, knew)

4. We saw a ___herd___ of cows in the pasture. (heard, herd)

Learning to Study

A **table of contents** is one of the first pages in a book. It shows the chapters that are in the book and on what page each one begins. Use the table of contents below to answer the questions.

How to Build a Robot
Table of Contents

1. How many chapters are in this book? ___five___

2. What is the third chapter called?
   ___Building the Robot___

3. On what page does the fourth chapter begin? ___23___

Reading and Thinking

1. Check the answer that tells what the story is mainly about.
   - ✓ saving a child from harm
   - ___ bouncing a ball
   - ___ climbing a tree

2. Who was Kevin? ___a boy who lived in Carlos's neighborhood___

3. Why did Kevin run back toward his house? ___He was afraid of Mosh.___

4. Check two sentences that tell about both Susan and Kevin.
   - ✓ They lived near Carlos.
   - ✓ They were playing outside.
   - ___ They cried when they ran away from Mosh.

5. What might have happened if Mosh had not scared Kevin? _____
   ___(Answers will vary.)___

51

Knowing the Words

Write the words from the story that have the meanings below.

1. moved shoulders up and down ___shrugged___
   (Par. 1)

2. looked quickly ___peeked___
   (Par. 2)

In each row below, circle the three words that belong together.

3. (garage) (car) sky (driveway)
4. (curb) (concrete) (street) grass
5. ladder (minutes) (time) (clock)
6. (tag) (game) (fun) mess
7. (shovel) (snow) (ice) night

Learning to Study

An **index** is a part of a book. It lists a book's topics in alphabetical order. It also lists page numbers so you can find those topics. An index is usually found at the back of a book. Use the index below from a book of games to answer the questions.

rules, 24
tag, 6, 12, 21
tennis, 5, 10–11
volleyball, 2–4, 11, 13

1. On what pages could you find out how to play tag? ___6, 12, and 21___

2. On what pages could you find out about tennis? ___5 and 10–11___

3. On what page could you find rules? ___24___

Reading and Thinking

Write **T** if the sentence is true.
Write **F** if the sentence is false.

1. ___T___ Carlos was upset when Mosh was missing.

2. ___F___ Lizzy took Mosh to hurt Carlos's feelings.

3. ___F___ Carlos told Mosh to take things out of Lizzy's garage to help her.

4. ___F___ Carlos watched Lizzy put everything back in her garage.

5. How do you think Mosh got in Lizzy's yard? ___Lizzy took it there.___

6. What game did Lizzy want to play with Mosh? ___tag___

Write the best word to complete each sentence below.

7. Agnes ___searched___ all over the house to find her clay. (heard, touched, searched)

8. We rode our ___bikes___ to the store. (airplanes, bikes, kites)

53

Knowing the Words

Write the word from the story that has the meaning below.

1. ability to move without slipping ___traction___
   (Par. 4)

Check the meaning that fits the underlined word in each sentence.

2. <u>Swing</u> at the baseball with the bat.
   - ✓ strike at
   - ___ seat that moves back and forth

3. Don't <u>dump</u> that dirt in the driveway.
   - ✓ unload
   - ___ place for trash

4. I ate a <u>roll</u> with my dinner.
   - ___ turn over and over
   - ✓ bread

Working with Words

Write a compound word using the underlined words in each sentence.

1. A <u>storm</u> in which <u>snow</u> falls is a ___snowstorm___

2. A <u>drift</u> made of <u>snow</u> is a ___snowdrift___

Circle the correct word in ( ) and write it in the blank.

3. Three inches of ___snow___ fell yesterday. (saw, (snow))

4. Please ___scoop___ out two cups of oatmeal. ((scoop), skip)

Reading and Thinking

1. Check the answer that tells what the story is mainly about.
   - ___ drawing in the snow
   - ✓ shoveling snow
   - ___ getting too cold

2. Number the sentences to show the order in which things happened.
   - 3 Carlos drew a face in the snow.
   - 2 Carlos put chains on Mosh's wheels.
   - 4 Mosh dumped snow down Carlos's back.
   - 1 Marie's hands got cold.

3. Marie wanted Mosh to help because ___her hands were cold___

4. Why did Carlos put chains on Mosh's wheels? ___so Mosh could move in the snow___

5. Where did Carlos get the chains for Mosh? ___from an old swing___

6. What was Carlos going to draw in the snow after he drew the silly face? ___Mosh___

7. What do you think Carlos did after Mosh threw the snow on him? _____
   ___(Answers will vary.)___

55

Knowing the Words

Write the words from the story that have the meanings below.

1. leader of a city ___mayor___
   (Par. 3)

2. carving; statue ___sculpture___
   (Par. 3)

3. deciding in a contest ___judging___
   (Par. 6)

Working with Words

Rewrite the following groups of words using 's or s' to show who owns something. The first one is done for you.

house that belongs to Susan
Susan's house

1. announcement made by the mayor
   ___mayor's announcement___

2. sculpture that belongs to the kids
   ___kids' sculpture___

3. eyes that belong to the sculpture
   ___sculpture's eyes___

Circle the correct letters to complete each word and write them in the blank.

4. I felt bett__er__ after my nap.
   or   ar   (er)

5. Snow fell early this m__or__ning.
   (or)   ar   er

6. Who will c__ar__ve this soap?
   or   (ar)   er

Reading and Thinking

Write **T** if the sentence is true.
Write **F** if the sentence is false.

1. ___T___ This story takes place in the winter.

2. ___F___ The snowstorm knocked down the telephone lines to Carlos's house.

3. ___T___ Susan made up a new word.

4. ___F___ The kids took more than two hours to finish their snowbot.

5. Write **M** next to the sentence that tells about something make-believe.
   - ___ You could make a robot out of snow.
   - ___M___ Robots can cry like people.
   - ___ Tennis balls can be colored green.

Write the best word to complete each sentence below.

6. I made a ___sculpture___ of a horse in art class. (mayor, marker, sculpture)

7. What color was the ___ribbon___ that you won? (ribbon, sound, yard)

57

Knowing the Words

Write the word from the story that has the meaning below.

1. someone who rides with someone else __passenger__
   (Par. 11)

Circle the pair of antonyms (opposites) in each row.

2. (slower) (faster) bigger larger
3. (closed) dragged ordered (opened)
4. (huge) (tiny) under down

Working with Words

When a word ends with e, the e is usually dropped before adding -ed or -ing. For example, like + ed = liked. Add -ed or -ing to the word in ( ) to make a word that completes each sentence.

1. My mom __rescued__ the cat from the tree. (rescue)
2. Why are you __staring__ at the wall? (stare)
3. We should start __closing__ the doors now. (close)

The prefix un- means "not." Unsure means "not sure." Add un- to the words below. Use the new words to complete the sentences.

    even   happy

4. Barb was __unhappy__ about losing the game.
5. The top of that table looks __uneven__.

Reading and Thinking

1. Check the answer that tells what the story is mainly about.
   ____ rolling through the snow
   ____ running into a snowdrift
   _✓_ sledding down the hill

2. Where did the kids go sledding?
   __a hill on Pine Street__

3. What helped Mosh roll through the snow? __chains on its wheels__

4. What might have happened if Carlos and Mosh had not run into a snowdrift? _____
   __(Answers will vary.)__

5. What do you think Carlos and Susan did when they were done sledding?
   _____
   __(Answers will vary.)__

59

Knowing the Words

Write the words from the story that have the meanings below.

1. was able __managed__
   (Par. 2)
2. got out __escaped__
   (Par. 2)
3. monster __beast__
   (Par. 5)

Choose the correct word to fill in the blanks for each pair of sentences.

    duck   light   close

4. Who left the __light__ on in the garage?
   The canoe was __light__ enough to carry.

5. The __duck__ flew over the pond.
   Kim needs to __duck__ to get through the opening.

6. Please __close__ the window.
   Do not get too __close__ to the parade.

Reading and Thinking

1. Number the sentences to show the order in which things happened.
   _3_ Carlos saw the thing that had been chasing him.
   _1_ Carlos ran into the house.
   _2_ Carlos ran into a cave.
   _4_ Carlos woke up.

Write T if the sentence is true.
Write F if the sentence is false.

2. _F_ Carlos was camping out.
3. _T_ Carlos woke up during the night.
4. _T_ Mosh put the desk in front of the bedroom door.
5. _F_ Carlos really caught a butterfly in his net.

Learning to Study

Number each list of words below in alphabetical order.

1. _1_ cold   3. _1_ sleep
   _4_ corner   _4_ still
   _3_ cool   _5_ stop
   _5_ cozy   _3_ small
   _2_ comb   _2_ slip

2. _5_ desk   4. _4_ woods
   _1_ deck   _2_ window
   _3_ delight   _1_ will
   _4_ depend   _3_ won
   _2_ deer   _5_ worry

61

Knowing the Words

Write the words from the story that have the meanings below.

1. directions for preparing food __recipe__
   (Par. 2)
2. mixture __batter__
   (Par. 5)
3. tool used in cooking __measuring cup__
   (Par. 6)

In each row below, circle the three words that belong together.

4. (cookbook) (recipe) milk (directions)
5. (bowl) peel (spoon) (cup)
6. (flour) (sugar) (eggs) oven
7. mash (batter) (pan) (bread)
8. (mix) (stir) (pour) eat

Write the word with the correct meaning to complete each sentence below.

9. Who __threw__ that ball? (threw, through)
10. Connie tried __some__ of the fresh bread. (sum, some)
11. Please __pour__ the milk now. (poor, pour)
12. Can you __add__ ten and twelve? (add, ad)
13. Val __made__ pizza in school today. (made, maid)
14. The __flower__ grew through a crack in the street. (flour, flower)

Reading and Thinking

1. Write three things that were needed to make banana bread. __bowl, spoon,__
   (Accept any three answers.)
   recipe, bananas, flour, sugar,
   milk, eggs, pan, oven, measuring cup

2. How did Carlos know how to make bread? __He had a recipe.__
   _____

3. What room do you think Carlos and Mosh were in? __the kitchen__

Learning to Study

Use the table of contents below to answer the questions.

Robot Recipes

Table of Contents

1. What is the fourth chapter called?
   __Vegetable Dishes__

2. On what page does the chapter about soups begin? __41__

3. In what chapter could you find how to make nut bread? __Breads or__
   __Chapter One__

63

Knowing the Words

Write the words from the story that have the meanings below.

1. keep from happening __prevent__
   (Par. 1)
2. forgive __excuse__
   (Par. 2)
3. spoiled __ruined__
   (Par. 7)

Synonyms are words that have the same or nearly the same meaning. Circle the pair of synonyms in each row.

4. (ended) (finished) begun baked
5. wish (wash) (clean) learn
6. (laughing) crying (chuckling) sleeping
7. showed (cooked) (baked) made

Learning to Study

Use the cookbook index below to answer the questions.

    baking, 6–10
    banana nut bread, 27
    biscuits, 38–40
    buns, 28, 31, 33

1. On what page would you look to find out about making banana nut bread? __27__

2. On what pages would you find recipes for buns? __28, 31, and 33__

3. On what pages could you find out about how to bake? __6–10__

4. On what pages could you find out how to make biscuits? __38–40__

Reading and Thinking

1. Check the answer that tells what the story is mainly about.
   _✓_ surprising Mr. Garza
   ____ watching TV
   ____ mopping up water

2. Carlos said "Excuse us" when he left the table because __he was being__
   __polite (Answers may vary.)__

3. Why did Mosh pour water on the candles? __to put the fire out__
   __(Answers may vary.)__

4. Check three words that tell about Mr. Garza.
   _✓_ pleasant   _✓_ patient
   ____ frantic   _✓_ kind

5. What kind of person do you think Mrs. Garza is? Explain your answer.
   _____
   __(Answers will vary.)__

Write the best word to complete each sentence below.

6. Sean tries to __prevent__ accidents by being careful. (watch, prevent, surprise)

7. Joy got muddy when she stepped in the __puddle__. (candle, pool, puddle)

65

Knowing the Words

Write the words from the story that have the meanings below.

1. upset __bothered__
(Par. 1)

2. given too much __spoiled__
(Par. 1)

Working with Words

Circle the correct letters to complete each word and write them in the blank.

1. Did the elephants sc __are__ you?
ur (are) ear

2. I forgot to t __ur__ n off the radio.
(ur) are ear

3. Our dog b __ar__ ked all night.
er or (ar)

4. Jo cut her fing __er__ on the broken glass.
(er) or ar

5. My shoes are very d __ir__ ty.
or (ir) ar

The suffix **-ful** means "full of." *Careful* means "full of care." Add **-ful** to the words below. Use the new words to complete the sentences.

help   joy   fear

6. The team members were __joyful__ that they won the game.

7. I try to be __helpful__ by cleaning up my room.

8. Stacy is __fearful__ of loud noises.

Reading and Thinking

1. Number the sentences to show the order in which things happened.

__4__ Mosh rolled into the corner and turned off its lights.

__3__ Mr. Garza opened the closet door.

__2__ Aunt Laura screamed.

__1__ Carlos tried to go to sleep.

2. What was Mosh getting out of Carlos's room? __a book__

3. Who is Sweetie? __Aunt Laura's dog__

4. What do you think Carlos did when he got back to the den after being in Aunt Laura's room? _____
(Answers will vary.)

5. What do you think Aunt Laura did after everyone left her room? _____
(Answers will vary.)

67

Knowing the Words

Write the words from the story that have the meanings below.

1. chain or rope used to walk a dog __leash__
(Par. 3)

2. answered __replied__
(Par. 10)

Working with Words

Write the two words that were used to form each of these contractions.

1. wouldn't __would not__

2. haven't __have not__

3. didn't __did not__

Write a compound word using the underlined words in each sentence.

4. A book used to cook with is a __cookbook__

5. A ball made of snow is a __snowball__

Circle the correct word in ( ) and write it in the blank.

6. The __huge__ balloon floated over the fairgrounds. (hug (huge))

7. The first __page__ has a picture of a lion on it. ((page) pig)

8. A robin's __egg__ is a beautiful color of blue. ((egg) edge)

Reading and Thinking

Write **T** if the sentence is true.
Write **F** if the sentence is false.

1. __T__ Carlos felt sad that Mosh had to stay in the garage.

2. __F__ Mosh had hurt Sweetie.

3. __F__ Sweetie was licking Mosh because he enjoyed the taste of metal.

4. __T__ Mosh and Sweetie spent a lot of time together after the first walk.

5. Check the sentence that tells how Mosh and Sweetie are alike.
____ They both had wheels.
____ They both barked.
__✓__ They both belonged to people.

Circle the name or names that each underlined word stands for.

6. "I want that robot out of here," said Aunt Laura.
Carlos   Mosh   (Aunt Laura)

7. "We can go for a walk," Carlos told Mosh.
Mosh and Sweetie   (Carlos and Mosh)
Carlos and Aunt Laura

8. "They are my friends," Carlos said, pointing to Susan and Mosh.
(Susan and Mosh)   Susan and Carlos
Carlos and Mosh

9. "You can ride along," Carlos said to Marie.
Carlos   (Marie)   Mosh

69

Knowing the Words

Write the word from the story that has the meaning below.

1. in good health __well__
(Par. 1)

Check the meaning that fits the underlined word in each sentence.

2. Please fill my glass with milk.
__✓__ container for holding liquids
____ a mirror

3. That is a great idea for a story.
____ very large
__✓__ excellent

4. Fall begins in September.
__✓__ season
____ to hit the ground

Working with Words

The ending **-er** sometimes means "more." It may be used to compare two things. The ending **-est** means "most." It is used to compare more than two things.

In each sentence below, add **-er** to the word before the blank if two things are being compared. Add **-est** if more than two things are being compared.

1. That was the great __est__ movie I have ever seen.

2. An ant is small __er__ than a bee.

3. Lynne is old __er__ than I.

4. Heather is the quiet __est__ person in our class.

5. An orange is sweet __er__ than a lemon.

Reading and Thinking

1. Check the answer that tells what the story is mainly about.
____ eating soup
__✓__ having a robot nurse
____ staying home from school

2. Carlos had to stay home from school because __he was ill__
(Answers may vary.)

3. What did Mosh bring instead of juice? __water__

4. Who was taking care of Carlos? __Mosh and Mrs. Wilson__

Write the best word to complete each sentence below.

5. I have an __extra__ pen you may use. (extra, eager, ill)

6. I was so __thirsty__ I drank a large glass of cold milk. (hungry, thirsty, sleepy)

7. The __juice__ was made from fruit. (water, juice, milk)

71

Knowing the Words

Write the words from the story that have the meanings below.

1. lying around __spread__
(Par. 6)

2. scattering water __splashing__
(Par. 6)

3. wonderful __marvelous__
(Par. 9)

Circle the pair of antonyms (opposites) in each row.

4. (morning)   noon   (night)   late

5. soapy   (clean)   (dirty)   terrible

6. (messy)   lucky   careful   (neat)

Working with Words

The words below have been divided into syllables. Put a mark above the first vowel to show the sound it stands for. Mark the long vowels with ¯ over the letter. Mark the short vowels with ˘.

1. mĭn/ute   5. răp/id   9. rō/bot

2. bā/by   6. fī/nal   10. măn/age

3. ō/ver   7. pā/per   11. sĕc/ond

4. lā/ter   8. văn/ish   12. fĭn/ish

Fill in each blank with the correct letters to make a word that completes each sentence below.

mb   kn   wr

13. Did you see a __wr__ en fly by the window?

14. The plu __mb__ er fixed the leaky pipe.

15. The sharp __kn__ ife cut through the meat.

Reading and Thinking

Write **T** if the sentence is true.
Write **F** if the sentence is false.

1. __T__ Carlos had not expected Mosh to do such a good job mopping.

2. __T__ Mosh tried to wash the dishes and the floor the same way.

3. __T__ Marie thought it was funny that Mosh was making a mess.

4. Carlos did not stay to watch Mosh mop the floor because __he had to clean his room__

5. Do you think Mosh will ever be asked to wash the dishes again? Explain your answer. _____
(Answers will vary.)
_____

6. What do you think Carlos did after he finished washing the dishes?
_____
(Answers will vary.)

73

Knowing the Words

Write the words from the story that have the meanings below.

1. used for baking ___baking soda or soda___
   (Par. 5)
2. mistakes ___mix-ups___
   (Par. 11)
3. told of trouble ahead of time ___warned___
   (Par. 12)

Working with Words

Circle the correct word in ( ) and write it in the blank.

1. Mosh is a robot and not a ___toy___.
   ((toy) today)
2. The bath ___powder___ made Joyce sneeze. (pour, (powder))
3. I forgot to wear my ___coat___ to school today. (cat, (coat))
4. Justin ___bought___ his lunch. ((bought) boat)

To form the plural of a word that ends in f or fe, the f or fe is changed to v, and es is added. Form the plural of each word below.

5. life ___lives___
6. calf ___calves___
7. scarf ___scarves___
8. loaf ___loaves___
9. elf ___elves___

Reading and Thinking

1. Number the sentences to show the order in which things happened.
   _3_ Mosh put out the candles.
   _2_ Carlos took the guests' coats.
   _4_ The guests came to the table.
   _1_ The guests arrived.

2. Write the name of one of the Garzas' guests. ___Mrs. Chung___

3. What two things were in the middle of the dinner table? ___candles and flowers___

4. The flames on the candles went out because ___Mosh put baking soda on them___.

Write the best word to complete each sentence below.

5. Sara ___invited___ me to her birthday party. (laughed, poured, invited)
6. Last night we had potatoes for ___dinner___. (breakfast, dinner, lunch)
7. Alice ___arrived___ just when the bell rang. (arrived, liked, lit)
8. The loud horn ___warned___ us that a tornado was coming. (heard, whispered, warned)

75

Knowing the Words

Write the words from the story that have the meanings below.

1. missing ___gone___
   (Par. 3)
2. chest of drawers ___dresser___
   (Par. 10)
3. pleasant ___delightful___
   (Par. 12)

Synonyms are words that have the same or nearly the same meaning. Circle the pair of synonyms in each row.

4. look ((find) (discover)) lose
5. ((idea)) problem ((thought)) question
6. found forget ((gone)) ((missing))

Working with Words

Rewrite the following groups of words using 's or s' to show who owns something.

1. coats that belong to the guests
   ___guests' coats___
2. bedroom that belongs to Carlos
   ___Carlos's bedroom___

Circle the correct letters to complete each word and write them in the blank.

3. Where is your oth___er___ glove?
   ar (er) or
4. Will you please f___or___give me?
   ar er (or)
5. Are you going to the p___ar___ty?
   (ar) er or

Reading and Thinking

1. Check the answer that tells what the story is mainly about.
   _✓_ finding the lost coats
   ___ apologizing to the guests
   ___ forgetting the party

Write **T** if the sentence is true.
Write **F** if the sentence is false.

2. _T_ Carlos did not want the guests to know their coats were lost.
3. _F_ Marie thought it was funny that the coats were missing.
4. _T_ Marie helped find the coats.
5. _T_ Mrs. Chung is a polite person.
6. Where did Carlos and Marie find the coats? ___in drawers___
7. What did it mean when Mr. Garza winked? _____ (Answers will vary.)
8. What do you think Carlos did after the guests left? _____ (Answers will vary.)
9. Do you think the Garzas will have another party? Explain your answer. _____ (Answers will vary.)

77

Knowing the Words

Write the words from the story that have the meanings below.

1. all things not made by humans ___nature___
   (Par. 1)
2. not comfortably ___uneasily___
   (Par. 2)
3. long walk ___hike___
   (Par. 4)
4. chase away ___shoo___
   (Par. 13)

Write the words with the correct meaning to complete each sentence below.

5. Kathy lost a ___shoe___ down by the pond. (shoo, shoe)
6. I ___know___ where to find deer. (know, no)
7. There are ___four___ pears on the ground. (four, for)
8. I have ___to___ walk home after school. (too, to, two)
9. We will return in ___one___ hour. (won, one)
10. The children lost ___their___ balloons. (there, their)

Reading and Thinking

1. Carlos thought the frogs were croaking loudly because ___they didn't like the cold water___

2. Why wouldn't Carlos let Mosh go on the hike? ___It would be too hard for Mosh to move.___

3. How else might the boys have gotten the frogs out of the tent? _____ (Answers will vary.)

Write the best word to complete each sentence below.

4. Roger was ___waving___ at the people on the ship. (waving, complaining, hiking)
5. The ___frog___ hopped off the rock and into the water. (snake, tent, frog)

Learning to Study

A dictionary entry shows the words divided into syllables. A space or a dot shows where the word can be divided at the end of a line of writing.

Read the words below. Next to each, write the number of syllables it has.

1. na ture _2_   4. stom ach _2_
2. un eas y _3_   5. min ute _2_
3. wa ter _2_   6. grum ble _2_

79

Knowing the Words

Write the words from the story that have the meanings below.

1. wanders ___roams___
   (Par. 3)
2. more nervous ___jumpier___
   (Par. 8)

Working with Words

When a word ends in a consonant followed by y, the y is changed to i before **-er** and **-est** is added. Change the y to i in each word in ( ). Add **-er** or **-est** to make a word that completes the sentence. The first one is done for you.

Hope's tale was _scarier_ than Jeff's. (scary)

1. I am ___hungrier___ now than I was an hour ago. (hungry)
2. That is the ___ugliest___ bug of all. (ugly)
3. A rose is the ___prettiest___ flower I've ever seen. (pretty)

The suffix **-less** means "without." Joyless means "without joy." Add **-less** to the following words. Use the new words to complete the sentences.

sleep   care   home

4. The ___homeless___ kitten looked hungry and cold.
5. I had a ___sleepless___ night because of a barking dog.
6. Because Donna was ___careless___, she got paint on her clothes.

Reading and Thinking

1. Number the sentences to show the order in which things happened.
   _3_ Carlos saw glowing green spots.
   _1_ Jake told a scary story.
   _2_ Jake fell asleep.
   _4_ The boys found out that the creature was Mosh.

2. Carlos was afraid because ___he had heard a scary story___

3. Who was camping with the boys? ___Mosh or Mr. Jones or both___

4. What did Carlos hear that frightened him? ___an owl hoot___

5. How did Carlos feel when he saw the shadow? Explain your answer. _____ (Answers will vary.)

6. How do you think Carlos felt when he found out that the creature was Mosh? Explain your answer. _____ (Answers will vary.)

81

Knowing the Words

Write the words from the story that have the meanings below.

1. visit to someplace with a group __field trip__
   (Par. 2)

2. jumped __leapt__
   (Par. 2)

3. tasty __delicious__
   (Par. 3)

Working with Words

Sometimes the plural form of a word is made by changing the spelling of the word. The plural form of *goose* is *geese*. Use the plural words below to complete the sentences.

mice   women   feet   children

1. Two __mice__ live in a cage in our classroom.

2. These tennis shoes are too small for Kay's __feet__.

3. Twenty __children__ rode on a bus to the zoo.

4. My older sister and my mother are __women__.

Fill in each blank with the correct letters to make a word that completes each sentence below.

ph   wr

5. There is a __wr__ inkle in my shirt.

6. Can you say the al __ph__ abet backwards?

Reading and Thinking

Write **T** if the sentence is true.
Write **F** if the sentence is false.

1. __T__ Carlos had overslept.

2. __T__ It took Carlos five minutes to get dressed.

3. __T__ The class might have seen an ostrich at the zoo.

4. __F__ Susan thought a Mosh special looked delicious.

5. __T__ Carlos thought the sandwich would be tasty.

6. What did Mosh put in the sandwich?
   __tuna fish, peanut butter,__
   __bananas, mustard, and pickles__

7. What do you think the class did when they finished eating? _____
   __(Answers will vary.)__

8. Do you think Mosh will be allowed to make another sandwich? Explain your answer. _____
   __(Answers will vary.)__

83

Knowing the Words

Write the word from the story that has the meaning below.

1. pleased __impressed__
   (Par. 1)

Synonyms are words that have the same or nearly the same meaning. Circle the pair of synonyms in each row.

2. box   (gift)   paper   (present)
3. (terrible)   (awful)   sad   brave
4. hope   (imagine)   tease   (think)

Working with Words

Write a compound word using the underlined words in each sentence.

1. The <u>day</u> of your <u>birth</u> is your __birthday__

2. A <u>fish</u> the color of <u>gold</u> is a __goldfish__

3. <u>Paper</u> with <u>sand</u> on it is called __sandpaper__

4. An <u>ache</u> in your <u>head</u> is a __headache__

5. <u>Light</u> from the <u>moon</u> is called __moonlight__

In each word below, draw a line to divide the word into syllables.

6. con|fuse   9. pil|low
7. rib|bon   10. jour|ney
8. al|most   11. les|son

Reading and Thinking

1. Check the answer that tells what the story is mainly about.
   ____ saying good-bye to Mosh
   ____ selling Mosh to Mrs. Chung
   _✓_ having a party for Mosh

2. What did Marie give to Carlos for Mosh? __lights for eyes__

3. What was Mrs. Garza's gift? __a battery and a note__

4. What do you think Carlos and Mosh did after the party? _____
   __(Answers will vary.)__

Write the best word to complete each sentence.

5. The crowd __cheered__ loudly for the team. (teased, thought, cheered)

6. When I close my eyes, it is easy to __imagine__ I am a bird. (imagine, sell, mention)

7. A small __package__ came in the mail today. (hug, cheer, package)

8. Can you __explain__ how to wrap a present? (explain, want, open)

9. After the long walk, Marge was very __tired__. (nice, tired, brave)

85

Knowing the Words

Write the words from the story that have the meanings below.

1. jumping __bounding__
   (Par. 3)

2. pipe that water comes out of __faucet__
   (Par. 4)

3. ran quickly __scrambled__
   (Par. 4)

4. turned quickly __whirled__
   (Par. 6)

Some words sound alike but have different spellings and meanings. Write the word with the correct meaning to complete each sentence below.

5. Those __stairs__ lead to the attic. (stares, stairs)

6. Please __close__ the garage door. (close, clothes)

Working with Words

Circle the correct word in ( ) and write it in the blank.

1. Do not get __soap__ in your eyes when you wash. (soup, (soap))

2. They __caught__ the butterfly in a net. ((caught), cat)

3. I'll need a __broom__ to clean up this powder. ((broom), brim)

4. Can you __reach__ that bottle of shampoo? (rich, (reach))

Reading and Thinking

1. Check the answer that tells what the story is mainly about.
   ____ a pile of dirty clothes
   _✓_ a bath for Herbie
   ____ two messes

2. Herbie ran away because __he hated water__.
   __(Answers may vary.)__

3. Put a check beside something that was probably in Tracy's basement.
   ____ a car
   _✓_ a washing machine
   ____ a mailbox

4. Put a check beside the two answers that tell where Herbie hid.
   ____ in the living room
   _✓_ in the pile of dirty clothes
   _✓_ beside the refrigerator

5. What did Tracy mean when she said that there were two messes to clean?
   __They had to clean Herbie and__
   __the floor.__

6. How do you think Rick and Tracy will clean the basement floor? _____
   __(Answers will vary.)__

87

Knowing the Words

Write the words from the story that have the meanings below.

1. tennis shoes __sneakers__
   (Par. 1)

2. made less tight __loosened__
   (Par. 1)

3. strings used for tying __laces__
   (Par. 1)

4. tiny pieces of wood __splinters__
   (Par. 7)

Check the meaning that fits the underlined word in each sentence.

5. <u>Roll</u> the ball across the floor.
   ____ bread
   _✓_ move by turning

6. Did you hurt your <u>foot</u>?
   _✓_ part of the body
   ____ twelve inches

7. I have <u>sand</u> in my shoe.
   ____ to make smooth
   _✓_ tiny bits of stone

Working with Words

An *'s* at the end of a word may be used to show that something belongs to someone. Add *'s* to each name below and write the new word in the correct blank.

Mr. Levi   Skipper   Elsa

1. __Mr. Levi's__ lumber

2. __Elsa's__ skateboard

3. __Skipper's__ doghouse

Reading and Thinking

1. Number the sentences to show the order in which things happened.
   _4_ Elsa rolled down the street on her skateboard.
   _2_ Mr. Levi gave the girls a piece of wood.
   _1_ Elsa discovered that her skates didn't fit.
   _3_ The girls attached the skate wheels to the board.

2. Check the sentence that tells why Elsa couldn't get her skates on.
   ____ Her skates had shrunk.
   ____ Her socks were too thick.
   _✓_ Her feet had grown.

3. Check two words that tell about Mr. Levi.
   _✓_ helpful   ____ selfish
   ____ grouchy   _✓_ friendly

4. Check two sentences that tell how Elsa's skateboard and roller skates were alike.
   ____ They both had laces.
   _✓_ They both had screws.
   _✓_ They both had wheels.
   ____ They both were made of wood.

89

Knowing the Words

Write the words from the story that have the meanings below.

1. large truck _____van_____ (Par. 1)

2. noise _____racket_____ (Par. 1)

Abbreviations are shortened forms of words. The abbreviation for *inch* is *in.* Match each word from the first list with its abbreviation from the second list.

3. _b_ street   **a.** mi.

4. _c_ Mister   **b.** st.

5. _a_ mile   **c.** Mr.

Learning to Study

A **table of contents** is on one of the first pages in a book. It shows the chapters that are in the book and on what page each one begins. Use the table of contents below to answer the questions.

All About Dogs
Table of Contents

Kinds of Dogs 1
Dogs as Pets 21
Caring for Your Dog 30
Feeding Your Dog 45

1. How many chapters are in the book?

_____four_____

2. What is the first chapter called?

_____Kinds of Dogs_____

3. On what page does "Dogs as Pets"

begin? _____page 21_____

Reading and Thinking

1. Check the answer that tells what the story is mainly about.
   - ✓ meeting new neighbors
   - ___ watching movers
   - ___ noises in the alley

2. Check the two sentences that tell about Tracy.
   - ✓ She likes to meet people.
   - ✓ She is a good neighbor.
   - ___ She does not like dogs.

Write **T** if the sentence is true.
Write **F** if the sentence is false.

3. _F_ Dale knocked the garbage can over.

4. _F_ Tracy could easily walk to Oak Hill.

5. _T_ Tracy thought Rags was lost.

6. _F_ Tracy wanted to keep Rags.

7. How far had Lindsay and Dale moved from their old home?

_____about 100 miles_____

Write the best word to complete each sentence below.

8. The _____furniture_____ in the kitchen is new. (barn, furniture, noise)

9. The _____comic_____ book is funny. (comic, metal, leftover)

10. We rode in the _____van_____ to the game. (toast, pup, van)

91

Knowing the Words

Write the words from the story that have the meanings below.

1. worried _____troubled_____ (Par. 2)

2. special things _____treats_____ (Par. 2)

3. teach _____train_____ (Par. 6)

Some words are spelled the same but have different meanings. For example, *yard* can mean "the land around a building" or "thirty-six inches."

Look at the list of words below. For each pair of sentences, one word from the list will correctly complete both. Choose the correct word to fill in the blank for each pair of sentences.

    bark   bowl   can

4. I like to _____bowl_____ with my friends.

   I poured cereal and milk into

   my favorite _____bowl_____.

5. Floppy doesn't _____bark_____ at people she knows.

   The tree _____bark_____ was bumpy.

6. Kevin _____can_____ play the piano.

   The soup _____can_____ was empty.

Match each word from the first list with its abbreviation from the second list.

7. _b_ minute   **a.** ft.

8. _c_ Monday   **b.** min.

9. _a_ feet   **c.** Mon.

Reading and Thinking

Words such as *he, she, you, it, we,* and *they* are used in place of other words. Read these sentences. *Rags is a puppy. He is owned by Lindsay and Dale.* Instead of repeating the name *Rags* in the second sentence, *he* is used in the place of *Rags.*

Read each set of sentences below. Fill in each blank.

1. Lindsay told Rags to sit. She used a firm voice.

   She stands for _____Lindsay_____

2. Lindsay and Dale are training Rags. They enjoy the work.

   They stands for _____Lindsay and Dale_____

3. The collar wasn't very heavy. It was made for a puppy.

   It stands for _____the collar_____

4. Rags was not eating his food at home

   because _he was eating somewhere else_

Learning to Study

Number each list of words below in alphabetical order.

1. _3_ problem   3. _2_ treats
   _1_ pretend   _3_ tried
   _2_ pride   _1_ train

2. _1_ happy   4. _3_ ran
   _2_ him   _1_ Rags
   _3_ house   _2_ rain

93

Knowing the Words

Write the words from the story that have the meanings below.

1. something nice that is said _____praise_____ (Par. 2)

2. strong _____firm_____ (Par. 2)

3. waiting without getting upset _____patient_____ (Par. 6)

Words that mean the same, or nearly the same, are called **synonyms.** Circle the pair of synonyms in each row.

4. (command) ask know (order)

5. firm (bright) shy (smart)

Learning to Study

At the top of each page in a dictionary are two words in dark print called **guide words.** They can help you find other words in the dictionary. The first guide word tells what the first word is on the page. The second guide word tells what the last word is on the page.

The words in a dictionary are listed in alphabetical order. To find a word, decide if it comes in alphabetical order between the guide words. If it does, the word will be on that page. Check each word that could be found between these guide words.

scatter/scout

1. ✓ science   5. ✓ scissors

2. ___ scramble   6. ✓ school

3. ✓ scene   7. ___ scrub

4. ✓ scratch   8. ✓ scent

Reading and Thinking

1. Check the answer that tells what the story is mainly about.
   - ___ getting tired
   - ___ a long afternoon
   - ✓ how to train a dog

2. Did Rags mean to misbehave? _____

   Explain your answer. _____

   (Answers will vary.)

3. What other things might Lindsay and Dale train Rags to do? _____

   (Answers will vary.)

4. What did the children do when Rags obeyed their command? _They patted Rags on the head and praised him._

5. Write **R** next to the two sentences that tell about real things.
   - ___ Puppies can talk.
   - _R_ Puppies can bark.
   - _R_ Puppies can be trained.

6. Put a check next to the two answers that tell what a person needs to do when training a puppy.
   - ✓ praise the puppy
   - ___ give up
   - ✓ give a command
   - ___ yell loudly

95

Knowing the Words

Write the word from the story that has the meaning below.

1. place to go in _____entrance_____ (Par. 2)

Words with opposite meanings are called **antonyms.** Circle the pair of antonyms in each row.

2. (narrow) small (wide) long

3. door (entrance) (exit) tunnel

Working with Words

The endings **-y** or **-ly** can be added to some words. Write the correct word to complete each sentence below.

1. The mountain trail was _____rocky_____ and difficult to climb. (rock, rocky)

2. This _____rock_____ is smooth, flat, and round. (rock, rocky)

3. I _____quickly_____ grabbed my jacket and ran home. (quick, quickly)

4. _____Quick_____ action kept the fire from spreading. (Quick, Quickly)

A word that means one of something is **singular.** A word that means more than one is **plural.** Most singular words are made plural by adding s. Most words that end in s, ss, x, ch, and sh are made plural by adding es. Form the plural of each word below by adding s or es.

5. hammer _s_   8. mess _es_

6. porch _es_   9. bush _es_

7. box _es_   10. seed _s_

Reading and Thinking

1. Check the answer that tells what the story is mainly about.
   - ___ a picnic
   - ✓ frightened explorers
   - ___ people who live in caves

Write **T** if the sentence is true.
Write **F** if the sentence is false.

2. _T_ Rick was frightened in the cave.

3. _F_ Elsa had a picnic in the cave.

4. _F_ Someone was living in the cave.

5. Some things are real and some are make-believe. Write **M** next to the sentence that tells about a make-believe thing.
   - ___ Caves are dark and damp.
   - ___ Animals live in caves.
   - _M_ Monsters live in caves.

Write the best word to complete each sentence below.

6. I dropped the _____flashlight_____ and ran. (flashlight, shelter, tunnel)

7. I have a secret _____hideout_____ in the attic. (hideout, shadow, cave)

8. We could not sleep outside because

   the ground was _____damp_____. (green, damp, soft)

9. Stay on the _____pathway_____ so you don't get lost. (doorway, entrance, pathway)

97

Knowing the Words

Write the words from the story that have the meanings below.

1. bird __blue jay__ (Par.1)

2. broke into little pieces __crushed__ (Par. 2)

3. very sad __heartbroken__ (Par. 5)

4. flew gently __fluttered__ (Par. 7)

In each row below, circle the three words that belong together.

5. (beak) (feather) shoe (wing)
6. (smash) flutter (crush) (pound)

Working with Words

A **contraction** is a short way to write two words. An apostrophe (') shows that one or more letters have been taken out. Write a contraction from the story for each pair of words below.

1. I am __I'm__ (Par. 2)

2. we have __we've__ (Par. 8)

3. did not __didn't__ (Par. 8)

Most words that end in a consonant followed by *y* are made plural by changing *y* to *i* and adding *es*. Write the plural form of each word below.

4. grocery __groceries__

5. library __libraries__

6. city __cities__

Reading and Thinking

1. Number the sentences to show the order in which things happened.

   __3__ Tracy and Dale fed Screamer.

   __4__ Screamer flew to a tree.

   __1__ Tracy and Dale found a blue jay.

   __2__ Dale put the bird in a shoe box.

2. Tracy and Dale named the blue jay Screamer because __he let out a loud scream__.

3. Tracy and Dale mixed __milk__ and __birdseed__ to feed to Screamer.

Write the best word to complete each sentence below.

4. This __yarn__ will make warm socks. (cereal, yarn, seed)

5. Stir the __mixture__ till it is smooth. (blue jay, mixture, scream)

6. The kids __agreed__ that Screamer was young. (agreed, tugged, drifted)

99

Knowing the Words

Write the words from the story that have the meanings below.

1. covered with a reddish-brown coating __rusty__ (Par. 3)

2. turns to play __innings__ (Par.4)

3. held something up so that it swung loosely __dangled__ (Par. 6)

4. not straight __crooked__ (Par. 8)

Match each word from the first list with its abbreviation from the second list.

5. __b__ seconds   a. wk.
6. __c__ Friday   b. sec.
7. __d__ inch   c. Fri.
8. __a__ week   d. in.
9. __e__ feet   e. ft.

Learning to Study

Check each word that could be found between the dictionary guide words.

1. **colt/crooked**   3. **fiddle/flakes**
   __✓__ crash   ____ fly
   __✓__ crept   __✓__ finger
   __✓__ crisp   ____ flow
   ____ coconut   __✓__ fierce

2. **scare/shy**   4. **whole/write**
   ____ slept   ____ wrote
   __✓__ shore   __✓__ wink
   __✓__ sense   __✓__ won
   __✓__ scream   ____ wheat

Reading and Thinking

1. Check the answer that tells what the story is mainly about.

   ____ trimming the bushes

   ____ looking for a lost watch

   __✓__ learning to play horseshoes

Write T if the sentence is true.
Write F if the sentence is false.

2. __F__ Mr. Levi's watch fell off his wrist.

3. __F__ Horseshoes is a game that could be played indoors.

4. __T__ Mr. Levi knew his watch was missing.

5. The number of innings in a game of horseshoes is __twenty-five__.

6. Write two words from Paragraph 4 that are also used in the game of baseball. (Accept any 2 of these answers.) __players, pitch, points, score, innings, game__

Write the best word to complete each sentence below.

7. A __yardstick__ can be used to measure the door. (chain, yardstick, hammer)

8. Brad __complained__ about the rain. (pounded, whistled, complained)

9. The fence was __crooked__ because it was old. (straight, tall, crooked)

101

Knowing the Words

Write the words from the story that have the meanings below.

1. understood clearly __realized__ (Par. 3)

2. gave an idea __suggested__ (Par. 5)

3. small shelf under a window __windowsill__ (Par. 7)

4. wishing something might happen __hopefully__ (Par. 9)

Check the meaning that fits the underlined word in each sentence.

5. The <u>back</u> door of the house is locked.
   __✓__ opposite of front
   ____ part of the body

6. I think I have a spot of gravy on my <u>tie</u>.
   ____ to fasten together
   __✓__ a piece of clothing

Learning to Study

Two pairs of dictionary guide words and their page numbers are shown in dark print. Beside each word below, write the number of the page on which it would be found.

   thick/trim   p. 302
   trouble/try p. 310

1. __p.310__ trumpet   5. __p.302__ thread
2. __p.302__ tremble   6. __p.310__ trust
3. __p.310__ truth   7. __p.302__ tight
4. __p.310__ truck   8. __p.302__ trap

Reading and Thinking

1. Check the answer that tells what the story is mainly about.

   ____ old tin cans

   ____ the secret talk

   __✓__ making a telephone

2. How is a tin can phone different from a real telephone? _____

   (Answers will vary.)

Write T if the sentence is true.
Write F if the sentence is false.

3. __T__ Sounds can travel through a string.

4. __T__ A tin can telephone will not work if the string goes around a corner.

5. __F__ Tracy could make a long-distance call on the tin can telephone.

6. __F__ A tin can telephone will not work with a knot in the string.

7. What had been in the cans before they were emptied? __soup__

Write the best word to complete each sentence below.

8. She __threaded__ the yarn through the needle. (snatched, threaded, connected)

9. There is a __knot__ in this rope. (phone, string, knot)

103

Knowing the Words

Write the words from the story that have the meanings below.

1. something planned __project__ (Par. 1)

2. a place to get water __fountain__ (Par. 3)

3. where things are sold __stand__ (Par. 4)

4. large shelf __counter__ (Par. 5)

Synonyms are words that have the same or nearly the same meaning. Circle the pair of synonyms in each row.

5. (dye) orange (coloring) water
6. radio (tune) (song) piano

Working with Words

Use each group of words in a sentence that tells who owns something.

1. Elsa's glass jars _____
   (Answers will vary.)

2. man's fruit juice stand _____
   (Answers will vary.)

Some words are easier to read if they are divided into parts called **syllables.** Some words have two consonants between two vowels. These words can be divided into syllables between the consonants, as in *for/got*.

In each word below, draw a line to divide the word into syllables.

3. for|ward   5. foun|tain   7. car|ry
4. ar|rive   6. prob|lem   8. en|joy

Reading and Thinking

1. Check the answer that tells what the story is mainly about.

   ____ music in City Park

   __✓__ solving a problem

   ____ a fruit juice stand

2. Why didn't Elsa use plain water in the jars? __She wanted her project to be colorful.__

Write T if the sentence is true.
Write F if the sentence is false.

3. __T__ The man thought Elsa's plan was a good one.

4. __F__ Elsa could not pay for the fruit juice.

5. __F__ Elsa could play eight different notes on the jars.

6. What do you think Elsa will do with the fruit juice after the music festival is over? _____

   (Answers will vary.)

Write the best word to complete each sentence below.

7. The class __project__ was finished. (flavor, dye, project)

8. A __colorful__ rainbow appeared after the storm. (fresh, colorful, musical)

9. Would you like __juice__ with breakfast? (juice, cup, spoon)

105

Page 107

Write the words from the story that have the meanings below.

1. people who buy ___customers___
   (Par. 3)

2. two-way radios ___walkie-talkies___
   (Par. 5)

3. make others believe ___convince___
   (Par. 10)

4. a small bit of liquid ___drop___
   (Par. 12)

Choose the correct word below to fill the blanks for each pair of sentences.

pitcher   right

5. Is this the ___right___ answer?

   Stomp your ___right___ foot.

6. Pour milk into the ___pitcher___

   Who is the team ___pitcher___ ?

Say *city*. Circle the words below that have the sound *c* stands for in *city*.

1. cave   (cent)   (face)   clown
2. (center) (dance) calm (twice)

When a word ends with *e*, the *e* is usually dropped before adding **-ed** or **-ing**. Add **-ed** or **-ing** to the word in ( ) to make a word that completes each sentence.

3. Mom's plane is ___leaving___ at three o'clock. (leave)

4. Tim ___noticed___ the plants were dry. (notice)

1. Check the answer that tells what the story is mainly about.
   ___ a thirsty man
   ___ Michael's walkie-talkies
   _✓_ selling lemonade

Write **T** if the sentence is true.
Write **F** if the sentence is false.

2. _F_ Heather and Michael washed the used cups.

3. _F_ Heather and Michael bought the lemonade at the store.

4. _T_ Michael had money to buy more cups.

5. What did the children have to buy to get started? ___lemons___

6. Why did Michael go back to the store? ___to get more cups___

7. What do you think Heather and Michael will do now that the thirsty man has gone? ___
   (Answers will vary.)

107

Page 109

Write the words from the story that have the meanings below.

1. something used for drying ___towels___
   (Par. 3)

2. things needed for a project ___supplies___
   (Par. 4)

3. able to make things ___inventive___
   (Par. 8)

Write the word with the correct meaning to complete each sentence below.

4. A ___piece___ of chalk fell to the floor. (peace, piece)

5. The ___blue___ coat is my favorite one. (blue, blew)

A **suffix** is a group of letters added to the end of a word that changes the meaning of the word. The suffixes **-ful** and **-ous** mean "full of." *Fearful* means "full of fear." *Joyous* means "full of joy."

Add **-ful** or **-ous** to the words below. Use the new words to complete the sentences.

power   humor   thought

1. It was very ___thoughtful___ of you to remember my birthday.

2. The ___powerful___ engine pulled the train.

3. The ___humorous___ story made us all laugh.

1. Number the sentences in the order that tells how a salt jar can be made.
   _2_ Rub chalk over some salt.
   _3_ Pour the salt into the jar.
   _1_ Gather supplies.
   _4_ Put the lid on the jar.

2. Why did the children give Mr. Levi a present? ___for his birthday___

3. Write one way in which the three salt jars were alike. ___
   (Answers will vary.)

4. Write one way in which the three salt jars were different. ___
   (Answers will vary.)

5. Check the word that tells how you think the children felt when Mr. Levi opened the box.
   _✓_ proud   ___ curious   ___ sad

6. What did Mr. Levi do with the gifts?
   ___He put them on a windowsill.___

109

Page 111

Write the words from the story that have the meanings below.

1. a little frightened ___nervous___
   (Par. 6)

2. word said when a trick is being done ___hocus-pocus___
   (Par. 7)

3. helpers ___volunteers___
   (Par. 8)

4. thin sheet of metal ___aluminum foil___
   (Par. 8)

Say the word *show* and notice the sound *ow* stands for in the word. Circle the words below that have the sound *ow* stands for in *show*.

1. (know) down   (blow)   cow
2. (slow) (arrow) town (throw)
3. (hollow) tower   how   (glow)

A **compound word** is made by combining two smaller words. Write a compound word using the underlined words in each sentence.

4. The yard in the <u>back</u> of a house is a ___backyard___

5. The time of day <u>after</u> the <u>noon</u> hour is ___afternoon___

6. <u>Seed</u> given to a <u>bird</u> is ___birdseed___

7. A paper that reports the <u>news</u> is a ___newspaper___

1. Number the sentences to show the order in which things happened.
   _2_ Kids arrived for Rick's show.
   _1_ Rick made a poster.
   _4_ Rick did a trick with aluminum foil.
   _3_ Rick did his first trick.

2. How were Rick's two tricks alike? ___
   (Answers will vary.)

3. How were Rick's two tricks different? ___
   (Answers will vary.)

Write **T** if the sentence is true.
Write **F** if the sentence is false.

4. _F_ The word *hocus-pocus* made the tricks happen.

5. _T_ The audience enjoyed Rick's performance.

6. _F_ Rick's tricks were magic.

7. A **fact** is something that is known to be true. An **opinion** is what someone thinks or feels. Check two sentences that give facts.
   _✓_ Messages can be put on posters.
   ___ Lifting ice on a string is a good trick.
   _✓_ Tricks can be learned from books.

111

Page 113

Write the words from the story that have the meanings below.

1. a ride at a fair ___Ferris wheel___
   (Par. 3)

2. feeling better ___relief___
   (Par. 9)

3. high places ___heights___
   (Par. 10)

4. money that people pay to ride somewhere ___fare___
   (Par. 11)

Write the word with the correct meaning to complete each sentence below.

5. The city bus ___fare___ is sixty cents. (fair, fare)

6. I'll ___meet___ you downtown this evening. (meet, meat)

7. I had ___four___ tickets for rides. (for, four)

The word you look up in a dictionary is called an **entry word.** Many words with endings are not listed as entry words. To find these words, look up the word to which the ending was added. To find the word *teased*, look up *tease*.

Write the word you would look under to find each of these words in a dictionary.

1. tickets ___ticket___
2. arrived ___arrive___
3. waiting ___wait___
4. completely ___complete___

1. Check the answer that tells what the story is mainly about.
   ___ a long bus ride
   _✓_ a visit to the fair
   ___ how a Ferris wheel works

2. Andy didn't want Rick to leave the fair without him because ___Rick had the bus fare___

3. How were Heather and Andy alike? ___
   (Answers will vary.)

Write **F** if the sentence gives a fact.
Write **O** if the sentence gives an opinion.

4. _F_ Riding a bus is one way to travel.

5. _O_ It is scary at the top of a Ferris wheel.

6. _O_ Ferris wheels are fun to ride.

7. _F_ Ferris wheels have seats.

8. If Heather and Andy had been left behind, how might they have gotten home? ___
   (Answers will vary.)

113

Knowing the Words

Write the words from the story that have the meanings below.

1. mistaking one thing for another _____confusion_____
   (Par. 1)

2. parts of your hands _____thumbs_____
   (Par. 3)

3. whole _____entire_____
   (Par. 3)

In each row below, circle the three words that belong together.

4. (thumb) (stomach) (ear) shirt
5. (wave) stripe (pat) (wiggle)
6. (ham) (cheese) plate (bread)

Working with Words

Write the two words that were used to form each of these contractions.

1. they've _____they have_____

2. I'll _____I will or I shall_____

3. that's _____that is or that has_____

Say *children*. Circle the words below that have the sound *ch* stands for in *children*.

4. (chose) (handkerchief) ache
5. (sandwich) (chuckle) stomach

Reading and Thinking

1. Check the answer that tells what the story is mainly about.
   _____ meeting new neighbors
   _✓_ playing a game
   _____ making sandwiches

2. What was Lin's sign? _____
   scratching her ear

3. What were the children having for lunch? ham and cheese
   sandwiches

4. Rick came over to Tracy's house because he wanted Tracy
   to meet Lin and Tat .

5. What do you think the children did after Tracy explained why she
   pointed to her mouth? _____
   (Answers will vary.)

Write the best word to complete each sentence below.

6. The zebra is a _____striped_____ animal. (confused, striped, tiny)

7. Please _____repeat_____ this word. (repeat, motion, scratch)

8. Don fixed a _____sandwich_____ for lunch. (sign, shirt, sandwich)

9. The bear was _____growling_____ (chuckling, reading, growling)

115

Knowing the Words

Write the words from the story that have the meanings below.

1. gather _____collect_____
   (Par. 4)

2. person who delivers mail _____mail carrier_____
   (Par. 7)

3. cardboard box _____carton_____
   (Par. 8)

Synonyms are words that have the same or nearly the same meaning. Circle the pair of synonyms in each row.

4. (delivered) came (brought) went
5. win (collect) buy (gather)
6. eleven some (dozen) (twelve)
7. frown (chuckle) sneeze (laugh)

Working with Words

The ending **-er** sometimes means "more." It may be used to compare two things. The ending **-est** means "most." It is used to compare more than two things.

In each sentence below, add **-er** to the word before the blank if two things are being compared. Add **-est** if more than two things are being compared.

1. Apple juice is sweet _____er_____ than lemonade.

2. Ken is the young _____est_____ of three sons.

3. The lamp is bright _____er_____ than the flashlight.

4. Kay is the fast _____est_____ swimmer on the team.

Reading and Thinking

1. Write **O** next to two sentences that give opinions.
   _O_ Cereal tastes best for breakfast.
   _____ Cereal is in the bread food group.
   _O_ A ten-speed bicycle is a good prize.

2. Why did Tat and Lin eat so much cereal? to collect box
   tops *or* to win a contest

3. How many box tops did Tat and Lin send in? _____sixteen_____

4. How many boxes of cereal did Tat and Lin win? two dozen *or* 24

5. How do you think the children felt when they saw what they had won?
   _____
   (Answers will vary.)

Write **T** if the sentence is true.
Write **F** if the sentence is false.

6. _T_ Tat and Lin won even more cereal than they had eaten.

7. _F_ Crunchy Munchies was like oatmeal.

8. What do you think Lin and Tat will do with the cereal they won?
   (Answers will vary.)
   _____

117

Knowing the Words

Write the words from the story that have the meanings below.

1. kind of dog _____Saint Bernard_____
   (Par. 2)

2. gently talked into doing something _____coaxed_____
   (Par. 6)

3. very wet _____soggy_____
   (Par. 6)

4. gave a job for pay _____hired_____
   (Par. 8)

Check the meaning that fits the underlined word in each sentence.

5. The <u>collar</u> was too big for the poodle.
   _____ part of a shirt
   _✓_ something a dog wears

6. <u>Park</u> the car in that empty space.
   _✓_ stop for a time
   _____ a place to play

7. Bootsie hid my brother's <u>block</u> under the couch.
   _✓_ a toy
   _____ area bordered by four streets

Learning to Study

Write the word you would look under to find each of these words in a dictionary.

1. spending _____spend_____

2. businesses _____business_____

3. weighed _____weigh_____

4. copies _____copy_____

Reading and Thinking

1. Check the answer that tells what the story is mainly about.
   _____ jumping in a fountain
   _✓_ walking a Saint Bernard
   _____ seeing a robin

Write **T** if the sentence is true.
Write **F** if the sentence is false.

2. _F_ Wee Willie is a lazy dog.

3. _T_ Wee Willie likes water.

4. _F_ Michael could carry Wee Willie in his arms.

5. What three kinds of dogs did Michael walk before he walked Wee Willie?
   bulldog, poodle, beagle

6. What do you think Michael said when Ms. Silva offered to hire him to walk Willie every day?
   (Answers will vary.)
   _____

Write the best word to complete each sentence below.

7. Ann has a _____poodle_____ named Puff. (collar, screen, poodle)

8. Ms. Kay _____manages_____ a gift shop in town. (spends, hires, manages)

9. A bird was _____splashing_____ in the birdbath. (splashing, leaping, laughing)

119

Knowing the Words

Write the words from the story that have the meanings below.

1. a piece of clothing _____sweatshirt_____
   (Par. 3)

2. rushed in suddenly _____burst_____
   (Par. 7)

Circle the pair of antonyms (opposites) in each row.

3. (buy) spend (sell) trade
4. door (enter) agree (exit)
5. (open) drop loose (close)
6. (found) rolled (lost) heard
7. (now) near (later) gold

Working with Words

Some words that have one consonant between two vowels are divided into syllables after the first vowel. The first vowel sound in these words is most often long, as in *ti/ger*.

Other words that have one consonant between two vowels are divided after the consonant. In these words, the first vowel sound is most often short, as in *trav/el*.

The words below have been divided into syllables. Put a mark above the first vowel in each word to show if the vowel stands for a long or short sound. Mark the long vowels with ¯ over the letter. Mark the short vowels with ˘.

1. lĕm/on   4. sī/lence   7. clōs/et
2. wăg/on   5. frō/zen   8. stō/len
3. mō/tor   6. cŏp/y   9. căb/in

Reading and Thinking

1. Number the sentences to show the order in which things happened.
   _1_ Heather dropped a quarter.
   _2_ The man dropped a coin.
   _3_ The man grabbed the quarter.
   _4_ The man returned the quarter.

Write **T** if the sentence is true.
Write **F** if the sentence is false.

2. _T_ Heather had been in Mr. Taylor's store before.

3. _F_ Heather had one dollar to spend in Mr. Taylor's store.

4. _F_ Mr. Taylor had never seen a gold piece before.

5. How much was the gold piece worth?
   twenty dollars

6. What might Heather buy with her money? (Answers will vary.)

7. How do you think Heather felt when the man gave her two quarters?
   (Answers will vary.)

Write the best word to complete each sentence below.

8. Jim found a _____coin_____ in his pocket. (shirt, shelf, coin)

9. Three _____quarters_____ equal seventy-five cents. (quarters, pieces, cards)

121

Page 123 (top left)

Write the words from the story that have the meanings below.

1. in charge of ___responsible___
   (Par. 1)
2. more than usually ___especially___
   (Par. 1)
3. holding too much ___overcrowded___
   (Par. 1)

In each row, circle the three words that belong together.

4. (desk) clothes (bed) (chair)
5. (stood) said (stooped) (bent)
6. laugh (agree) (argue) (talk)

Working with Words

Circle the correct word in ( ) and write it in the blank.

1. The ___boys___ talked for a long time. (buys (boys))
2. Did you ___clean___ out the garage alone? ((clean) clothes)
3. Rick ___stood___ in line for thirty minutes. (stand (stood))
4. When Andy went ___away___, Rick was lonely. ((away) awake)

Reading and Thinking

1. Check the answer that tells what the story is mainly about.
   ___ clothes on the floor
   ___ a divided room
   _✓_ cleaning a room together

2. Rick and Andy divided the room because ___neither one wanted___ ___to clean more than half___.

3. Check three words that tell what Rick and Andy divided in half.
   _✓_ desk   _✓_ bulletin board
   _✓_ floor   ___ toy box

Write F if the sentence gives a fact.
Write O if the sentence gives an opinion.

4. _O_ Cleaning is difficult work.
5. _F_ Vacuum cleaners can be used to sweep rugs.
6. _F_ A bed is a piece of furniture.
7. _O_ Cleaning should be done once a week.
8. Were Rick and Andy still arguing at the end of the story? Explain your answer. _____
   (Answers will vary.)
9. What might Rick and Andy do after they clean their room? _____
   (Answers will vary.)

123

Page 125 (top right)

Knowing the Words

Write the words from the story that have the meanings below.

1. a strong cloth ___canvas___
   (Par. 1)
2. a long seat with cushions ___couch___
   (Par. 2)
3. said unhappily ___grumbled___
   (Par. 8)
4. covered with hair ___furry___
   (Par. 9)

Synonyms are words that have the same or nearly the same meaning. Circle the pair of synonyms in each row.

5. shades (curtains) windows (drapes)
6. (swallow) chew lick (gulp)

Learning to Study

Some words have more than one meaning. In a dictionary, the different meanings of a word are numbered.

Read each word in dark print and the dictionary meanings that follow. Then read each sentence below and decide the meaning of the underlined words. Write the number of the correct meaning in the blank.

coun try 1 nation 2 land outside a city

1. _2_ Dave works on a farm in the country.
2. _1_ Each country has its own flag.

room 1 area with walls inside a building 2 space

3. _2_ We have room for one more.
4. _1_ The girls gave the room a new coat of paint.

Reading and Thinking

1. Check the answer that tells what the story is mainly about.
   _✓_ looking for a pet
   ___ a visit to the country
   ___ the blue canvas bag

2. Do you think Tracy meant it when she said she did not care about Herbie? Explain your answer.
   (Answers will vary.)
   _____
   _____

Write **T** if the sentence is true.
Write **F** if the sentence is false.

3. _F_ Tracy's aunt and uncle live down the street from her.
4. _T_ Tracy knew she would miss Herbie while she was gone.
5. _F_ Aunt Ruth and Uncle Stan probably met Tracy at the airport.
6. What do you think Tracy did with Herbie after she found him? _____
   (Answers will vary.)

125

Page 127 (bottom left)

Knowing the Words

Write the words from the story that have the meanings below.

1. something used to control a horse ___reins___
   (Par. 3)
2. awfully ___terribly___
   (Par. 5)

Write the word with the correct meaning to complete each sentence below.

3. Spring ___rains___ help flowers to grow. (reins, rains)
4. ___There___ are horses out in the pasture. (Their, There)
5. Who ___won___ the race? (one, won)

Working with Words

Write a compound word using the underlined words in each sentence.

1. A bowl in which a fish lives is a ___fishbowl___.
2. A knob used to close a door is a ___doorknob___.

The words below have been divided into syllables. Put a mark above the first vowel in each word to show if the vowel stands for a long or short sound. Mark the long vowels with ¯ over the letter. Mark the short vowels with ˘.

3. nā/tion   6. min/ute   9. nĕv/er
4. rē/cess   7. fĭn/ish   10. stā/tion
5. vĭs/it   8. pī/lot   11. fī/nal

Reading and Thinking

1. Check the answer that tells what the story is mainly about.
   ___ riding to town on a horse
   _✓_ a riding accident
   ___ how to ride a horse

2. Check three answers that tell about both Tracy and Aunt Ruth.
   _✓_ had a scary accident
   ___ lives in the city
   _✓_ rides horses
   _✓_ is no longer afraid of horses
   ___ is an adult

3. Check two words that tell how Tracy felt when Big Gabe threw her.
   _✓_ scared   ___ pretty
   ___ hungry   _✓_ angry
   ___ sleepy   ___ proud

4. Do you think Tracy will ride Big Gabe after today? Explain your answer.
   (Answers will vary.)

Write the best word to complete each sentence below.

5. Pull the ___reins___ to make the horse stop. (saddle, reins, rider)
6. Because of her ___bravery___ the woman was given a medal. (fear, bravery, stable)

127

Page 129 (bottom right)

Knowing the Words

Write the words from the story that have the meanings below.

1. something that happens because of something else ___results___
   (Par. 1)
2. a post ___stake___
   (Par. 3)
3. closed in on all sides ___surrounded___
   (Par. 3)

Circle the pair of antonyms (opposites) in each row.

4. (pull) (push) drop fall
5. month (night) year (day)
6. race watch (asleep) (awake)
7. (found) planned missed (lost)

Choose the correct word to fill in the blank for each pair of sentences.
   rose   felt   row

8. David's costume was made from yellow and purple ___felt___.
   The sidewalk ___felt___ hot under my feet.
9. Ty helped ___row___ the boat yesterday.
   The ___row___ of beans is straight.
10. The sun ___rose___ in the East.
    Kevin found a ___rose___ near the edge of the garden.

Reading and Thinking

1. Number the sentences to show the order in which things happened.
   _2_ Tracy hung aluminum pans around the garden.
   _4_ The thief was caught.
   _1_ Tracy noticed that some beans were missing.
   _3_ Clyde rattled the pie pans.

2. Why did Tracy hang aluminum pans from a string? ___to get the thief to make some noise___

3. How do you think Tracy felt when she saw who the thief was? _____
   (Answers will vary.)

4. Why did Tracy say she would share the ripe beans with Clyde?
   (Answers will vary.)

5. What do you think will happen to Clyde now? _____
   (Answers will vary.)

Learning to Study

Number each list of words below in alphabetical order.

1. _1_ flavor   2. _2_ caught
   _2_ fresh   _1_ catch
   _3_ friend   _3_ corner

129

Write the words from the story that have the meanings below.

1. a high table used for work ____workbench____
(Par. 2)

2. said in a low voice ____murmured____
(Par. 2)

Synonyms are words that have the same or nearly the same meaning. Circle the pair of synonyms in each row.

3. (gazed) laughed cried (stared)

4. called (finished) (completed) tripped

5. wrote (murmured) read (said)

6. garage (city) (town) window

A **prefix** is a group of letters added to the beginning of a word that changes the meaning of the word. The prefixes **un-** and **dis-** mean "not" or "the opposite of." *Distrust* means "the opposite of trust." *Unfair* means "not fair."

Complete each sentence by writing **un-** or **dis-** in the blank.

1. It is ___un___ safe to climb on that rock.

2. Sean's wool socks were causing him some ___dis___ comfort.

3. Dan and I ___dis___ agree.

4. I was ___un___ able to go to the movies because I was sick.

1. Check the answer that tells what the story is mainly about.
____ how birds fly
__✓__ Tracy's project
____ talking with Uncle Stan

Write **T** if the sentence is true.
Write **F** if the sentence is false.

2. __F__ Uncle Stan has no hobbies.

3. __T__ Tracy likes to help.

4. __T__ Tracy is tired of the rain.

5. Write three things Tracy had done to keep herself busy. read, painted, wrote a letter

6. Write **R** next to two sentences that tell about real things.
__R__ A girl could fly in a plane.
____ A boy could fly like a bird.
__R__ A bird could fly through the clouds.

Write the best word to complete each sentence below.

7. Bob ____imagined____ he was on a ship. (pleased, imagined, sang)

8. The ____garage____ is big enough for two cars. (skate, garage, workbench)

9. The plant on the ____windowsill____ gets lots of sunshine. (closet, river, windowsill)

131

Write the words from the story that have the meanings below.

1. leftover pieces ____scraps____
(Par. 3)

2. cook who is in charge ____chef____
(Par. 7)

Synonyms are words that have the same or nearly the same meaning. Circle the pair of synonyms in each row.

3. (garbage) collect (trash) truck

4. jar (bucket) water (pail)

5. hope (ready) (prepared) leave

6. (begin) clean stay (start)

Write a compound word using the underlined words in each sentence.

1. A <u>room</u> with a <u>bed</u> in it is a ____bedroom____

2. A <u>bench</u> at which to <u>work</u> is a ____workbench____

The suffix **-ment** means "the act of." *Enjoyment* means "the act of enjoying." Add **-ment** to the following words. Use the new words to complete the sentences.
amuse agree

3. Joel has an ____agreement____ with his brother about sharing toys.

4. The joke was told for our ____amusement____

1. Check the answer that tells what the story is mainly about.
__✓__ making vegetable soup
____ Mr. Hastings's dog
____ eating in a restaurant

2. The soup and beef scraps got mixed up because they were in jars that looked alike

3. What did Mr. Hastings plan to do with the beef scraps? feed them to his dog

Write **T** if the sentence is true.
Write **F** if the sentence is false.

4. __F__ Mr. Hastings is a cab driver.

5. __F__ It was evening when Rick went to work with his father.

6. __T__ Rick's dad made a lot of soup.

7. What was in the soup besides vegetables? ____beef____

8. Number the sentences in the order that tells how the soup was made.
__4__ The mixture was cooked.
__1__ Water was boiled.
__3__ Vegetables and beef were put in the pot.
__2__ Vegetables and beef were cut up.
__5__ The soup was put into jars.

133

Write the words from the story that have the meanings below.

1. having many leaves ____leafy____
(Par. 2)

2. moved slowly and quietly ____crept____
(Par. 3)

3. moved without anyone knowing ____sneaked____
(Par. 4)

4. picturing in one's mind ____imagination____
(Par. 5)

In each row below, circle the three words that belong together.

5. (forehead) closet (elbow) (shoulder)

6. (sneaked) (crept) (tiptoed) stuffed

7. tease (moan) (shout) (whisper)

To write the plural of a word that ends in *f* or *fe*, the *f* or *fe* is changed to *v*, and *es* is added. Write the plural form of each word below.

1. leaf ____leaves____

2. wife ____wives____

3. half ____halves____

4. shelf ____shelves____

Say *large*. Circle the words below that have the same sound *g* stands for in *large*.

5. (danger) gathered grab (engine)

6. (sponge) (ginger) (giant) dragon

1. Number the sentences to show the order in which things happened.
__4__ Andy waited for Heather.
__2__ Heather telephoned Andy.
__3__ Rick hid beside some bushes.
__5__ Rick scared Andy.
__1__ Rick tied branches to himself.

2. Check the sentence that tells about Rick.
____ He was always mean to Andy.
____ He wanted to hurt Andy.
__✓__ He wanted to teach Andy a lesson.

3. Do you think Rick and Andy will make a deal? What kind? ____
(Answers will vary.)

4. Write **R** next to two sentences that tell about real things.
____ Bushes can talk and moan.
__R__ Fear can make people tremble.
__R__ People can imagine scary things.

135

Write the words from the story that have the meanings below.

1. the OK to do something ____permission____
(Par. 1)

2. got comfortable ____snuggled____
(Par. 3)

3. breathing loudly while sleeping ____snoring____
(Par. 7)

Synonyms are words that have the same or nearly the same meaning. Write **S** after each pair of synonyms. Write **A** after each pair of antonyms (opposites).

4. zip-unzip __A__   **7.** tired-sleepy __S__

5. old-new __A__   **8.** better-worse __A__

6. early-late __A__   **9.** nearby-close __S__

A dictionary shows words divided into syllables. A space or a dot shows where the word can be divided at the end of a line of writing.

Read the words below. Next to each write the number of syllables it has.

1. let ter __2__   **5.** gi raffe __2__

2. ac ci dent __3__   **6.** morn ing __2__

3. an oth er __3__   **7.** ceil ing __2__

4. chuck le __2__   **8.** prob a bly __3__

1. Check the answer that tells what the story is mainly about.
____ shadows on the roof
____ the howling dog
__✓__ camping out

2. Andy thought Michael's reason for going home was he was frightened by the noises

3. Did Andy own a real tent? Explain your answer. ____
(Answers will vary.)

4. Was Michael used to sleeping outdoors? Explain your answer.
(Answers will vary.)

5. Write two things Andy and Michael did before they went to sleep.
made shadows, told jokes and funny stories

Write the best word to complete each sentence below.

6. A ____bulldozer____ was used to clear the land. (alligator, bulldozer, yawn)

7. The ____giraffe____ ate leaves. (beagle, giraffe, shadow)

8. You will need a ____blanket____ on your bed. (tent, blanket, story)

137

Knowing the Words

Write the words from the story that have the meanings below.

1. part where power is __control__ (Par. 4)

2. moving back and forth __rocking__ (Par. 4)

Circle the pair of antonyms (opposites) in each row.

3. (long)   large   (short)   huge
4. (whispered)   (yelled)   laughed   sang
5. new   tall   (fast)   (slow)

Working with Words

Write the two words that were used to form each of these contractions.

1. wasn't __was not__

2. you're __you are__

3. it'll __it will or it shall__

4. it's __it is or it has__

The suffix **-less** means "without." *Hopeless* means "without hope." Add **-less** to the following words. Use the new words to complete the sentences.

breath   cloud   spot

5. The windows were __spotless__ after Jeff washed them.

6. The __cloudless__ sky was a beautiful color of blue.

7. Adam was __breathless__ after running the race.

Reading and Thinking

1. Check the answer that tells what the story is mainly about.
   ____ a pet cat
   ____ playing tag
   _✓_ a result of carelessness

2. Why didn't Tracy put the car in a safe place? __She was__ __in a hurry.__

3. How did Herbie make the car move? __He stepped on the control box.__

4. Check two words that tell how Tracy might have felt when she saw the broken lamp.
   _✓_ angry   ____ tired
   _✓_ sorry   ____ thrilled

Write **T** if the sentence is true.
Write **F** if the sentence is false.

5. _T_ Tracy bought the car with her allowance money.

6. _F_ Herbie broke the car.

7. _F_ Tracy didn't know how the lamp got broken.

8. Write **O** next to three sentences that give opinions.
   _O_ Cats are too curious.
   ____ A toy car could be put on a table.
   _O_ Toys should always be put in a toy box.
   _O_ Cats should not be left alone.

139

Knowing the Words

Write the words from the story that have the meanings below.

1. following closely __tagging__ (Par. 1)

2. said in a low voice __muttered__ (Par. 2)

3. things __items__ (Par. 3)

4. answer __solution__ (Par. 3)

Working with Words

When a word ends in a consonant followed by *y*, the *y* is changed to *i* before an ending is added. Change the *y* to *i* in each word in ( ). Add **-ly** to make a word that completes the sentence.

1. Mark spoke __angrily__ to the naughty pup. (angry)

2. Max __easily__ won the race. (easy)

3. Jan walked __lazily__ through the field. (lazy)

Rewrite the following groups of words using 's or s' to show who owns something. The first one is done for you.

the nickel that Carmen owns

Carmen's nickel

4. the coins that belong to the girls
   __girls' coins__

5. the vacuum cleaner that Bill owns
   __Bill's vacuum cleaner__

Reading and Thinking

1. Number the sentences to show the order in which things happened.
   _3_ Elsa realized she didn't have enough money.
   _1_ Carmen asked to go to the store.
   _4_ Carmen gave Elsa a coin.
   _2_ The girls stood in line.
   _5_ Elsa gave Carmen a hug.

2. Why did Carmen say she had a penny when she really had a nickel? __She didn't know the difference__ __between a nickel and a penny.__

Write **T** if the sentence is true.
Write **F** if the sentence is false.

3. _T_ The store the girls went to was close by.

4. _F_ The girls were both upset when they left the house.

5. _F_ Elsa was angry with Carmen on the way home.

Write the best word to complete each sentence below.

6. The __total__ was twelve cents. (errand, clerk, total)

7. Mark __skipped__ to the bank. (laughed, skipped, stopped)

141

Knowing the Words

Write the words from the story that have the meanings below.

1. boxes __crates__ (Par. 1)

2. small jobs __chores__ (Par. 2)

3. without making trouble __patiently__ (Par. 4)

In each row, circle the three words that belong together.

4. (finger)   (thumb)   arm   (palm)
5. (job)   stool   (chore)   (work)
6. wall   (rug)   (carpet)   (mat)
7. (scraps)   (chunks)   (pieces)   chores

Learning to Study

Write the word you would look under to find each of these words in a dictionary.

1. patiently __patient__

2. smiling __smile__

3. stepped __step__

4. finest __fine__

Number each list of words below in alphabetical order.

5. _3_ blue   6. _3_ cat
   _4_ club   _4_ door
   _1_ angry   _5_ floor
   _5_ crate   _2_ can
   _2_ animal   _1_ camp

Reading and Thinking

1. Check the answer that tells what the story is mainly about.
   ____ Tracy's chores
   _✓_ Tracy's idea
   ____ a sign that said "Keep Out!"

2. Why had Tracy's dad saved the carpet scraps? __He knew they__ __would be useful.__

3. Check the answer that tells what Tracy was probably doing when she thought of making a patchwork rug.
   ____ washing the dishes
   ____ making her bed
   _✓_ sweeping the carpet

4. Tracy put up a sign and covered the windows because __she wanted to__ __keep what she was doing__ __a secret__

5. Check two sentences that tell how the clubhouse was like a house.
   _✓_ A poster hung on the wall.
   _✓_ The floor was carpeted.
   ____ The sign on the door said "Keep Out!"

143

Knowing the Words

Write the words from the story that have the meanings below.

1. the project of getting votes __campaign__ (Par. 2)

2. filled with something __stuffed__ (Par. 5)

Write the word with the correct meaning to complete each sentence below.

3. __Our__ poster is the most colorful. (Hour, Our)

4. Jake has a __pair__ of tickets for the movie. (pair, pear)

5. Dan has a __new__ red wagon. (new, knew)

6. Jo gets a letter in the mail every __week__. (weak, week)

Working with Words

Fill in each blank with the correct pair of letters to make a word.

wr   kn   mb   ph

1. co __mb__   3. __wr__ ote
2. __kn__ ob   4. ele __ph__ ant

Circle the correct word in ( ) and write it in the blank.

5. She __paid__ for the scarf with quarters. (pad, (paid))

6. Will you __join__ me for lunch? ((join), junk)

Reading and Thinking

1. Check the answer that tells what the story is mainly about.
   ____ being president
   ____ making a poster
   _✓_ running for president

2. Tell two things Tat did to get votes. (Accept any 2 of these answers.) __made a poster, made a campaign shirt,__ __talked to classmates, gave a speech__

3. Write **O** next to the sentence that gives an opinion.
   ____ There are usually five days in a school week.
   _O_ A poster is important to a campaign.

Learning to Study

Use the table of contents below to answer the questions.

1. How many chapters are in this book? __four__

2. On what page does "Nearing Elections" begin? __page 12__

3. What chapter tells how to give a speech? __Victory Speeches__

145

Knowing the Words

Write the words from the story that have the meanings below.

1. a bright light __spotlight__
(Par. 2)

2. best at something __champion__
(Par. 6)

3. a reward __medal__
(Par. 2)

4. world sports contests __Olympics__
(Par. 6)

Working with Words

Circle the prefix or suffix in each word. Then use the words to complete the sentences.

(re)read use(ful)
(un)zip sleep(less)

1. Old rags are __useful__ for cleaning dirty windows.

2. __Unzip__ your coat and hang it on a hanger.

3. Les will __reread__ the book because he likes it.

4. Tom had a __sleepless__ night because a storm kept him awake.

Write the singular form of each word.

5. patches __patch__

6. cities __city__

7. shelves __shelf__

8. boxes __box__

9. blueberries __blueberry__

Reading and Thinking

1. Check the answer that tells what the story is mainly about.
   - ___ a famous Olympic ice skater
   - ___ a trip to the library
   - _✓_ a dream that could come true

2. Write two places Rick's father went.
   __grocery store and library__

3. Why do you think Rick's dad brought Rick a book about a skater?
   __(Answers will vary.)__

4. Dreams are not real, but sometimes they can come true. Check two sentences that tell about dreams that could come true.
   - _✓_ Jim dreamed he was a famous artist.
   - ___ Jeff dreamed he lived in a pumpkin.
   - _✓_ Kate dreamed she was an astronaut.

Write the best word to complete each sentence below.

5. The knife __blade__ is sharp. (handle, blade, cover)

6. "May I have your __autograph__ on this card?" the man asked the singer. (pillow, medal, autograph)

7. The small __package__ was on the desk. (package, smile, ice)

147

Knowing the Words

Write the words from the story that have the meanings below.

1. cooking directions __recipe__
(Par. 2)

2. a spice __cinnamon__
(Par. 3)

3. covered lightly with drops __sprinkled__
(Par. 3)

4. flashed off and on __flickered__
(Par. 6)

Match each word in the first list with its abbreviation from the second list.

5. _c_ minutes a. tsp.
6. _a_ teaspoon b. Sat.
7. _b_ Saturday c. min.

Working with Words

Use the following words to form compound words. Then use the compound to complete the sentences.

snow cook flake book

1. This __cookbook__ has a recipe for bean soup.

2. A __snowflake__ landed on my mitten and melted.

Circle the correct word in ( ) and write it in the blank.

3. Add __cinnamon__ to the brown sugar. (campaign, (cinnamon))

4. The fruit __juice__ spilled. ((juice) jack)

Reading and Thinking

1. Number the sentences in the order that shows how Tracy's muffins are made.
   - _2_ Pour the batter into baking cups.
   - _3_ Combine brown sugar and cinnamon.
   - _1_ Mix the egg, sugar, milk, and baking mix.
   - _4_ Put the topping on the muffins.
   - _5_ Bake the muffins for fifteen minutes.

2. Why didn't the muffins bake?
   __The electricity was off.__

Write T if the sentence is true.
Write F if the sentence is false.

3. _T_ Tracy made twelve muffins.
4. _F_ Tracy baked the muffins in a gas oven.
5. _T_ Tracy would need two eggs to make two dozen muffins.
6. _F_ Tracy made the muffins for Tat.
7. _F_ The muffins had fruit in them.

Write the best word to complete each sentence below.

8. The blue flame __flickered__ in the breeze. (flickered, bumped, leaned)

9. They __watched__ the muffins turn brown. (watched, decorated, baked)

149

Knowing the Words

Write the words from the story that have the meanings below.

1. filled with air __blown-up__
(Par. 2)

2. walking heavily __trudging__
(Par. 2)

3. not sure __doubtful__
(Par. 4)

Circle the pair of antonyms (opposites) in each row.

4. tube (inner) rubber (outer)
5. (doubtful) answer (certain) guess
6. beside (top) (bottom) near

Working with Words

Use each group of words in a sentence that tells who owns something.

1. children's ideas ___
   __(Answers will vary.)__

2. Elsa's basket ___
   __(Answers will vary.)__

3. friend's sled ___
   __(Answers will vary.)__

4. kids' races ___
   __(Answers will vary.)__

In each word below, draw a line to divide the word into syllables.

5. diz|zy 7. mi|nus 9. pen|cil
6. met|al 8. gar|bage 10. cra|zy

Reading and Thinking

1. Check the answer that tells what the story is mainly about.
   - ___ winning a race
   - ___ building a sled
   - _✓_ practicing for a race

2. Where were the sled races to be held?
   __at City Park__

3. Tracy, Rick, and Elsa had crazy sleds because __they didn't own regular sleds__.

4. Do you think the kids with the crazy sleds will win the race? Explain your answer. ___
   __(Answers will vary.)__

5. Check the answer that tells what Tracy thinks is most important about sledding.
   - ___ being the first-place winner
   - _✓_ having a good time
   - ___ having the best-looking sleds

In each sentence below, a word is underlined. Circle the name or names that the underlined words stand for.

6. "I will go first," said Elsa to Tracy.
   Tracy Rick (Elsa)

7. "You look cold," Tracy said to Rick.
   (Rick) Elsa Tracy

8. "We should leave," Rick said to Tracy.
   Rick (Rick and Tracy) Tracy

151

Knowing the Words

Write the words from the story that have the meanings below.

1. special way of writing __code__
(Par. 3)

2. figured out a secret code __decoded__
(Par. 3)

3. directions __instructions__
(Par. 5)

In each row, circle the three words that belong together.

4. (message) (note) drop (code)
5. (paper) read (pen) (pencil)
6. yard (den) (kitchen) (bedroom)
7. (chair) (lamp) coat (table)
8. (read) fold (solve) (think)

Learning to Study

Read each word in dark print and the dictionary meanings that follow. Then read the sentences below and decide the meaning of each underlined word. Write the number of the correct meaning in the blank.

den 1 small room in a house
     2 an animal's home

1. _2_ The fox was asleep in its den.
2. _1_ Is the TV in the den?

glass 1 something that holds liquid
       2 material that can break

3. _1_ I spilled the glass of water.
4. _2_ A piece of glass was in the tire.

Reading and Thinking

1. Number the sentences to show the order in which things happened.
   - _1_ Heather dropped a note near Michael's chair.
   - _3_ Michael decoded the message.
   - _5_ Michael met Heather in the kitchen.
   - _4_ Michael went to the den.
   - _2_ Michael found the first note.

Write T if the sentence is true.
Write F if the sentence is false.

2. _F_ Michael had never seen this code before.
3. _F_ It was the middle of summer.
4. _T_ All of the notes were inside the house.

5. How many notes did Heather write in all? __four__

6. How were all the notes alike?
   __(Answers will vary.)__

7. How was one note different from the others? ___
   __(Answers will vary.)__

BLF HLOEVW GSV XLWV!

153

Knowing the Words

Write the words from the story that have the meanings below.

1. a place where some insects grow ___cocoon___ (Par. 2)

2. insect ___moth___ (Par. 10)

Choose the correct word below to fill the blanks for each pair of sentences.

rest   fine

3. That is ___fine___ with me.

The thread was too ___fine___ to see.

4. Roger needs to ___rest___.

Did you get the ___rest___ of the programs?

Working with Words

Fill in each blank with the correct pair of letters to make a word. Then use each of the words in a sentence below.

sh   ch   wr   ph

1. bu ___sh___   3. hand ___wr___ iting

2. stoma ___ch___   4. autogra ___ph___

5. My ___stomach___ hurts.

6. Leo has beautiful ___handwriting___.

7. May I have your ___autograph___?

8. Look at the cocoon on that ___bush___.

Reading and Thinking

Write **F** if the sentence gives a fact.
Write **O** if the sentence gives an opinion.

1. ___O___ A moth is a pretty insect.

2. ___F___ The body of a moth looks furry.

3. ___F___ Some insects come out of cocoons.

4. ___F___ A moth is an insect.

5. Why do you think Tracy and Ms. Carr took the moth outside?

_____
(Answers will vary.)

6. What kind of person do you think Ms. Carr is? Explain your answer.

(Answers will vary.)

Learning to Study

You can look in an **encyclopedia** to find facts about different topics. You may need to look under more than one topic to find the facts you need. To learn more about cocoons, Tracy could have looked under *cocoon*. Also, she could have looked under *moth* or *insect*.

Read each sentence below. Write the names of two topics you might look under.

1. You want to know about blue jays. ___(Answers will vary.)___

2. You want to learn about forest animals. ___(Answers will vary.)___

Knowing the Words

Write the word from the story that has the meaning below.

1. a trip to see something special ___tour___ (Par. 3)

Check the meaning that fits the underlined word in each sentence.

2. My new shirt is <u>light</u> blue.
   ___✓___ pale
   _____ not heavy

3. We are planning a <u>trip</u> to England.
   ___✓___ vacation
   _____ to stumble

4. I left a <u>note</u> on the table.
   _____ a musical sound
   ___✓___ a short letter

Working with Words

Write the contraction for each pair of words below.

1. you have ___you've___

2. would not ___wouldn't___

3. what is ___what's___

4. you will ___you'll___

5. we are ___we're___

6. I will ___I'll___

7. do not ___don't___

8. I have ___I've___

Reading and Thinking

1. Check the answer that tells what the story is mainly about.
   _____ cold, damp walls
   _____ a secret stairway
   ___✓___ visiting a castle

2. Write **R** next to two sentences that tell about real things.
   ___R___ A person can drive to a castle.
   _____ A person can drive into the past.
   ___R___ Castles have walls.
   _____ Castles have dragons.

Learning to Study

Each book of an encyclopedia is called a **volume.** Write the number of the volume you could use to find the topics below.

1. castles ___3___   6. carriages ___3___

2. bicycle ___2___   7. gardening ___8___

3. history ___9___   8. horses ___9___

4. cotton ___4___   9. dolls ___5___

5. fish ___7___   10. England ___6___

Knowing the Words

Write the words from the story that have the meanings below.

1. invention ___device___ (Par. 7)

2. ended ___concluded___ (Par. 11)

Choose the correct word to fill in the blank for each pair of sentences.

drive   saw

3. Ed is too young to ___drive___.

___Drive___ the nail into the wood.

4. We ___saw___ you at the game.

Where did you put the ___saw___?

Learning to Study

Names of people are listed in an encyclopedia by the person's last name. Write the number of the volume you could use to find the topics below.

1. invention ___10___

2. computers ___4___

3. Mary Anderson ___1___

4. Thomas Edison ___6___

Reading and Thinking

Write **T** if the sentence is true.
Write **F** if the sentence is false.

1. ___T___ Tracy, Lindsay, and Rick had been to the library.

2. ___T___ Tracy pretended she was a news reporter.

3. ___F___ The class was not interested in the project.

4. Did Tracy really talk to Mary Anderson? Explain your answer.

___No, she just pretended to.___

5. Why did Mary Anderson make a device for cleaning a windshield?

___She wanted to make___

___driving safer.___

Read each set of sentences below. Fill in each blank.

6. Lindsay pretended she was Mary Anderson.

She stands for ___Lindsay___.

7. Rick said he liked the new invention.

He stands for ___Rick___.

8. The inventor thought she had a good idea.

She stands for ___the inventor___.

9. The class was surprised when it saw the report.

It stands for ___the class___.

Knowing the Words

Write the word from the story that has the meaning below.

1. moved from side to side ___shook___ (Par. 9)

Circle the pair of antonyms (opposites) in each row.

2. sing (cry) (laugh) applaud

3. (lost) helped looked (won)

4. (answered) said (inquired) grumbled

Working with Words

The suffix **-ly** helps tell how something was done. *Smoothly* means "done in a smooth way."

Add **-ly** to the words below. Use the new words to complete the sentences.

silent   friend   loose   clear

1. When he was in the library, Robert read a book ___silently___.

2. Amy tied the knot ___loosely___.

3. Pat was happy to see the ___friendly___ puppy.

4. The announcer spoke ___clearly___.

Say *gather*. Circle the words below that have the sound g stands for in *gather*.

5. (began) edge giant (against)

6. (get) (goldfish) message charge

7. (forget) (eager) magic bridge

8. cage (goose) (give) (together)

Reading and Thinking

Write **T** if the sentence is true.
Write **F** if the sentence is false.

1. ___T___ Dale wanted to help with the puppet show.

2. ___F___ Dale did not try very hard to find his stuffed elephant.

3. ___T___ Dale thought of a new way to solve his problem.

4. ___F___ Dale finally found the toy himself.

5. Dale was going to make a sock puppet because ___he couldn't___ ___find his stuffed elephant___

6. What do you think Dale will do now that his elephant has been found?

___(Answers will vary.)___
_____

Write the best word to complete each sentence below.

7. James ___wondered___ why the tire was flat. (wondered, jumped, searched)

8. The ___elephant___ was bigger than a car. (mouse, robin, elephant)

Write the words from the story that have the meanings below.

1. asked forgiveness __apologized__
(Par. 1)

2. common sickness __cold__
(Par. 3)

Check the meaning that fits the underlined word in each sentence.

3. It is very <u>cold</u> outside.
   - _✓_ low temperature
   - ___ sickness

4. This is the third <u>act</u>.
   - ___ to behave in a certain way
   - _✓_ part of a show

An **index** is a part of a book. It lists a book's topics in alphabetical order. It also lists page numbers so you can find those topics. An index is usually at the back of a book. Use the index below to answer the questions.

    performances, 1–5
    plays, 4, 21
    puppets, 4, 8–10
    stages, 11–15

1. What topic would you find on pages 1–5? __performances__

2. What could you learn from pages 11–15?
   __about stages__

3. On what pages would you look if you wanted to make a puppet? _4, 8–10_

1. Number the sentences to show the order in which things happened.
   - _4_ The puppets did a trapeze act.
   - _5_ The elephant performed.
   - _3_ Tracy announced the first act.
   - _2_ The children went to Elsa's house.
   - _1_ Dale went to Tracy's house.

Write **F** if the sentence gives a fact.
Write **O** if the sentence gives an opinion.

2. _F_ An elephant's skin has wrinkles.

3. _O_ The trapeze acts are the most thrilling to watch.

4. _F_ An elephant can be trained to stand on its hind legs.

5. _F_ Many circuses have elephants.

6. _O_ A circus isn't exciting.

Read each sentence below. Fill in the blank.

7. The children knew they had made Carmen happy.

   They stands for __children__.

8. Dale believed he had done a good job.

   He stands for __Dale__.

9. Carmen applauded as she watched the performance.

   She stands for __Carmen__.

163

Write the words from the story that have the meanings below.

1. a season __spring__
(Par. 1)

2. said something was true __admitted__
(Par. 7)

3. moved up and down __shrugged__
(Par. 11)

4. saw __spotted__
(Par. 15)

Choose the correct word below to fill the blank for each pair of sentences.

    close   spring

5. __Spring__ begins in March.

   The __spring__ in my pen is broken.

6. Please __close__ the window.

   Do not stand too __close__ to the fire.

Number each list of words below in alphabetical order.

1.
   - _5_ shrug
   - _6_ sing
   - _4_ shoulders
   - _2_ piano
   - _7_ smile
   - _1_ memorize
   - _3_ question

2.
   - _5_ crowd
   - _6_ cry
   - _7_ cute
   - _3_ concert
   - _4_ crawl
   - _2_ believe
   - _1_ beg

Write **T** if the sentence is true.
Write **F** if the sentence is false.

1. _F_ Elsa was very nervous.

2. _T_ Rick and Elsa had practiced the song more than once.

3. _F_ The concert took place at the beginning of the school year.

4. Rick did not want to sing in the concert because __he was nervous__

5. Who was Mr. Barnes? __the music teacher__

6. Why did Mr. Barnes tell Rick he needed to believe in himself?
   __so Rick wouldn't be nervous__

7. How do you think Rick felt about himself after he sang the song?
   __(Answers will vary.)__

8. Do you think Rick will ever sing in a concert again? Explain your answer. __(Answers will vary.)__

165

Write the words from the story that have the meanings below.

1. good price __bargain__
(Par. 1)

2. might be __probably__
(Par. 1)

Check the meaning that fits the underlined word in each sentence.

3. Did you see the <u>play</u> Michael was in?
   - _✓_ a show
   - ___ to have fun

4. Did Ken <u>watch</u> TV yesterday?
   - ___ something that keeps time
   - _✓_ to look at

Circle the correct word in ( ) and write it in the blank.

1. I hope I __grow__ two inches this year. (group (grow))

2. The __sound__ of his scream frightened me. ((sound) sand)

3. Has Sam __thought__ of a name for his kitten? ((thought) that)

4. The __show__ begins at 8:30. (shoe (show))

5. Did you write __down__ the correct address? (dawn (down))

6. Jenny __showed__ us how to tie a knot. (should (showed))

1. Why was Tracy saving money?
   __for a bike__

2. Tracy had to call Rick because __she needed the customers' addresses__

3. How do you think Tracy felt about asking Rick for the addresses?
   __(Answers will vary.)__

4. What do you think Tracy did after she delivered her last paper?
   __(Answers will vary.)__

Read each question below. Write **dictionary** or **encyclopedia** to answer each one.

1. Where would you find the meaning of the word *newspaper*?
   __dictionary__

2. Where could you find the history of newspapers?
   __encyclopedia__

3. Where could you find facts on how newspapers are made?
   __encyclopedia__

4. Where could you find the word *newspaper* divided into syllables?
   __dictionary__

167

NOTES

NOTES